Lessons in
Liberty

★ ★ ★ ★

Lessons in Liberty

★ ★ ★ ★

Thirty Rules for Living
from Ten Extraordinary Americans

Jeremy S. Adams

BROADSIDE
BOOKS

HarperCollins books may be purchased for educational, business, or sales promotional use. For information, please email the Special Markets Department at SPsales@harpercollins.com.

Broadside Books™ and the Broadside logo are trademarks of HarperCollins Publishers.

Images are in the public domain, with one exception: the photograph of Ruth Bader Ginsburg is courtesy of Lynn Gilbert.

FIRST EDITION

Designed by Nancy Singer

Library of Congress Cataloging-in-Publication Data has been applied for.

ISBN 978-0-06-331107-7

24 25 26 27 28 LBC 5 4 3 2 1

To my endlessly supportive older brothers, Howard and Will . . .

if our fates are framed by the souls we love in this life, then being

your younger brother has been the greatest boon of all . . .

We are like dwarfs sitting on the shoulders of giants. We see more, and things that are more distant, than they did, not because our sight is superior or because we are taller than they, but because they raise us up, and by their great stature add to ours.

—John of Salisbury

And the most glorious exploits do not always furnish us with the clearest discoveries of virtue or vice in men; sometimes a matter of less moment, an expression or a jest, informs us better of their characters and inclinations, than the most famous sieges, the greatest armaments, or the bloodiest battles whatsoever.

—Plutarch, *The Lives of the Noble Grecians and Romans*

CONTENTS

Lessons in
Liberty

★ ★ ★ ★

INTRODUCTION

It was probably the most inspiring moment I have ever experienced in my years as a high-school teacher. Sadly, it didn't occur in my classroom. But it did take place during a school event. At the time, I was already in the stretch of my teaching career in which all-school rallies tested the endurance of my middle-aged eardrums. The gymnasium on my campus is ancient. The air-conditioning doesn't work particularly well, especially when a thousand students are jammed into the bleachers. The acoustics are horrendous. And to be honest, the unfettered buffoonery of the games and activities always left me feeling like a bit of a crank.

The rally began as all rallies do—with a student singing the national anthem. The students stood, the female student began to sing, but within a few seconds she ran into trouble. Not because she couldn't hit the high notes or remember the words. Her microphone had suddenly died. But instead of silence, something utterly astonishing happened. The students quickly picked up where she left off, not just mumbling the lyrics but collectively belting out "The Star-Spangled Banner" with an effusive pride and vitality that shocked and delighted my fellow faculty members. I can remember dropped jaws and whispered "wows" coming from more than a few teachers.

Even today, this memory from almost a decade ago never fails to stir the deepest emotions of my teacher soul, not simply because I recall the exhilaration of being inspired by the student body but because I cannot help but wonder today how modern students would respond to the same situation.

I'm quite certain the outcome would be colossally different and, yes, disappointing.

Would the students today even be standing? Would they know the words of the national anthem? Would they feel compelled to sing it?

I have spent my entire adult life teaching American civics to young Americans on the cusp of adulthood. It is impossible for me to become a fashionable cynic about the United States of America when I have witnessed thousands of her young people do extraordinary things with their lives, many of them from backgrounds of deep disadvantage, triumphing against despairing odds because they believed in themselves and the power of individual liberty.

I am, thus, an unapologetic romantic about the United States. This romanticism does not come from a naïve or Pollyannaish belief that America can do no wrong—far from it. My titanic affection for this nation arises from my hope of what it can and should be. It is inspired by an unshakable faith in the animating ideals that birthed our founding documents and spurred each successive generation to inch closer to a more perfect union.

But what I have witnessed in the past decade is a plaintive pivot away from empowering optimism and toward a contemptuous cynicism about American civilization and its history. This scorn has exploded on a scale and with a celerity that is difficult to fathom. The iconoclasm of our age has led to broad discouragement and civic embarrassment among American youth. A jaw-dropping forty percent of Gen Zers now characterize America's founders as "villains." Many of my current and former students now ask questions that betray a deep suspicion of national pride.

Should they stand or kneel during the national anthem?

Should they recite the Pledge of Allegiance or sit on their hands during the flag salute?

1619 or 1776?

Even though this fashionable self-flagellation may advertise itself as courageous honesty, its real effect is to tell young people that America was never great to begin with, and even if it was, they shouldn't see themselves as a part of it. Can you imagine a more deflating message to students striving to identify their place in a grander story of national purpose?

It's no coincidence that this fever of contempt for Americans from the past has emerged in an era of powerful personal and political misery. A slew of recent reporting tells the dispiriting tale of young Americans finding it difficult to have fun, maintain mental health or be happy, pursue a career or higher education, form friendships, pursue passions, or seek romance. In the past decade alone, the number of American teenagers who agree with statements such as "I do not enjoy life" and "My life is not useful" has roughly doubled. A quarter of eighteen-to-twenty-four-year-olds have seriously considered suicide. It is no surprise that cynicism has surged in the classroom. My students often describe themselves as helplessly overwhelmed, feeling as though they have no agency or ability to shape their own destinies. They're crippled by anxiety, guilt, perfectionism, and apathy.

Pundits blame a host of national ills for our youth's anxiety epidemic, many of them economic or sociological in nature. But what ails the American soul today is not material poverty but existential ignorance. Our moral shibboleths are weak, our focus is shallow, and the greatest goal presented to kids is living for yourself. This may seem like freedom, but it's not. Imagine a wasteland powered by energy drinks and processed foods, medicated to quell constant anxiety, hyperfocused on navel-gazing safetyism. That's not freedom.

This is why the primary project of our time is educational in nature. Americans want answers but keep looking in all the wrong places. We have a lot of entertainment. We have a lot of politics. We have a lot of pontification, online strutting, and braggadocio.

What we need is a healthy form of national pride. We need more moral authority and inspiration. We need to confront what Dostoyevsky called "the eternal questions."

As a teacher, a father, and a deeply worried citizen, I have been searching for a path out of this ruin, probing the national landscape for geysers of inspiration or wells of purpose. How can modern citizens recover hope in America and in themselves? How do they absorb the life lessons of the best American men and women who have ever lived? How do we apply these lessons in such a way that we can live better and more joyful lives?

While the United States is a physical place that can be objectively measured in a variety of ways—by its population, GDP and unemployment rate, public policies and abundant resources—truly understanding and loving America has to start not with cold, impersonal data but with American stories liltingly revealed and intimately studied. People connect with stories because they connect with people. And not just any people, but our people, our American brethren.

The Greek historian Plutarch is famous for *The Lives of the Noble Grecians and Romans*, a book that stirred so many Westerners to greatness—especially America's founding generation. A compelling and defensible case could be made that Plutarch wrote the most successful self-help book of all time. As Thomas E. Ricks notes, "There is no equivalent book today with which familiarity would be assumed by all members of a political elite. Even Washington, not much of a reader except in a handful of topics that intrigued him—notably agricultural innovation, and late in his life, the abolition of slavery—owned a copy of Plutarch's Lives."

At the outset of his narrative about Alexander the Great, Plutarch explicitly, albeit briefly, reveals the ultimate intention of his grand project. He writes, "Therefore, as portrait painters are more exact in the lines and features of the face, in which the character is seen, than in the other parts of the body, so I must be allowed to give my more particular attention to the marks and indications of the souls of men, and while I endeavor by these to portray their lives, may be free to leave more weighty matters and great battles to be treated by others."

Plutarch is not concerned so much with the grandiose headlines of life, not battlefields, not masterpieces, not wealth or the traditional springs of social accolade and political acclaim. Instead, he chooses to focus his attention on "the souls of men," for it is ultimately the character we sow or the virtue we cultivate that paves the road we sojourn in this life.

The American story—*our* story—is one of the richest and most fascinating tales in the history of human civilization. It still holds tremendous, even salvific, power. Despite young Americans disliking their own country at unprecedented levels, I have found that when the phones get turned off and my students take a deep breath and listen to the stories of the men and women who made this country, something extraordinary occurs. They show a steady and pronounced interest in the lives of the people who made America, the citizens brave enough to renew America, and those who continue today to add new colors and fresh contours to the national tapestry of our country. It is this interest that holds the key for helping our students and fellow citizens live better, deeper, more significant lives. In short, an Americanized version of Plutarch is needed now more than ever—it might not be a magical elixir, but it would be powerful medicine nonetheless.

What it has taken me two and a half decades to learn is that this engagement with these historic actors and actresses sells itself organically. It doesn't have to be coerced, lulled, or strong-armed. Students are authentically fascinated by the human element of the political institutions they are learning about. But this only works if we're willing to praise the good and heroic when we see it. As novelist and Laureate for Irish Fiction Sebastian Barry gorgeously frames the process, we must engage "the good gold of memories retrieved in a certain way."

Nowadays, sadly, we ignore "the good gold" and instead rush to condemn and denounce instead. As Roosevelt Montás observes in *Rescuing Socrates*, "As with all thinkers from the past, our moral censure has to be applied with discrimination and historical awareness. 'In what way are they right?' is almost always a more productive and a more difficult question than 'In what way are they wrong?'"

My argument is simple but powerful: Let us study the best

American men and women in our rich history and focus on the best they have to offer. Leaving these figures' flaws to able-minded scholars and academics, let the everyday American, the teacher and the truck driver, the pediatrician and the police officer, instead honor what is honorable, praise what is praiseworthy, and most of all, emulate what is highest and best so we can take advantage of the miracle of human freedom.

These ten extraordinary Americans aren't as remote as we might think, despite their historic stature or the centuries that sometimes separate us. In fact, it is their fallibility that makes them so wholly worthy of study and emulation, their crucibles of tragedy or foibles of excess—Washington's legendary self-control was necessitated by his mighty temper, Clara Barton's colossal achievements borne of her epic stubbornness, Ruth Bader Ginsburg's extraordinary commitment to her family the consequence of almost losing her husband to cancer.

What reveals the inner fabric of a man or woman is not selfies taken from a mountaintop—it's the private moments of doubt, turmoil, or debilitating disappointment. It's the moments we don't want to talk about. It's the private humiliation of standing on a scale when trying to lose weight and nothing has changed. It's the tragic inability to truly process the betrayal of a friend, a spouse, or a colleague. It's the hubris of writing a book we think will change the world and the world's response is a shrug. It's losing faith in a benevolent cosmos in the face of unspeakable private tragedy. Rest assured, these moments happen to us all, even those who end up in history books or on Mount Rushmore.

The men and women in this book were right about a lot of things, especially the things that deeply matter . . . how to love, how to build and renew a country, how to learn and prosper, how to win battles with others but also with ourselves, how to befriend adversaries and defeat true enemies, how to internalize inspiration and consider the galaxy of life's possibilities, but most of all, how to maximize the most finite and mysterious resource of all: *time.*

I don't want my fellow Americans to spend their lives suppressing a proud heritage because it's fashionable to engage in self-loathing. We should rest assured that freedom, greatness, and patriotism are all good things and possible, even now. The great question is not whether they're possible but how to achieve them. One of us could be the next Abraham Lincoln or Arthur Ashe . . . so why aren't we? To aspire to greatness, we have to look at the choices of great people and determine the surprising and sometimes counterintuitive insights which made them the heroes they ultimately became.

That's what we'll do in this book.

What lasts are the lessons whispered to us by those who have lived the types of lives we should all aspire to. What lasts is what men and women from our own history "got right." We live in a time when we ignore their insights at our peril. Their whispered wisdom can only be discerned if we study them with care.

Let us begin.

CHAPTER 1

George Washington

Have Good Manners in Every Setting

★

★

Curiously, of all the founders, George Washington is both the most omnipresent in our national life and also the most difficult to truly understand.

The nation's capital is named after him. The dollar bill bears his likeness. Hundreds of Washington statues, paintings, bridges, forts, and memorials can be found from Maine to California; there are even Washington statues in places as far away as Lima, Peru, and Trafalgar Square in London.

The financier Robert Morris proclaimed him "the greatest man on earth." When Washington's nemesis, King George III, heard of his plan to retire his military commission in the wake of defeating the British army, the vanquished monarch purportedly remarked "then he will be the greatest man in the world." He was unanimously selected for every significant position he ever held. In a generation brimming with eclectic talent and towering genius, Washington was universally lauded as the greatest.

However, as the historian Richard Brookhiser has observed, "If Washington's contemporaries were too willing to be awed, we are not willing enough."[1]

The man whose likeness is so often chiseled into marble and hillsides, who wins the loudest applause of the most impressive men and women from his era and beyond, appears to the twenty-first-century American to be rather inaccessible and mercurial. He seems more a figment of fiction than organic flesh and blood, more a mannequin donning laurels of impossible virtue than a real human being engaged in the challenges of living life.

It is easy for us to forget his humanity, to forget that he fell desperately in love with a married woman, had a volcanic temper, didn't like being touched (even by his friends), and was forever concerned with wealth and reputation. It is easy to forget his education was paltry, his military victories somewhat sparse, and his family relationships occasionally rocky.

Much of our estrangement from men of Washington's ilk and disposition can be attributed to the titanic chasm separating his political world from our own. Political power in our era is sadly divorced from the trappings of classical civic and personal virtue. It strains one's imagination to conjure the first president attending a modern political fundraiser, or sending out petty partisan tweets, or standing on a debate stage trying to outduel his political rivals by uttering outrageous nonsense. Washington would never attend the Iowa State Fair and eat deep-fried butter sticks or beclown himself in a congressional committee hearing.

To Washington, unapologetic ambition and the ostentatious drive for glory were impulses to suppress and hide at all costs. Such hubris of the soul was the path of despotism and destruction, of tyrants and autocrats, of Julius Caesar, Alexander the Great, and later dictators of the twentieth century. Washington wanted none of it. He knew the success of republics hinged on the successful suppression of vainglory. Today, aspiring political leaders make little effort to hide their quest for political success. There is little they will not do or say to assume the mantle of power. And sadly, few Americans expect much better in their political discourse.

There is a word for this deadweight of modern expectation: *cynicism.*

We live in a cynical age characterized by an endless zeal for "debunking," "deconstructing," and "demystifying" men and women from our past. Our iconoclastic zeal to hollow out and tear down exemplars from yesterday says much more about us than it does about them. What Washington offers us is something truly unique, even startling: a glimpse of power rooted in unimpeachable character. More than any figure in American history, Washington radiated a nimbus of incorruptibility. And because there is no American today who comes close to approaching the universal acclaim enjoyed by Washington during his lifetime and beyond, it raises a fascinating question: How did he do it, and how can we emulate him in our own lives?

Let's find out.

Lesson #1: Embrace the Ethic of Self-Help

Washington is not just the Father of our country; he is the most famous apostle of American self-help.

Of course, our first president never would have used the expression "self-help." In all likelihood he would have found the term feeble and vaguely narcissistic. Instead, the lexicon of the eighteenth century provided such weighty words as virtue, character, esteem, and honor to describe enriching one's inner nature and domesticating the unruly elements within. As a man of the Enlightenment, Washington ardently believed human beings were imbued with a special capacity to fortify their characters, ameliorate their minds, and in the process, assume the wheel of their own destinies.

A belief in self-help is really just optimism cloaked in the sheen of hard work and sacrifice. Optimism—because it requires us to believe we can be better than we currently are. Sacrifice—because improvement is always colossally difficult to achieve.

Many Americans have become fatalistic in their thinking. Our national mood is collectively gloomy. Although he may seem distant to us, Washington offers men and women of the modern age a powerful alternative. His cheerful conviction is that our failings are only temporary: Ignorance can give way to wisdom, rashness can embrace reflection, and sloth can always be transformed into vigor. If we are angry, we can learn to hold our tongues and suppress our emotional eruptions. If we are overweight, we can diet and hit the gym. If we don't read enough because we are obsessed with our phones, we can power down our devices and devote ourselves to traditional books instead. If we allow ourselves to be distant friends, selfish spouses, or distracted parents, then every day is a new opportunity to do better and be better. Any excess or deficiency of character can be remedied with the right aim and enough exertion.

Washington also reminds us that improvement is not just possible but vitally necessary. He was keenly aware of a concept sorely missing in many of us today, a concept that is ubiquitous in Greek philosophy as well as in Judeo-Christian teachings: the notion of human incompleteness. A belief in the fallibility of the self was utterly conventional in Washington's day, and yet today it often runs counter to the loud and fashionable messages of a narcissistic culture constantly telling us that we are fine as we are, that none of us need to participate in the arduous business of moral or intellectual improvement. We don't really need self-help, merely abundant self-love. Seen through a therapeutic lens, the path toward a good and just society is paved not with virtuous citizens continually striving for improvement and refinement but instead with infinitely tolerant residents mutually vowing to avoid judgment of one another.

Affirmation, not improvement, we are told, is the elixir to induce a true and abiding contentment. But Washington knew better.

We can't reject self-improvement because we all have our vices and flaws. But conversely, we can't reject the possibility of greatness, because *every* person who has ever achieved anything has been flawed. Young Washington knew early on that he aspired to a life of genuine consequence and grand significance. He had no longing for the well-worn paths of an ordinary life. Instead, he yearned for a life lived on the grandest of historic stages. He longed for the prestige afforded those deemed imminently worthy of acclaim.

Quite simply, Washington wanted to become a better version of himself. There are twenty thousand documents he did not destroy and some of the earliest preserved documents capture this zest for self-improvement. The historian John E. Ferling describes the youthful ambitions of Washington: "His tactics were simple: he read, studied, attended, and imitated. He fell into the habit of quiescence, watching, listening, seldom speaking, and all the while discreetly preparing and polishing his behavior and expression into an accommodating style."[2]

Every serious biographer of Washington notes his early embrace of "The Rules of Civility and Decent Behavior in Company and Conversation," a set of a hundred and ten rules and maxims conceived by the French Jesuits in 1595. The Jesuits' overarching purpose for writing the precepts is captured in the first rule: "Every action done in company ought to be with some sign of respect to those that are present." For the rest of his life, Washington exuded an Olympian awareness of how his actions would be perceived by others. In an era where honorability was considered one of the highest goods, if not the highest—as opposed to the infamous, the notorious, or the exceedingly outrageous—Washington mastered the trick of gaining power by foreswearing power.

Not all of the rules he copied are serious and high-minded. Many of them are amusingly practical, such as rule four: "In the presence of others, sing not to yourself with a humming noise . . ." or rule nine, "Spit not in the fire . . ." By sixteen, Washington had copied every single precept by hand in twenty pages of his notebook; the enormity of their influence on his life is impossible to understate. The Washington biographer Willard Sterne Randall observed of the axioms, "The Jesuit rules were to become a catechism to Washington, not only a code of conduct that he followed more faithfully than religious doctrine, but his own self-teaching school for manners."[3]

This youthful project was the genesis of a lifetime of self-help, not the sum total of it. Washington's belief in self-improvement and his stoic quest for unflinching civility was a constant throughout his life. Decades after copying "The Rules of Civility" as a teenage boy he was still purchasing books on politeness as an adult. As one historian explained, "A man capable of constant self-improvement, Washington grew in stature throughout his life. This growth went on subtly, at times imperceptibly, beneath the surface, making Washington the most interior of the founders."[4]

While young Americans would certainly benefit from emulating Washington's self-help ethic, they aren't the only ones who should observe his rules. Washington believed that all of us should be forever on the path of improvement, no matter our age, our imminence, or our station in life. There is never a bad time in life to crave an enlargement of the self.

To Washington, self-mastery was an essential ingredient in attaining genuine freedom. However, liberty meant something wholly and materially different to him than what it means to most Americans today. To modern ears and sensibilities, liberty is associated with the freedom to be ourselves, to say what we want, go where we want, wear what we want, and love whom we want. The realization of modern liberty requires little in terms of curbing excess or upholding tradition. It is often the embodiment of unbridled individualism.

Washington, on the other hand, associated liberty with the sentiment of Heraclitus—"Character is destiny." To Washington, liberty was more than simply the absence of external limitation. A more sophisticated and genuine freedom is attained when one is free from the excesses of the self—the very excesses preventing us from becoming the men or women we hope to be. A person who is lazy is not free to write the book he dreams of writing. A person who can't stop drinking or taking drugs can't live up to the personal commitments she has made. Just because no one is stopping me from losing weight or preventing me from yelling at the television doesn't mean I have the self-mastery to behave as I should—just ask my scale and my wife.

In short, Washington's ennobling view of freedom was closer in spirit to Aristotle than to Hugh Hefner.

Even in a generation as extraordinary as the American founding, our founders were often known for their excesses. Alexander Hamilton's vanity was legendary. Benjamin Franklin's amorous entanglements and bonhomie with the opposite sex were well known. Thomas Jefferson, by all accounts, had a taste for political duplicity and luxurious living beyond his means. John Adams was a man of high character who did his absolute best to be unlikable, alienating friend and foe alike with acute bouts of self-righteousness. These character traits made them fascinating people, lively and accessible to posterity.

But Washington was different. He followed the Jesuit rules with the aim of self-mastery. While some sensed cool detachment bordering on arrogance, Washington's supreme command of his inner desires made him imminently trustworthy when the nation needed him most. No one ever worried about him being bribed or seduced or unduly tempted by power. He lived in an era of deep historic drama, surrounded for

decades by the storms of war and revolution. Washington's inner trans-
formation was a moral ballast against the external hurricanes of his
time, bestowing him with a rare fortitude and serenity that dazzled
virtually everyone in his presence, calling to mind the opening lines
of Rudyard Kipling's immortal poem "If—" that asserts you are a man
"If you can keep your head when all about you / Are losing theirs and
blaming it on you."

Washington learned to always keep his head. But it wasn't easy. He
had his personal failings. Most famous was his reputation "as the posses-
sor of a fiery disposition" and "tremendous temper."[5]

During the Revolutionary War, Washington's anger occasionally
broke through his disciplined facade. Retreats on the battlefield elic-
ited everything from swearing at General Charles Lee at the Battle
of Monmouth to whipping his men with a riding cane in the face of
advancing British troops on the Harlem Heights. Adams hinted that
Washington's fury was generally only witnessed by aides who were
loyal. "Whenever he lost his temper, as he did sometimes, either love
or fear in those about him induced them to conceal his weakness from
the world."

The paradox of Washington's temper is that it unintentionally enhanced his reputation. Sensing that a large reservoir of fury was always
close at hand, those in Washington's presence learned to fear the fury
but adulate the strength of character that was keeping it forever at
bay. Men of brilliance, courage, and high achievement all deferred to
Washington because they knew he was in possession of unassailable,
yet hard-won integrity.

Lesson #2: Appearances Matter

No American has ever been more hyperaware of his appearance and the
acute power it can have on events and people than Washington.

This observation might seem to paint him with a shallow brush,
but nothing could be further from the truth. Like Odysseus, whom we

are told in the opening lines of *The Odyssey* was "skilled in all ways of contending," Washington understood that perfection of one's interior self would only go so far in a world that often overlooks the quiet virtues of the soul in favor of the external ornamentations of strength and elegance. He cultivated his appearance with extraordinary care, projecting an image of the patrician soldier whose honor and stature were demonstrated by his inordinate muscle and abundant social grace.

Both on the battlefield and in the political arena, a first impression can play a significant or even decisive role in deciding how one's friends and foes behave. Washington's aura radiated strength and authority. He was well aware of the effect his appearance had on people. Indeed, it could be said that he knowingly cultivated a mythology of the reticent warrior.

Of course, some people are just abundantly blessed by nature. Washington was certainly one of them.

He stood at a strapping six feet, four inches and weighed roughly two hundred nine pounds during the years of the American Revolution.[6] He had broad shoulders, muscular limbs, and was generally considered to be quite handsome. But it was his brute strength and physical stature that was the stuff of legend. On Interstate 81 in central Virginia a historic stop called Natural Bridge features an arch 215 feet above the ground, giving the appearance of being a natural bridge. In 1750, a young Washington surveyed the area, carved his initials into a rock (which can still be seen today), and then did something—admittedly the stuff of legend and lore—utterly extraordinary. He took a rock and launched it from the bottom of Cedar Creek to the top of the bridge. To give this feat its proper modern context, 215 feet is just under 72 yards, a mere 28 yards shy of a full-length football field. And unlike a football, which is generally thrown horizontally by quarterbacks, young Washington threw the rock vertically, straight up. He once admitted that he "never met any man who could throw a stone so great a distance as himself."[7]

His strength embodied itself in other ways—through superhuman endurance and epic bravery. Brookhiser recounts some of Washington's military exploits: "During the War, he could stay awake and on horseback for days at a stretch. On his first expedition to the Pennsylvania wilderness, he walked for a week through snowy pathless woods, fell off a raft into an ice-choked river, spent the night on an island, and then pressed on to a trading post. His traveling companion, a frontiersman, came down with frostbite: he did not."[8]

At times he seemed to exude the invincibility of Achilles. He escaped the massacre during the Battle of the Monongahela in 1755 despite riding his horse directly into harm's way. Four musket balls breached his coach and he lost two horses when they were shot out from underneath him. In the summer of 1777, Washington was engaged in reconnaissance of an enemy position when the best marksman in the British army, Major Patrick Ferguson, had him in his sights. But as the historian Stephen Brumwell explains, "Something stopped him from squeezing the trigger."[9] At the Battle of Princeton, Washington personally led a charge to within thirty yards of British troops before giving the command to his men to fire. He was surrounded by so much gunfire his aide-de-camp at the time, Colonel John Fitzgerald, placed his hat in front of his eyes to avoid witnessing Washington's death by friendly fire. As Ron Chernow vividly describes the scene, "Fitzgerald finally peeked and saw Washington untouched, sitting proudly atop his horse, wreathed by eddying smoke." As was often the case with Washington, he seemed to be "protected by an invisible aura."[10]

Even when he was not on the battlefield, his movement evoked awe in onlookers. Their impressions present a man who possessed a fluid gait, moved through the world with seemingly perfect posture, and seemed to assume his destination would obediently wait for him no matter when he arrived. He never galumphed, trounced, or stomped. Like a star imbued with an abnormally strong gravitational force on all the objects in its orbit, Washington possessed what the Greeks called "charisma," quietly winning adoration from all quarters of society.

Many considered him to be the finest horseman of his era, Jefferson chief among them.

But his physical stature alone does not explain the power wielded by Washington. His fellow citizens marveled not only at his physical virtues. They were equally impressed with his flawless manners and social grace. His appearance at social and political events was always impeccable and thoughtfully manicured. It did not escape notice that he was the only delegate to wear a military uniform when the Continental Congress convened in 1775, and that he had the foresight to pack an old military uniform without knowing what the congress would ultimately decide.

The historic record is filled with anecdotes of Washington's refined manners and unblemished civility. Almost a decade after Washington's death, Adams wrote a pugnacious and unintentionally humorous letter to his friend Benjamin Rush in which he enumerates ten of Washington's characteristics that contributed to his status as an iconic American hero. He begins the letter by asking, "Talents? You will say, what Talents? I answer." All ten are astute observations, but item number eight rings especially true when trying to grasp Washington's social genius: "He possessed the Gift of Silence. This I esteem as one of the most precious Talents."[11] If Adams were being especially honest and self-reflective, he would admit he considered this the "most precious" trait because Adams could never stop talking.

Besides his physical majesty, manners, and bravery, Washington was ever mindful of how his actions would impact his reputation and honor. Appearances matter, not just in presentation and interaction but in the motives of one's actions.

When he was appointed commander in chief of the Continental Congress at the outset of the war, he refused any salary, asking only to be reimbursed when the war concluded. In the aftermath of the conflict, the Virginia Assembly decided to reward him with a hundred fifty shares of the James River and Potomac companies. But Washington, ever fearful of appearances, and asking the question "How would this matter be viewed then by the eyes of the world?," decided it would be an insult to refuse the shares so he gave them to a fledgling college in Lexington, Virginia, called Liberty Hall Academy, which promptly changed its name to Washington Academy. At the time, it was one of the largest donations to an educational institution. Washington Academy would later rename itself Washington College, and after the Civil War, Washington and Lee University. To this day, his donation is a part of the university's operating budget.[12]

Washington's legacy is proof that appearances matter. Everyone in his orbit felt the force of his presence. Indeed, one has to use words that are seldom evoked nowadays—stoicism, gravitas, sobriety—to fully grasp and appreciate the allure of our first president. Few of us have the force of will or discipline of character to even approach Washington's level of achievement. The sheer poetry of his movement, the power of his presence, and the potency of his character are the reasons why there is only one George Washington in human history and why this nation was blessed beyond measure or description to have him at the helm for two decades during the fragile infancy of our republic.

Above all else, to know Washington is to feel a tug of inspiration to be better. To be physically and mentally stronger. To be mindful of how our words and actions are interpreted by others. To question our own motives and actions. To listen more than we talk. To yearn for more than wealth or fame or accolades in abundance. To rise above our time and live beyond the horizons of our own place in the world. To be the shoulders upon which future generations can stand.

Lesson #3: Emulate Cato but Prefer Cincinnatus

Much has been written in the past half century about the founding generation's endless fascination and celebration of ancient Rome. Their knowledge of and familiarity with the Roman Empire and the men and women who populated it was nothing short of encyclopedic, perhaps even a bit obsessive. The heroes and villains of the ancient Roman world were as well known and real to the founders in their time as *Star Wars* characters were to my generation, or Marvel characters are to my students and children today.

Instead of Luke Skywalker, Yoda, and Obi-Wan Kenobi, the men of the founding generation populated their official speeches, private correspondence, and public debates with references to Cicero, Cincinnatus, Publius, Scipio, Lucius Junius, Antony, and Octavian, to name just a few. Instead of Darth Vader and Emperor Palpatine the founders referenced Catiline, Caesar, and Brutus.

Everyone seemed to have a favorite Roman character. Adams revered Cicero above all others. Hamilton, at least according to his nemesis Jefferson, believed Caesar was "the greatest man that ever lived." James Madison's pseudonym in his debates with Hamilton about the nature of presidential power was Helvidius, the Roman stoic who believed emperors can only act with the consent of the senate.

But the most famous love affair between an ancient Roman and a founding father was Washington's reverence for the Roman senator Marcus Porcius Cato Uticensis, more widely known as Cato. What's ironic is that while Washington's emulation of Cato's death-defying courage gained him fame, it was only by embracing the opposite virtue—the humility of Cincinnatus—that he ensured his own immortality.

Volumes, from his own time through ours, have been written about the tumultuous and consequential life of Cato. The source of Washington's adoration of Cato was largely informed by a popular and widely performed play at the time, *Cato, a Tragedy* by Joseph Addison. Many of the lines of the play were borrowed and tweaked during the revolutionary era and became used as rhetorical ammunition in the conflict against the tyranny of George III. Even the most famous quote of the era, Patrick Henry's immortal "Give me liberty or give me death!," can find its inspiration in the second act of the play: "It is not now time to talk of aught / But chains or conquest, liberty or death."[13]

Washington attended the play numerous times, most famously

allowing some of his officers to put on a version of it during the miserable winter spent at Valley Forge. For Washington, Cato exemplified both the steadiness of character and virtuousness of soul required for a republic to endure. Cato is most famous for heroically resisting the megalomania of Caesar, whose endless quest for power and prestige led to the eventual destruction of the Roman republic.

Caesar—who famously uttered "I had rather be first in a village than second at Rome"—was the living embodiment of the unquenchable thirst for glory. Such glory-seeking was incongruent with the building of a republic. On the other hand, Cato exemplified what was necessary to create and preserve a republic: citizens and leaders committed to principles and institutions, not narrow self-interests and petty enrichments. Cato famously committed suicide rather than submit to the despotic demands of a tyrannical Caesar.

So what exactly does it mean to emulate Cato? How did Washington do it and why should we?

Above all else, it means steadfast devotion to an ideal bigger than oneself. It means sacrifice, selflessness, and duty. It looks like loyalty to a cause, fidelity to a principle, and, above all else, always acting as a pillar that never goes wobbly. Washington was a perpetual pillar of the American cause—he stood cemented in the cold soil of America during the infancy of the republic as general of the Continental Army, sat gracefully aloft the Constitutional Convention as the presiding officer when it required an aura of legitimacy, and, finally, lent his steady and trustworthy hand to the newly created office of president of the United States for which there was no precedent in all of human history.

Emulating Cato is rooted in public and private virtue. Washington's power, like Cato's, lay in his trustworthiness to navigate perilous waters using principled patriotism as his North Star. Every time he was appointed to a powerful position, he gave the impression of the hesitant hero. While he was certainly ambitious, the republican spirit of the time prevented any outward demonstration of it. And every time he succeeded in using his power to further the interests and aims of the new nation, no one ever had to tell Washington when it was time to step aside.

In this way, Washington surpassed his hero. We take it for granted today that civilian and military power are constitutionally divided, but it came as a shock to most Americans when Washington traveled to Annapolis, Maryland, where the Continental Congress was seated at the time, and surrendered the totality of his power to a legislature short on power and even shorter on prestige. As one historian observed, "Few people alive at the time were prepared for such a bold gesture." Such ceremonial surrendering of power simply wasn't done in the chronicles of human history. No one could fathom any of the monstrous tyrants of history—Nero, Ivan the Terrible, Genghis Khan—even considering it.

This, of course, is where Washington's nickname, "the American Cincinnatus," comes from. Cincinnatus famously answered the call of the Roman senate to become a temporary dictator while plowing his land. In a mere fifteen days, he liberated the Roman army that had become trapped in the mountains by a neighboring tribe, the Aequi, and promptly returned to his farm, though the senate mandate allowed him to enjoy six months of absolute power. The parallels to Washington willingly surrendering power and joyfully returning to Mount Vernon were too obvious to overlook.

When it was apparent that the Articles of Confederation were faltering and in need of substantial reform, it was Washington who lent his reputation to the Philadelphia gathering, whose "presence would provide an invaluable veneer of legitimacy for extensive reform that was, strictly speaking, a violation of the mandate soon to be issued by the Confederation Congress."[14] In typical Washington fashion, he said little of substance during the vigorous debates surrounding the formation of a new Constitution, but his table and chair, both slightly and conspicuously elevated, cast a spirit reminiscent of parental oversight. During the convention Washington's chair had a half sun painted on the back of it. Franklin famously observed, "I have often looked at that [chair] behind the president without being able to tell whether it was rising or setting." Because of Washington's willingness to serve as the trustworthy custodian of the gathering, the sun became a rising sun.

Though the Constitution began as mere words on parchment conceived by endless compromise and hours of pragmatic oratory, once ratified it became the source of real-world practical power. The new executive office described in Article II of the Constitution became incarnate in a living, breathing, human being. Far from being occupied by "the most powerful man in the world," the American presidency started off as an office laden with ambiguity and uncertainty. It would be defined as much by its first occupant as by the theory it represented. Thus, Washington wrote to his friend, "I go to the chair of government with feelings not unlike those of a culprit who is going to the place of his execution."[15]

And yet, Washington served with honor and distinction, ensuring that the American presidency resisted any semblance to monarchical or aristocratic tendencies, famously ignoring Adams's humorous attempts to shape the nomenclature of the new presidency with awkward suggestions such as "His Mightiness" or "His Elective Majesty," settling instead for the modest and plain "President of the United States" or "Mr. President" instead.

His disdain of political parties also spoke to the Cato-esque spirit of upholding the public interest as paramount to ephemeral ideological squabbles. For the second time in his life, Washington would retire at the height of his power, refusing a third presidential term, believing a republic must be replenished not by the efforts of a single man but by the patriotic spirit of the men and women whose belief in the Constitution would perpetuate the principles and reinvigorate the institutions of a free society. He would leave it to the next generation and see if they were up to the challenge.

Which begs an uncomfortable but urgent series of questions: Are we Americans up to the challenge today? Do modern citizens particularly want a republic anymore? Or do we simply want lives of easy and breezy contentment? Republics require an active and informed citizenship. They require the robust teaching of common values and an ethic of shared responsibility.

Do modern Americans understand what a republic requires of its citizens, its leaders, or its institutions in order to survive and replenish its moral corpus? Is any of this knowledge ever taught in our schools? Do we comprehend the fragility of freedom and the republican responsibilities of those we elect into positions of power in the way Cato and Washington did? Or has our inherited wealth corrupted our republican virtue and rotted away our ardor for genuine sacrifice?

Washington certainly emulated Cato's love of classical republican principles. But in many ways Washington's model of republican leadership is superior to Cato's for a simple reason: Washington didn't die for his country; he stayed alive for it instead. He revered Cato for his courage and passion, but he modeled the simplicity and self-effacement of Cincinnatus. In forgoing his own future power, he ensured the future for the rest of us.

Unlike Jefferson and Adams, who both lived for decades after leaving the White House, Washington died three years into Adams's single term. It is almost as if Washington had just enough time to discern that his exit from the national stage wouldn't result in the abrupt end of the American experiment. He could die knowing that he had done everything in his power to guarantee the survival of the nation he sacrificed so much to birth.

It is difficult but possible to imagine an alternate American history without some of the greatest founders—the Declaration of Independence would lack the lyrical brilliance without Jefferson, the Constitution would certainly have been less innovative without Madison, and who knows how long it would have taken the Second

Continental Congress to declare independence from King George III without the fiery resolve of Adams.

But there is no independence without Washington. No Constitution. No United States. Such is the measure of his importance to the cause of human liberty and the forging of the nation dedicated to its creation and perpetuation.

CHAPTER 2

Daniel Inouye

Be a Joiner

There is a curious exhilaration a traveler experiences when searching for the baggage claim at the Honolulu International Airport for the first time.

Instead of a long indoor walk followed by a hasty descent down an escalator, visitors to Hawaii's capital city are treated to the welcoming rush of warm air as they walk outside before entering the area of the airport where the baggage-claim center is located.

The first time I visited Hawaii with my family, I looked up at the airport's tower while making this particular walk to the baggage area and under it was the word "Aloha," written in welcoming red cursive. The words underneath the Aloha sign were less friendly and more official—in black capital letters: DANIEL H. INOUYE INTERNATIONAL AIRPORT.

Little did I appreciate at the time that Inouye (pronounced *ih-NO-ay*) was much, much more than merely a long-tenured US senator with an airport named after him. While few Americans beyond history junkies, political aficionados, and Hawaiians know a lot about Inouye today, his name and life should be studied and celebrated in all fifty states, by young and old Americans alike. Inouye is one of the greatest and most extraordinary Americans of the twentieth century—to learn about his life, to study his words, and, most of all, to emulate his patriotic zeal is to learn what authentic and meaningful American citizenship looks and sounds like.

But more than that, Inouye's life seems uniquely positioned to help remedy the paralyzing political and social ailments of our dysfunctional time—the brash political tribalism, the fashionable self-loathing of our nation and its institutions, the empty oratory of those who claim to love America but despise broad swathes of its population. Inouye's words are a tonic. His actions, an elixir. It is almost as if he lived his life in order to bestow a particular brand of civic wisdom to us, who are a mere decade removed from his passing.

Inouye died in 2012, and yet the echo of his extraordinary biography can act as a megaphone to awaken our heedless times. History is certainly not hagiography, but the story of Inouye's life and career can inspire the most hardened cynic, reminding us that great nations don't just accumulate power and prestige—they also produce great human beings.

This isn't hollow hyperbole or poetic exaggeration.

Neal Milner, a retired political scientist at the University of Hawaii, captured the essence of Inouye by noting that he possessed "an original

power and a kind of aura."[1] This "power" and "aura" were clearly witnessed by Joe Biden, who was Inouye's Senate colleague for decades,
prompting the future president to observe, "I never met a man with as
much loyalty to his country, to his family and to his friends."[2] Senator
Lloyd Weicker of Connecticut, a Republican who was no easy judge
of his fellow legislators, bluntly said, "There is no finer man in the
Senate."

One rarely encounters in modern political life a public servant with
such a potent sense of unapologetic faith in the nation. Inouye consistently argued that American idealism was a kind of boundless well of
inspiration for current and future generations to draw from, as each era's
citizens are tasked with inching the nation toward its animating ideal of
reaching a more perfect union.

We live in a time when people of all political persuasions have lost
faith in institutions. We don't even trust the fundamental building
blocks of society: family, church, community, and, of course, political
parties, which are trusted least of all. The conservative political thinker
Yuval Levin has powerfully argued that this is due to a fundamental
shift in how we view institutions. In the past, people viewed institutions
as engines of character formation. Now, we see institutions as providing services to us or as serving as platforms for our own agendas. If
they don't offer things that appeal to our narrow interests, we simply
don't join. Of course, some objections to institutions are serious—we
see corruption, oppression, and abuse. It can be very easy to assume the
identity of "not a joiner," exaggerating even minor differences to the level
of existential ones.

Inouye shows us a better way. He undeniably encountered corrupt
institutions as a Japanese American born in 1924. Instead of becoming
an iconoclast, he hardened his resolve to join some of the very institutions that blocked him because of who he was. Through his participation
in those imperfect institutions, his character strengthened and the institutions changed to accommodate him.

In the wake of the Watergate scandal, Inouye delivered a powerful speech to graduating high-school seniors, where he sternly remarked, "Please stop telling me that you and I—that our nation—is doomed to eternal damnation. That the malaise which has been with us this past year is proof of our limitations. If it is proof of our limitations, our willingness and ability to do something about it is no less proof of our vital strength as a free people. If America can regain faith in herself, we can embark on our third century tempered by our mistakes, but enthusiastic about our future."[3]

The genesis of Inouye's soaring sense of faith in the country was rooted not in the banal pomp and circumstance of national holidays or the artificial adornments often associated with the traditions of the US Senate. No, Inouye bled and suffered for his country as few others have, at a time when his fellow Japanese Americans were being summarily rounded up and placed in camps. But he never became disenchanted about the ideals of his country.

How much did this man love America?

He participated in some of the most dangerous and daring missions in World War II. He helped save a lost battalion of the Texas National Guard that had become trapped behind enemy lines, and he was almost killed but for a silver dollar he had placed in his breast pocket, which deflected an enemy bullet. Enough to dramatically lose his right arm just eleven days before the Germans surrendered. Enough to win the Distinguished Service Cross (which was eventually upgraded to the Congressional Medal of Honor by President Clinton), the Bronze Star, the Purple Heart with a cluster, as well as twelve other citations and medals. Enough to spend two years in a hospital recuperating so that he could go on to live a meaningful and productive life.

And productive it was.

He was the first Asian American to serve in the US House of Representatives, the first Japanese American to serve in the US Senate, the first person of color to deliver the keynote address at a national party convention. He was the highest-ranking Asian American public official in American history when he became the president pro tempore of the Senate in 2010.

In the beginning of his career in Congress, Inouye was thrilled to meet the Speaker of the House, the much-venerated Sam Rayburn. Inouye said, "It's a very great honor to meet the most famous, widely recognized member of the Congress." Rayburn was purported to have affectionately replied, "Don't worry, you'll soon be the second most widely recognized member in the Congress." Inouye asked, "How do you figure, Mr. Speaker?" Without missing a beat Rayburn explained, "We don't have too many one-armed, Japanese congressmen here."[4] When Inouye later took the oath of office and was told to raise his right hand, people in the gallery gasped when he raised his left hand instead, not realizing the colossal sacrifice he had made for his country.

Inouye deeply and passionately loved a country that didn't treat him particularly well at times. He befriended and loved fellow legislators who were from the opposite party. He never sought the spotlight, and yet when it found him, he always managed to elevate the possibilities of American statecraft. He exuded optimism when others embraced cynicism and modeled institutional fidelity when others eschewed traditional pride in being US senators. He was a Democrat, but in many ways he embodied the greatest conservative values.

History is littered with soldiers who embraced conflict as a path to glory and honor—Inouye simply wanted to fight to make sure he did all he could to defeat America's enemies.

History is also littered with self-aggrandizing and calculating politicians who view the political arena as a portal to power and distinction—Inouye believed the American Creed was the essence of justice and worked as a lawmaker for five decades, quietly, diligently, and patiently, to extend it to as many citizens as possible, especially those who had yet to experience its blessings.

George Eliot once observed that much of what is good and right in the world is the consequence of those "who lived faithfully a hidden life, and rest in unvisited tombs."

How tragic it would be, and what a colossal loss for well-meaning modern Americans struggling to find purpose in their civic lives, if Inouye's life were to stay "hidden." He has much to teach us.

Let's listen.

Lesson #1: A Patriot Is Not Blind

> But in the truest sense of the word, a patriot is not blind. He does not believe his country is perfect. A patriot has the courage to keep his eyes open even when the most painful events occur in his midst. He may cry out in distress—but if he closes his eyes to injustice, he is not a patriot—he is a coward.[5]
>
>   —Daniel Inouye, 1975

Historians in the future will note that in the early 2020s, Americans—especially the young—began to forcefully question traditional gestures of patriotism, such as reciting the Pledge of Allegiance or standing for the national anthem. These historians might even pinpoint events like the football player Colin Kaepernick's high-profile act of kneeling during an NFL preseason game; the combustible social upheaval that followed the shooting of Michael Brown in Ferguson, Missouri; or the murder of George Floyd by a Minneapolis police officer in late May 2020.

What seemed to unite these gestures of protest and grandiose grievance was a new and troubling notion that the American soul was not merely flawed and imperfect, not merely tarnished by the injustices of the moment or the wrongs echoing from the past, but that the American polity itself was now suddenly irredeemable and forever tainted.

Somehow, during these years, veneration of the nation's symbols (the flag) or participation in its customs (reciting the Pledge of Allegiance or singing the national anthem) was interpreted by some as tantamount to blind indifference to the flaws and frailties of the body politic. Young Americans made superficial denunciations of the nation and its founders, condemning any historical narrative that purported to unite the diverse social fabric of the nation.

Inouye died in 2012 so we can never know for certain what he would have made of these protests and acts of gleeful national prostration—the tearing down of statues and monuments en masse, the narratives advanced by the likes of the 1619 Project, or the cottage industry of critical race theorists and commentators.

But if anyone was hyperaware of the contradiction between the nation's soaring ideals and the biting reality of its bigotry, it was Inouye. And yet, his patriotism never wavered.

On the day of the Japanese attack on Pearl Harbor, a seventeen-year-old Daniel Inouye was dressing for church and listening to the radio when the broadcast suddenly stopped. The disc jockey began yelling that Pearl Harbor was being bombed by the Japanese.[6] Daniel and his father ran outside just as three Japanese planes unmistakably marked with red dots flew over their heads. Dark plumes of smoke and exploding shells erupted in the distance.[7] At the time, Daniel dreamed of becoming a doctor and volunteered as a Red Cross aide while in high school.

In the aftermath of the attacks, he went to the harbor to offer assistance and ended up treating so many victims that he didn't come home for five days.

Inouye was a proud American citizen and desperately wanted to serve in the American military. Instead, in March 1942, the United States military designated him, and any American of Japanese descent, to be 4-C: an "enemy alien."[8] Inouye was a nisei or second-generation Japanese American; like so many American immigrants, he had a foot in two different worlds. His family used chopsticks when eating Japanese food and forks and knives when dining on American cuisine. He learned Japanese before English but attended American schools.[9]

But never for a moment did he consider himself to be anything but a proud American. His banishment from service left him utterly devastated: "That really hit me. I considered myself patriotic, and to be told you could not put on the uniform, that was an insult."[10]

Inouye's response to this colossal slight was not to condemn his country or to recast it in the most damning terms possible but instead to sign a petition with thousands of others asking the government to let him serve. His response to injustice was not indignation and cynicism but insistence on the very ideal for which the nation now claimed to fight. And as is often the case in the story of America, righteousness eventually triumphed over myopia.

In early 1943, President Roosevelt issued an executive order honoring the petition's request for service. When issuing the order, Roosevelt made one of the most powerful statements about American identity in our entire national history, a quote Inouye could recite verbatim for the rest of his life: "Americanism is not and never has been a matter of race or color. Americanism is a matter of mind and heart."[11]

This spirit of ebullient "Americanism" was responsible for the formation of the famous 442nd Regimental Combat Team, a segregated unit made up of nisei from Hawaii and even men who had been in camps on the West Coast. This unit, also known as the "Go for Broke" unit, went on to become the most decorated fighting unit in the history of the US Army, receiving 9,400 Purple Hearts and 53 Distinguished Service Crosses (19 of which were eventually elevated into Congressional Medals of Honor). The regiment only had space for 4,500 soldiers, yet in the course of the war, 12,000 men served in the unit because the casualty rate was so high.[12]

In total, Inouye lived through six major campaigns, but not before losing his right arm in a daring raid that is the stuff of a Hollywood screenplay. In fact, Hollywood producers would probably reject such a screenplay on the grounds that it was utterly unrealistic, even cartoonish, in its depiction of the hero's battlefield exploits.

On April 21, 1945, Inouye participated in an attack on a German-occupied ridge near San Terenzo, Italy, that would become the defining event of his life.

Inouye and his fellow soldiers were on the left flank of the assault when they came under heavy fire from three German machine guns. Inouye was shot in his abdomen with the bullet exiting through his back, just missing his spine. Undeterred, he destroyed two of the machine guns with a flurry of grenades. Though profusely bleeding, he continued to press forward, making his way to the flank of the third machine gun. Right as he was about to throw another grenade—he had pulled the pin and cocked his right arm—a German soldier just ten feet in front of him fired a rifle grenade, all but tearing off the arm holding the grenade.

As Inouye later described it, his arm had been "shredded." This is when his bravery and dedication became the stuff of legend. He assumed the grenade he had almost thrown was now lying somewhere on the ground. When he began looking for it, he realized the grenade was miraculously still in his deadened right hand, which had become frozen in place with enough grip strength to prevent the grenade from being dropped. He quickly grabbed it with his left hand and threw it in the face of the German soldier who was trying to reload.

At this point, Inouye blacked out, and when he came to he found himself at the bottom of the hill. What he didn't know, and what his fellow soldiers later had to tell him, is that with his right stump and back bleeding, he had managed to pick up a tommy gun with his left hand and continued charging the third machine gun. He only stopped his advance toward a fourth gun post when he was shot in the right leg. A fellow soldier later remarked, "I couldn't believe what I saw, because you were a crazy man."[13]

This "crazy man" is not just an American hero. He is a guide for modern Americans who mistakenly believe patriotism is inappropriate, even misguided, in the face of imperfection. He understood, even as a young man, what is incomprehensible to many young Americans today: A nation does not have to be perfect to be worthy of veneration. Inouye wasn't waiting for the country to reach perfection before signing up to defend it. And he certainly did not believe that his ardent desire to defend America was somehow synonymous with blind indifference toward the transgressions of the past; defending his nation did not mean defending his nation's treatment of him and other Japanese Americans. Quite the opposite. As President Obama observed in his eulogy, Inouye was "a man who believed in America even when its government didn't necessarily believe in him."[14]

Inouye's inspired faith in America speaks to the utter uniqueness of our civic identity—America, unlike virtually any other nation in the history of human civilization, orients itself around a particular political truth and idea, a truth rooted in what is considered natural, eternal, and unchanging: natural law and universal precepts about the character of political justice.

The American ideal can outlive every generation, and even reach greater heights of genuine justice for all, but only if there are patriots acting to defend it. Inouye's father certainly captured this truth in the words he dramatically uttered to his son before dropping him off to war: "My father just looked straight ahead, and I looked straight ahead, and then he cleared his throat and said: 'America has been good to us. It has given me two jobs. It has given you and your sisters and your brothers education. We all love this country. Whatever you do, do not dishonor your country. Remember: Never dishonor your family. And if you must give your life, do so with honor.'"[15]

Inouye listened to his father. He defended his nation. And in the process, he modeled for all of us what it means to be a patriot who is not blind.

Lesson #2: Love the Institutions That Bind Us

What should concern us is something far more fundamental. The true dimension of the challenge facing us is loss of faith . . . I mean a loss of faith in our country, in its purposes, and in its institutions . . . If we cut down our institutions, public and private, and with indifference starve the systems which have given us our achievements, who will feed the hungry?[16]

—Daniel Inouye, 1968

It was one of the most touching moments in modern political history. A few days before Christmas 2012, in the midst of a crippling political impasse about tax increases and spending cuts that were set to take effect in just a few days, dozens of House and Senate members from both parties stood shoulder to shoulder to witness the first Asian American to ever lie in state in the Capitol Rotunda. Here, Inouye rested on a catafalque constructed for President Lincoln's memorial service in 1865.[17]

But the most poignant moment of the historic proceeding didn't involve a serving senator or congressman. It involved a man Inouye met more than six decades earlier in an army hospital in Michigan, a man who was also recovering from wounds incurred in battle, which would prevent him from using his right arm for the rest of his life—these two men were wounded "a day apart and a mile apart."[18] Advanced in age by the time Inouye passed away, Bob Dole used a wheelchair to get around. But on this day, he rejected such assistance saying, "I wouldn't want Danny to see me in a wheelchair."

Instead, Dole timidly walked up to the casket on his own, briefly touched it, and then saluted it with his left hand.

In this moment, the ineffable enormity of their friendship, patriotism, and mutual reverence for the US Senate submerged the inconsequential fact that they were on opposite sides of the political aisle for half a century. Dole had actually planted the seed of public service in Inouye's mind during their stay at the same hospital. As Inouye humorously noted, he "followed the Dole Plan" of running for Congress one day. And, in fact, he was actually elected before Dole.

Dole wasn't the only across-the-aisle friendship in Inouye's life. Inouye's best friend in the Senate was a different World War II vet who also happened to be a Republican: Senator Ted Stevens of Alaska. Stevens had been awarded the Yuan Hei Medal from the Republic of China for his service as a fighter pilot in the Army Air Corps.[19] When he became embroiled in a controversy late in his career about making false claims on a Senate disclosure form, Inouye made sure to attend the court hearings and even sent personal checks to help cover Stevens's mounting legal costs. Inouye was criticized by liberal activists at the time for his gestures of friendship for the man he called "brother."[20]

Stevens tried to explain their bond to a country that was increasingly baffled by their deep affection for each other: "The aisle between the two sides is now a canyon . . . And people on either side accuse me and Dan Inouye of being freaks because we're friends."[21]

The insoluble bond between Inouye and Stevens can only be seen as a motley union of "freaks" by those who do not comprehend the utter joy of attaching oneself, or even devoting one's entire life, to an institution that serves an ideal nobler than mere self-aggrandizement. It's hard to look at the modern Senate, and the broader Congress, and not conclude that the real work of changing the nation is done elsewhere, while Congress has descended into an extravaganza mirroring the hollow shenanigans of reality television, where shallow influencer-like politicians engage in dueling and unhinged one-upmanship, playing to and fundraising from an increasingly narrow subset of the public.

Even more broadly, cynicism abounds in the modern American soul these days about a variety of institutions that once served to improve the everyday lives of Americans. Citizens are skeptical about the efficacy and trustworthiness of a broad spectrum of once-trusted American institutions: law enforcement, organized religion, public education, medicine, business, and, of course, the media.

Inouye's life exemplifies the notion that we can revere and serve imperfect institutions. His devotion to the cause of the country took the form of intensive institutional love for the US Senate.

This devotion to the Senate informed and elevated his expectations of how a senator ought to behave, conferring a moral bond with his fellow senators, like Dole and Stevens, forever transcending the momentary transactions of party politics or the cheap triumph of ideologically pure isolation. This reverence for the institution he served is why Inouye was both operationally bipartisan and personally collegial. It explains why he was beloved in both chambers of the US Congress and by Republicans and Democrats alike. It highlights why he never needed to valorize his own résumé or seize the superficial imprimatur of trendy party polarization to get things done.

Inouye was unapologetic in his love of the Senate—not because of its once-soaring prestige, not because he was a member of what James Buchanan called "the world's greatest deliberative body," and certainly not because he wanted his place in the "millionaires club." He loved the Senate because its multivalent traditions quietly helped to preserve an august sense of gravity about the animating issues of the day. He was known as the keeper of Senate traditions, exercising a "taciturn authority" to marshal bipartisan attention to issues that deserved the weight of broad consensus born of genuine compromise. He believed debate should elevate a legislative institution, not debase it.

Thus, he never demagogued complex issues or threw rhetorical grenades at fellow senators across the aisle. The rostrum of the Senate is not a shrine or an altar, and yet it is democratically sacrosanct to men of Inouye's ilk for a simple reason: The institutional heartbeat of the Senate is responsible for pumping the national blood of the body politic—it acts as a forum for discerning the common good of the entire nation, transcending the raw and rowdy regionalism of popular sentiment given voice by the House of Representatives. The attainment of this common good requires leaders of a particular disposition—stately, dispossessed of ego, institutionally minded—leaders who know how to participate in the arduous but serious task of governing a country as large and diverse as ours.

The conservative columnist George Will cleverly explained Inouye's senatorial temperament by noting, "Some senators are closed books you have no desire to open; others are open books always reading themselves to you. Inouye is well worth reading, but, not being a self-advertiser, he is not as well-known as he should be."[22] The veteran journalist James Fallows labeled Inouye "A Genuine Hero" when he passed away and noted that Inouye's "dignified," "fair-minded," and "non-showboating" demeanor was a model he wished all members of the Senate would follow.[23]

Forty-three hours of tapes released from the LBJ Presidential Library in 2008 revealed that in 1968 President Johnson forcefully encouraged

the Democratic nominee, Hubert Humphrey, to pick Inouye as his running mate. Johnson remarked to Humphrey that Inouye had "cold, clear
courage" and he would appeal to minority voters because "he is one."[24]
But Inouye purportedly told Humphrey he wasn't interested in the job
for a simple reason: He wanted to spend his working life in the Senate.
Years later he explained: "I do not want to be Vice President of the United
States. I have never in my wildest dreams seen myself in that role, and I
don't see it now. What I'd like are two more terms in the Senate. Nothing
more."[25]

On occasion, the national spotlight did find Inouye, and in such
moments, he seemed not only to shine but to command broad respect
from the entire nation for the grace with which he performed his senatorial duties. Nothing exemplified this better than his participation in
the Watergate hearings. In an interview with *Parade* in late 1973, Inouye
related a story about the moment he knew his profile and standing were
different because of Watergate. A group of schoolchildren rushed up to
him when he was walking with Senator Ted Kennedy. "I stepped back,"
he explained, "because I knew from experience that everybody wants
Ted's autograph. But this time it was different. The kids didn't want his
autograph. They wanted mine. I knew then that Watergate had changed
my life."[26]

Five times Inouye turned down the Senate Watergate committee assignment, but because he was not particularly partisan and didn't harbor presidential ambitions, the Democratic leadership insisted he was
a perfect fit for the high-profile assignment. "I tried every way I knew
to get out of the assignment," he remembered. The nationally televised
hearings granted Inouye a level of national exposure that allowed him
to make a lasting and positive impression on the American people. His
evenhanded but firm questioning of John Dean, H. R. Haldeman, John
Ehrlichman, and John Mitchell won him accolades from the American
public. When the hearings concluded, Gallup measured Inouye's national favorable rating at a meteoric eighty-four percent.

When Inouye went to law school in Washington, DC, he would

sometimes go and watch the proceedings of the US Congress. Perhaps he had prophetic visions as a young man of what he could achieve as a member of the Senate. Maybe he felt a youthful surge of inspiration simply knowing he was sitting in the same building where men like Daniel Webster, Henry Clay, and John Quincy Adams worked to tilt the country toward a more perfect union. Maybe he simply knew there were wrongs to right and injustices to correct and this institution was the American republic's best hope to achieve it.

Whatever he imagined, as he sat in the galleys of Congress, Inouye probably could not have imagined he would spend half a century in the Senate representing the people of Hawaii, casting 16,300 votes in the process, eventually standing third in line to the presidency as president pro tempore of the Senate until the day of his death.

But none of it would have been possible without a form of secular faith in the institution he served, without wedding his industry and his idealism to an institution designed to serve the nation.

Lesson #3: Have Faith in the American Dream

Inouye delivered his maiden speech as a US senator on January 31, 1963. It immediately made a powerful impression:

> I understand the hopelessness that a man of unusual color or feature experiences in the face of constant human injustice. I understand the despair of a human heart crying for comfort to a world it cannot become a part of, and to a family of man that has disinherited him. For this reason, I have done and will continue to do all that one man can do to secure for these people the opportunity and the justice that they do not now have.[27]

For the next fifty years this "one man" made the American dream into a living reality for thousands of Americans whose hearts had intimately known injustice. As he reminded his fellow senators on the day of this speech, "I am a member of a minority, in a sense few Senators have ever been."

To distill a political career into a single soaring achievement is difficult and also a little unfair, especially for a public servant of Inouye's longevity and policy breadth. But anyone studying his life and achievements cannot help but be struck by his dogged and consistent mission of delivering justice for citizens who had been marginalized or mistreated by the United States.

Americans who celebrate the march of justice and are convinced the arc of American history bends toward justice for all, should remember that marches must be led and arcs must be bent by someone. If you are an Asian American who was interned, if you are a Filipino who helped the United States during World War II, if you are a Native American suffering from poverty, or if you are a native Hawaiian or Alaskan who felt left behind by American civil society, then you should know that one of the people leading the march and bending the arc for fifty years was Inouye.

Inouye's approach to expanding civil rights was grounded in a form of eloquent humility about the capacity of laws to transform society. While he was always an ardent supporter of civil rights, he understood that true bigotry would never be abolished through legal remedies and statutory solutions. Legislation could only go so far in helping America reach its goal of making the American dream available to all of its citizens. He explained his support for the 1964 Civil Rights Act by observing, "Laws cannot change the hearts of men, and we will not change the hearts of men by this law if indeed we enact it . . . The rest must be provided in the churches, in the schools and in the consciences of the people."[28]

If a nation has a voice, however, it is heard through its laws.

Time and time again Inouye proposed laws that sought to right the wrongs of the past. He was tenacious, determined, and ever-faithful that his nation would always serve the cause of justice. But it was rarely easy or fast. His fight for redress for Japanese Americans during World

War II was an arduous process that spanned twelve years and three separate presidencies.

When Japanese Americans were released from the camps, they were given a $25 train ticket and told to make their own way back home. For decades the consensus in the Japanese American community was to move on from President Roosevelt's Executive Order 9066 by proving to the American people through hard work and social contribution that their internment had been a dreadful mistake. But as the decades passed and the nation began to address civil rights issues related to African Americans and women, the time to discuss restitution in the form of an apology and compensation finally found momentum in the Japanese American community.

Inouye not only was instrumental in but also was politically savvy about the drive toward redress.

He recognized that the first step toward meaningful redress was not to make too many demands too fast. The first step was to educate the American people. Thus, he introduced a bill to create the Commission on Wartime Relocation and Internment of Civilians, which was signed into law by President Carter in 1980 and which received testimony about life in the camps from almost eight hundred witnesses. In June 1983 the commission recommended that the president and Congress formally apologize and offer monetary compensation of $20,000 for each living internee. House and Senate bills embracing these recommendations were offered in 1983 and again in 1985 to no avail.

But Inouye persisted.

Finally, on September 17, 1987, on the two hundredth birthday of the US Constitution, the House passed a bill adopting the recommendations of the commission with the Senate passing its own version a few months later. In August 1988, President Reagan signed the Civil Liberties Act of 1988 and formally apologized on behalf of the United States, stating, "Yet we must recognize that the internment of Japanese-Americans was just that: a mistake. For throughout the war, Japanese-Americans in the tens of thousands remained utterly loyal to the United States."[29]

Inouye was far from done.

In 1986, he assumed the chairmanship of the Senate Select Committee on Indian Affairs. He ended up on the committee by accident. As a member of the steering committee that made committee assignments, he had trouble finding anyone to do it. But as the years wore on and he learned the full extent of injustice toward Native populations, he commented, "By God, did we do all these things? We should be embarrassed and ashamed of ourselves."[30]

He resolved to do something about it.

In the previous decade, Native American poverty had skyrocketed from twenty-six to thirty-nine percent. In response, Inouye introduced the landmark Indian Gaming Regulatory Act in the hopes of empowering Native Americans to have more economic agency. The law stipulated that gaming businesses be owned by tribal governments and the revenue be invested in the general welfare of the community in which the facility operated.[31]

In 1994, the Tribal Self-Governance Act took the colossal step of recognizing tribes as independent and separate nations, which enabled them to create and implement their own programs and services.[32] The most high-profile contribution was Inouye's sponsorship of a law that culminated in the opening of the National Museum of the American Indian in 2004 as a part of the Smithsonian in Washington, DC. His commitment to Native Americans was so authentic and intense that when he had the opportunity in 1998 to become a ranking member of the prestigious Senate Committee on Rules and Administration, he declined so he could focus on Native American affairs.

He worked to give citizenship to Filipinos who had fought to defend the United States during World War II. He fought to broaden the definition of a Native American to include Hawaiians and Alaskans so that they may be eligible for federal funds. He supported statehood for the District of Columbia.

Inouye's work on behalf of the marginalized and mistreated bolsters the notion that the American dream doesn't belong to only some citizens, it belongs to all citizens. Thus, democracy is more than merely taking a vote and giving the majority what it wants. He eloquently put his finger on this deeper, richer, and more meaningful pulse of democracy when he observed that there is a "strange, strange power that occasionally appears in the American soul in times of struggle and strife."[33]

This "strange, strange power" is rooted in a particular recognition about American politics, that in times of struggle and strife Americans often rise to the occasion because deep down, below the banal substrata of daily headlines and faux outrage, most Americans sense that their place in the torrent of history is an anomaly—for it is oppression not liberation, poverty not material abundance, upheaval not harmony, that are the more dominant realities of human history.

And this is Inouye's life lesson to us: If the American dream belongs to all citizens, the responsibility of making it truly possible falls on all of us. We can consciously choose to be joiners, not isolated perfectionists. We can join a club, even—especially—if it's not filled with people just like us. Take the initiative to meet your standoffish neighbors. Run for the school board. While most of us can't write laws and right historic wrongs, we can volunteer in our communities and churches. Church attendance isn't about having a spiritual revelation every week. It's about being in community with a group of people who are also imperfectly striving toward improvement. You might just get better by being reminded of the eternal once a week. You might just step in to fill a need for the masses of lonely Americans around you. There are churches, community groups, and political institutions in your city that are lessened by the absence of so many talented people who have decided it's not a worthwhile use of their time.

How we use our time and money and conversation can be ways of making a choice to "join" society. We can donate to righteous causes whose mission is to improve the lives of those who are struggling. We can talk to our children about history and civics and American idealism. We can broaden our awareness of the deep disadvantages suffered by many Americans whose lives often seem powered by hardened cycles of familial and cultural decay instead of the highest notions of personal empowerment.

Inouye was that rarest of Americans who didn't require a war, a pandemic, or an economic downturn to feel the "strange power" of America, to use this power to buck the trendlines of history and deliver the possibility of the American dream to his fellow citizens. Thus, he was part Homeric hero, part Roman senator, and wholly a loyal America with a talent for meaningful citizenship rarely encountered in our troubled times. It is a tragedy that he is not universally known and celebrated by the country he helped to save and renew. But even more tragic is that we are forgetting the wisdom his life can teach us.

Inouye's last word on his deathbed was "Aloha."[34] In Hawaii, the word can be used as both a greeting and a farewell. While Inouye was bidding farewell to his life, we Americans should embrace the other meaning of the word and familiarize ourselves with the life and legacy of this extraordinary American.

CHAPTER 3

Clara Barton

It's Not Someone Else's Problem

Clara Barton began her life as a Christmas present to her parents and ended it as an American icon.

Nothing in her background suggested she was fated for anything other than an ordinary life. Born on December 25, 1821, her four siblings were all much older. Raised in a modest household, what Barton called a "small environment," by an affectionate father and emotionally distant mother, by the time she reached the age of forty she was known to no one beyond her immediate orbit of family, friends, and school colleagues. As she entered middle age, no one would have described her as a beauty, a savant, or a saint.

And yet, there was a voice within her that never flagged or failed, wavered or waffled. It was an inner whisper that cannot be taught or acquired by superficial means. It is a voice that often occupies the visionary, the driven, and the inspired. It is the voice within us that sometimes whispers "I matter" in moments of agonizing doubt, the voice that sometimes cries out "By God I will not give up!" in moments of audacious resolve. It is the voice that can be colored by Muses and lifted by memory.

Two decisive questions must be answered when trying to grasp the lessons of Barton's life: Where did this voice come from, and how did she use it?

In much the same way that the founders discovered inspiration in the heroes of Plutarch's *Lives*, Barton's inner voice came alive in early encounters with inspiring stories. Her childhood seemed to both prepare and inspire her for patriotic greatness. Her father, Stephen Barton, was a captain in the Indian Wars and spent many evenings by the fire as a paternal raconteur, regaling young Clara with stories of service and sacrifice. She reveled in family lore about a much earlier Barton generation taking part in the famed English Wars of the Roses. Later in life, Clara could remember the stirring words of her father who taught her that "next to Heaven, our highest duty was to love and serve our country and honor and support its laws."[1]

What makes Barton both fascinating to study and an exemplar for modern Americans to emulate is her absolute refusal to bow to convention or engage in obsequious reverence for pallid customs or archaic traditions. If her father inspired the anchoring of a determined inner voice, what that voice actually said was utterly clear. If ever there was an animating creed or personal canon in her mind, it was perfectly stated in the book Barton penned late life, *The Story of My Childhood*: "I have an almost complete disregard of precedent, and a faith in the possibility of something better. It irritates me to be told how things have always been done. I defy the tyranny of precedent. I go for anything new that might improve the past."

Defying this "tyranny of precedent" informed her early and forward-thinking views on women's rights and her hearty embrace of abolitionism. It fortified her belief that a high-quality education is a right that ought to be enjoyed by all Americans, no matter their position in society. This spirit of optimistic defiance pushed her to lobby endlessly for nurses to travel to the front lines of bloody Civil War battles in order to better provide care for the wounded and comfort dying soldiers. It inspired her to challenge the rigid gender hierarchies of her time and to force men to reevaluate the potential of women to contribute to a richer cross-section of American civil society. This American faith in the perpetual potential for progress even positioned her to challenge some of the most long-standing and sacred doctrines of American foreign policy—chiefly, that the United States doesn't join international organizations.

Again and again, Barton exhibited a soaring, even Olympian sense that her efforts were on the right side of progress—not just an arbitrary, amorphous, highly subjective sense of progress as movement without aim, but a thoroughly American spirit of progress shaped by an unremitting devotion to human dignity, human liberty, and human equality.

We should find inspiration in the life of Barton not simply because of her extraordinary achievements but because these feats were carried out by a human being with no pretense of being anything other than deeply flawed, subject to daily drama and disappointment. For those of us who struggle to triumph over our frailties and mend our flaws—*all of us!*—Barton's life story is more crooked twig than upright oak.

She was often depressed and listless as she searched for new projects and probed for new paths to pursue. She was no titan of superhuman strength as she fell ill for long periods of time. Buried beneath the headlines about revolutionizing nursing and bringing the Red Cross to America is a woman who was often egotistical and dogmatic, rapacious for the spotlight, and so stubborn it actually triggered a congressional investigation into her running of the American Red Cross. She carried out an affair with a married man in the midst of the Civil War, doing little to hide the illicit behavior as the couple took refuge from the carnage of the war by reciting the poetry of Elizabeth Barrett Browning together at night.

As her biographer Cathy East Dubowski powerfully observed, "Clara Barton was one of the great women of American history. She was not a saint, but a flesh and blood woman with strengths and weaknesses, convictions and insecurities. Yet it was her shortcomings as well as her special talents that made her the unique person that she was."[2]

Many of us have the same voice inside of us that spoke to Barton throughout her life. But most of us choose to ignore it. We convince ourselves that the problems of the world are too big and we are too small. The problems are too complicated and our capacities too meager. We assume "someone else" will confront the gathering storms of our particular moment in history. Or maybe, if we are being honest, we simply want our lives to be pleasant and comfortable. We yearn for the carefree luxury modernity has reliably granted us, hoping to avoid the heartbreaks and hassles befalling the likes of Barton.

However, while George Washington and Daniel Inouye showed us heroism in more traditional venues—in uniform and in civil service— Barton shows us that heroism is possible in every sphere of life. She found agency where no one believed it was possible. She always took ownership of the problems that landed in her way. She didn't stop to consider whether it was appropriate for a five-foot-tall woman to face violence, peril, ugliness, and personal confrontation with men in positions of authority. She just saw problems that needed fixing, and she would not back down.

Lesson #1: If You See a Problem, Be the Solution

It was a family tragedy from her childhood that presented Barton with the greatest joy of her adult life: the deep and soulful satisfaction of being needed by others. From a young age, she yearned to serve others, especially the vulnerable and the suffering, discovering one of the great-est nourishments of the human soul.

To modern Americans, the life of Barton can appear more than merely foreign—to be blunt: It is off-putting. In our era of narcissism and luxury, of easy prosperity and moral indifference, a life spent in constant pursuit of solving problems and righting wrongs can have a dizzying effect. For Barton, the endless pursuit of humanitarian virtue was not just a way to pass the time; it was a way of existing in the world, a way of answering the basic existential question we all must confront if we are to experience any hope of authentic human joy: What ought we to do with the finite time allotted to each of us?

The answer to this question didn't fall out of the sky, but for Barton, it did involve a fall that was almost fatal. In the summer of 1832, her family was in the process of building a barn. Clara's brother David was standing on top of the barn when he fell and hit the ground feetfirst. Within a few days he developed debilitating headaches and a fever. Thus began a two-year ordeal in which eleven-year-old Clara slowly and pains-takingly nursed her brother back to health.

For modern Americans raising eleven- and twelve-year-old children, struggling to get them to read a book or clean their rooms, the notion of a preteen spending almost every waking moment for two years inten-sively nursing a relative back to health is awe-inspiring. What it required of her was much more than making soup or walking her brother to the bathroom. During this period, it was commonly believed that applying black leeches to the veins of patients was a panacea that could somehow remove the excessive "bad blood" that was responsible for making the patient ill.

As one can imagine, the leeches were terrifying to young Clara. But her unflinching love and loyalty to her brother eclipsed the potency of her terror. She remembered, "My little hands became schooled to the handling of the great, loathsome crawling leeches which were at first so many snakes to me . . . and thus it came about, that I was the accepted and acknowledged nurse of a man almost too ill to recover."[3]

Leeching, of course, was a false medicine, worsening David's condition. But in the meantime, he came to rely almost exclusively on his little sister. Eventually, the leeches were replaced with a new and more effective treatment and David completely recovered. By nursing her brother back to the land of the healthy—slowly, if not glacially—Clara experienced the birth pangs of a form of joy that would define the rest of her life: the unfettered ecstasy of easing the suffering of her fellow human being.

This particular form of joy—being of genuine service to the agonized and the wounded—was the genesis of perhaps her most humane and enduring contribution: revolutionizing the way soldiers are cared for in the midst of battle. The same spirit that nursed her brother back to health when she was a child was reborn during the American Civil War.

Barton's central insight about the Civil War had nothing to do with troop movements, grand strategies, or advances in weaponry. Her revolutionary insight was that medical care for injured soldiers could be infinitely improved if they were treated where they lay wounded. Too often, soldiers were incapacitated and languished for days on end waiting for water, food, and removal from the front lines. The military hired people to take water and brandy to wounded soldiers, but these same people usually got lost and ended up drinking the brandy themselves.[4]

Thousands of soldiers died waiting for assistance. In fact, in the early days of the Civil War, the War Department was more interested in supplying weapons and ammunition than providing clean water and ample medical supplies. Surgical equipment was filthy, vermin teemed in the camps, and more soldiers died of illness and infection than barrages of enemy gunfire. Barton correctly wagered that giving medical assistance, food, and water to wounded soldiers soon after a battle concluded would bolster their chances of survival.

But there was a deep and cavernous problem: Absolutely nobody in the early days of the war believed battlefields and front lines—theaters of infinite gore, twisted and bloodied human tissue, and grotesque amputations—were appropriate places for women to contribute to the cause, even as nurses.

Barton changed this prevailing, almost universal bias.

Her first instinct was to solve the problem herself. She adeptly organized women's groups from New Jersey and Massachusetts to help provide many of the supplies, such as bandages, food, and clothing, that were woefully underprioritized by the War Department. Throughout the war she continued to solicit supplies and paid for so much of them out of her own pocket that after the war Congress reimbursed her. She eventually raised three warehouses chock-full of supplies.

But the highest hurdle in her quest to transform the medical care of wounded soldiers was the deep and abiding bias against women traveling to and serving on the front lines. Women, it was believed, were ill-equipped for the unspeakable horrors of war. The idea that women, who during this era rarely went unescorted in public, would be welcomed to the closest thing to Hell on Earth stood in the face of virtually every cultural gender norm of the time.

To reverse this deeply ingrained prejudice, Barton exercised a significant degree of grit and even cleverness. She wrote to the War Department for passes to the front. She begged her political allies for help. She asked her well-connected friends for assistance. Again and again, she failed to change the appropriate minds. In February 1862, she went home to visit her ailing father who lovingly sanctioned her aspiration of serving on the front lines, despite the disapproval it was sure to elicit from most quarters of polite society.

After her father's death, she doubled her efforts. She wrote to the Massachusetts governor John A. Andrew who found her cause compelling. He agreed to help her. Despite more roadblocks she eventually won a meeting with the quartermaster Colonel H. Rucker. The decisive meeting took place in the maelstrom of Rucker's wartime office, which was inundated with soldiers and their family members airing grievances or asking for favors. When Rucker finally spoke to Barton, she was so overcome by an attack of anxiety that tears started to stream down her face. Rucker was unmoved by the tears but once she solemnly revealed the deep reserve of supplies she had painstakingly accumulated, he suddenly changed his tune, immediately granting her the permission she had long sought.

She quickly earned the moniker of "Angel of the Battlefield" after the Battle of Cedar Mountain when she arrived at a struggling field hospital in the middle of the night with a four-mule team carrying fresh supplies. After the Second Battle of Bull Run, she calmed a raving soldier who had been shot through the abdomen and was hysterical and hallucinating, yelling at his imagined sister, "Mary, don't let me die here alone . . ." Barton kissed his head, pulled the soldier onto her lap, and pacified his delirium. The next morning, she convinced the surgeon to allow the boy to go home where he had two days with his mother and sister before dying of his wounds.[5]

The Battle of Antietam, known as the bloodiest single day in American history, left roughly twenty-three thousand Americans killed or wounded. It was fought at close range, with the armies a mere hundred yards or less from each other. Barton traveled all night to get there, ordering her supply wagons to pull ahead of military medical units, prompting one of the field surgeons to exclaim, "God indeed has remembered us! How did you get here so soon?"

As the battle ravaged both sides, Barton stood firm, working without respite as the clouds of menacing smoke gathered around her. Her close proximity to the battle facilitated frequent brushes with death. A thirsty soldier lying on the ground asked Barton for water. Just as she bent down a Confederate bullet ripped through her sleeve and instantly killed the soldier she was attempting to help. She gruesomely remembered, "He fell back dead. There was no more to be done for him and I left him to rest. I have never mended that hole in my sleeve."

Her heroics at Antietam didn't end there. A soldier with a bullet lodged deep his cheekbone pleaded with Barton to "take the ball out for me." Armed with only a pocket knife and a deep reservoir of gumption, she performed an extemporaneous surgery, removing "the ball" and winning the eternal gratitude of the soldier.

Antietam stopped Robert E. Lee's assault on Northern territory, denied the South any support from European nations, and in the process helped to turn the tide of the war toward the cause of the Union. It is no coincidence that just a few days later, President Lincoln issued a preliminary version of the Emancipation Proclamation.

Barton's reputation and fame grew as the war progressed. Her contributions continued at the Battle of Fredericksburg and she lamented her absence at Gettysburg. Years later, when her casket was being carried from Maryland to Massachusetts, the wagon driver was rendered utterly agog when he learned whose body he was transporting. "My God, is this the body of Clara Barton?" he cried. During the war the driver's father had been shot in the neck and was bleeding to death. "Miss Barton found him on the battlefield and bound up his wounds in time to save his life."[6]

How many lives were spared because of Barton's dogged determination to look trial and tribulation square in the face? How many children were able to be raised by their fathers? How many spouses enjoyed additional decades of matrimony? Such is the immeasurable impact she had on the lives of her countrymen because she insisted on being a part of the solution to the problems she encountered.

Lesson #2: Never Stop Searching for New Challenges

Barton's achievements may give the faulty impression that she had nerves of steel and a powerful charisma from a young age. The opposite is true. What she did have, however, was a strong distaste for apathy and complacency, from her youth all the way through her life.

Legions of middle-aged Americans can attest to the nagging parade of reminders that our best days are probably behind us—the tyranny of aching joints, the wealth of sprouting gray hairs, the sinister slowing of one's metabolism to a trickle, and, most of all, the death of one's parents.

We come to intimately know the meaning of the words "finitude" and "mortality." We learn to accept the sprawling chasm dividing our actual lives from the lives we dreamed of when we were younger. Such acceptance can become a poisonous complacency. The obvious markers of midlife discontent can easily become middle-age minefields, filled with unfulfilled ambitions, stagnant relationships, and decaying bodies, what the Bible describes as "the plague that ravages at noon." Or, as the MIT philosophy professor Kieran Setiya describes the issue in *Midlife: A Philosophical Guide*, "stalled career, fading youth, and listless marriage."[7] In the midst of life's disappointments, the prospect of fresh challenges and new hurdles just seems too overwhelming.

Which is why one is struck when studying the extraordinary life of Barton just how frequently she sought new challenges, how immune she was to the soft seductions of comfort and the congenial banalities of routine. The sharp twists and rapid turns of her life were no accident, however. She never allowed herself to stay in one place or profession for too long, never afforded herself the steady exhilaration of a single love or profession or cause. If we are awed by the magnitude of her achievements, it is only because we live in a time brimming with an excess of device scrolling, television gazing, and sporting obsession.

Before she was even eighteen years old, Barton began her career as a teacher. But there was a problem. At this point in her life, she did not exude the towering forces of grit and determination that would come to define her in later years. In fact, she was painfully shy, so timid that her own mother worried that her shyness was getting worse as she aged. When she entered a one-room schoolhouse she encountered forty sets of curious eyes, some of whom had a reputation for wicked shenanigans, having mistreated the previous term's teacher by locking her out and taking over the school.[8]

She refused to be intimidated by her male students, participating in sports with them during recess, drawing on the athletic prowess to run, throw, or ride a horse that her brothers had instilled in her from a young age—"My four lads soon perceived that I was no stranger to their sports or tricks." She came to have a powerful reputation for discipline and also for imbuing a love of learning in her students. For most of her twenties, she taught at a variety of schools in her hometown of Oxford, focusing on solving specific problems at different schools.

But as she approached thirty, she was ready for a new challenge. She wanted to further her education and decided to enroll in one of the few coeducational facilities of the time, the Clinton Liberal Institute, where she tackled her studies with aplomb and devotion, gaining academic depth in the subjects of mathematics, history, and philosophy. Sadly, after only three terms, she ran out of money and had to return home.

Soon after, on a visit to Bordentown, New Jersey, she stumbled upon a group of young boys walking down the street in the middle of the day. She asked why they were not in school and one of them replied, "Lady, there is no school for us. We would be glad to go if there was one." In that moment Barton's newest challenge began to take shape.

She had always been bothered by the inherent inequality of a "subscription school" system in which families had to pay for the education of their children. Barton's conviction that education ought to be free and universal was a founding and animating principle of her home state of Massachusetts. When John Adams drafted the Massachusetts Constitution in 1780 there were provisions for universal education as a right and in 1789 Massachusetts became the first state to pass a comprehensive education law.[9]

The people of New Jersey were not as enthusiastic. Barton didn't care.

Her inner conviction that she was right and majority sentiment was wrong, coupled with her hyperkinetic verve to convince the appropriate people and institutions that her vision should come to fruition, emboldened her to realize her aspiration. She offered her teaching services for free at the school she was proposing to open. Having taught students from all walks of life and with different intellectual capacities and interests, she was thoroughly convinced that education was a universal balm for both individual citizens and democratic society writ large. After winning the approval of the chairman of the local school committee and the editor of the local newspaper (which, conveniently, happened to be the same person), she was now authorized to open the first public school in New Jersey.

Her school was everything she had hoped it would be. She quickly grew it from the six students who showed up on the first day to more than two hundred, with hundreds more requesting her services. She hired additional teachers. She broadened the curriculum. She gained a degree of fame and recognition from the community. She won more funding to open new schools.

But there was a problem that would eventually clash with Barton's uncompromising and at the time avant-garde belief that professions should not be defined by gender stereotypes. When the new school opened, Barton was passed over for the principalship. The norms and expectations of the time dictated that a large institution required an administrative capacity that was thought to be reserved for men. Barton would be relegated to "female assistant" and given half the pay of the male principal.[10]

Things quickly fell apart. She didn't work well with the new principal and didn't agree with his policies. Staff members began taking sides. And in a pattern that would repeat itself throughout her life, the stress and unhappiness began to adversely affect her health. She lost too much weight. She lost her voice.[11] Finally, she resigned from the school she had founded.

The next decade would become the most eventful of her life. She found a job working in the US Patent Office, which she later lost for partisan reasons but eventually reacquired. When the Civil War broke out, she began her campaign to transform medical care on the front lines. After the war was over, she embarked on a new challenge that would have shocked her younger self: She became a much-celebrated and sought-after public speaker. As she noted, "I would rather stand behind the lines of artillery at Antietam, or cross the pontoon bridge under fire at Fredericksburg, than to be expected to preside at a public meeting."

Yet for two years she embraced the new challenge of bringing the story of the war to eclectic and eager audiences. She used her platform to electrify her fellow Americans all over the Northeast and Midwest. Audiences were mesmerized by her authentic and sometimes gruesome accounts of what it was like to be a nurse during the Civil War. She often "thrilled crowds with stirring descriptions of charge and retreat and intimate portraits of dying soldiers whispering last thoughts of mother or sweetheart."[12] Some writers and orators have an almost divine capacity to pluck the perfect word or craft the perfect phrase out of the abundant corpus of the English language—Barton was no Shakespeare or Keats, but she could certainly turn a phrase with vigor and dexterity. Decades later, when speaking to veterans on behalf of the candidacy of James A. Garfield, she quipped, "defend by your votes what you saved by your arms."[13]

Nineteenth-century Americans considered lectures, speeches, and orations to be necessary prerequisites of a rich civic and democratic life. They were also sources of vibrant entertainment. Famous orators in lyceums, churches, and lecture halls were the celebrities of their time and worked hard to cultivate larger-than-life personas.[14] The long speeches of Daniel Webster in the well of the Senate or the famed Lincoln-Douglas debates captured the imagination of the broader public. It was within this cultural milieu that Barton made a name for herself on the speaker's circuit of nineteenth-century America.

Thus, her time as a popular public speaker not only educated and enthralled the public; it gave her a measure of personal wealth that would last for the rest of her life. She sometimes made $100 a night and spoke up to fourteen times a month.[15] It also positioned her to make important political and social connections. During this time, she came into contact with both Elizabeth Cady Stanton and Susan B. Anthony, who helped to publicize her speeches. In return Barton became more vocal in her support on behalf of women's suffrage.

Embracing new challenges is not just about keeping boredom at bay. It is a form of faith that there are rich and meaningful layers of potentiality within us all that will remain forever dormant if we don't occasionally tilt our minds or position our bodies in new and adventuresome ways. Barton started life as a timid young woman, often ignored by her mother and underestimated by those around her. But instead of settling for a life of safe redundancy and familiar horizons, she intentionally oriented herself toward the squalls and the tempests, discovering new capacities and palatial talents she didn't know were there.

Which prompts a defining question: What untapped treasures lie within us, and do we have the courage to find them?

Lesson #3: Want Happiness? Be Useful to Others

In early 2022, Gallup released a series of alarming findings about the level of American happiness and contentment.[16] The findings were consistent with the disquieting sense that Americans are not a particularly happy people these days, that a nation founded by a propositional commitment to use individual agency in pursuit of personal happiness had become infected by an expansive and deflating pessimism, reflecting declining confidence in the nation, its institutions, and its moral compass. A significant segment of the population—thirty percent—claimed to be broadly dissatisfied with the overall quality of their lives.

Just two decades earlier, in 2001, that number was a paltry ten percent.

In other words, within two decades, American unhappiness has exponentially skyrocketed despite living through profound technological innovation, a booming stock market, and relative peace. There were recessions but not depressions, wars but not world wars. Freedom has never been more robust and widely available, legal equality less abstract and more real. It would not be hyperbole to suggest we are living through an epochal paradox: At the apogee of civilization's achievements, we are, for various reasons, at the nadir of personal well-being. Instead of basking in the radiance of American abundance and success, we seem paralyzed by a lack of real meaning and higher purpose in our lives.

Modern Americans would be wise to remember that the stretches of Barton's life where she battled unhappiness and sadness were the times when she did not know how to be useful, calling to mind one of the central insights about human happiness articulated by C. S. Lewis: "I'm not sure God wants us to be happy. I think he wants us to love, and be loved. But we are like children, thinking our toys will make us happy and the whole world is our nursery. Something must drive us out of that nursery and into the lives of others, and that something is suffering."

Barton had a prodigious capacity to empathize with the suffering of others—the physical suffering of her older brother when he was ill or the torment suffered by abandoned soldiers on Civil War battlefields. But she was also deeply attuned to the emotional suffering of others; what drove her "out of that nursery and into the lives of others" was a desire to assuage a unique form of suffering—the suffering endured by those whose loved ones had simply vanished without a trace during the long conflict between the North and the South.

To lose a child, a spouse, or a close sibling is perhaps the deepest and most penetrating torment that can ever pinch our souls. But as Barton discovered, there is, perhaps, something even worse: the abyss of ignorance that haunts those whose loved ones simply disappeared—no notice of death from the War Department, no letter from a fellow soldier, no testimony from a commanding officer. Nothing. Just eternal silence and perennial absence. Tens of thousands of men simply disappeared or were buried in unmarked graves. The viciousness of this particular genus of suffering is the stuff of a Greek or Shakespearean tragedy or a Russian novel. It besieges those whom it ensnares.

There was no official record or method of keeping track of missing soldiers. With the explicit assistance of President Lincoln, who released a letter supporting her project of finding the lost soldiers of the Civil War, Barton established the Bureau of Records of Missing Men of the Armies of the United States, a kind of "clearinghouse for information."[17]

Her plan was both audacious and somewhat convoluted. When she received letters from the public, she "placed the missing soldier's name on a master list, which was subdivided by state. She decided that she would periodically publish the list in newspapers, display them in post offices, and circulate them through organizations such as the Masons. She would then ask the veterans to check the lists for any name about which they had knowledge and to send that information to her."[18] Between 1865 and 1869, she received more than sixty-nine thousand letters and was able to identify more than twenty-two thousand missing soldiers.[19]

An interesting twist in the course of this enterprise occurred when Barton was occasionally contacted by lost soldiers who did not wish to be found. Many wanted to remain missing because they were deserters or had found a "Southern sweetheart," or simply wanted to use the war as a pretext for beginning their lives anonymously anew.[20] In response to a missing solider who had written to her complaining of appearing on one of her lists, she tartly replied by writing, "It seems to have been the misfortune of your family to think more of you than you did of them, and probably more than you deserve from the manner in which you treat them."

An extraordinary development emerged as Barton continued her work. She received a letter from a former soldier named Dorence Atwater who wrote to tell her about Andersonville, a Confederate prison in Georgia where he had been a prisoner for twenty-two months. The conditions were nothing less than subhuman—twenty-five thousand men kept in an exposed enclosure with little water, minimal food, raging disease, and widespread sickness. He had been assigned to the hospital and told to keep track of the name, rank, and cause of death for each fatality at the prison. Once deaths began surpassing seven hundred a week, he decided to make a duplicate list for fear the Confederate authorities would hide the evidence of their atrocities.

Atwater's list ultimately contained a staggering fourteen thousand names. When the secretary of war Edwin Stanton discovered the existence of the prison, he dispatched a party to Georgia, including Barton, to investigate Atwater's claims so that the graves could be properly marked. In the course of his work, Atwater revealed that the graves were not designated by the soldier's name but by impersonal sticks with numbers written on them. Fortunately, his list could help identify the names of the men buried in the unmarked graves.

The aim of Barton's journey to Andersonville was not merely to appropriately bury the dead but to transform a mass graveyard into a new national cemetery. Headboards were made, walkways constructed, and, most important of all, almost thirteen thousand lost soldiers were finally given a respectful burial with correctly marked gravestones.[21] The work was relatively straightforward, though Barton continually and bitterly quarreled with an army officer who was also part of the expedition.

Despite the success of bringing emotional closure to thousands of families, Barton continued to empathize with and reflect on the families of the four hundred soldiers who were never correctly identified, tragically buried with only "Unknown US Soldier" chiseled on their headstones. The memory of loved ones killed in battle is transformed over time—the death of a soldier becomes stitched into the history of a nation, perpetually linked to the cause for which the life was given. Sacrifice echoes through the ages as posterity is blessed with the perspective of knowing how a soldier's death altered the character of the nation, how the single dot of a soldier's sacrifice changed the color and content of the national canvas. Barton was haunted by the cruelty of these anonymous graves, knowing not just that they died, not just that their families would suffer for the rest of their lives, but that these men would remain forever anonymous in the recollection of the nation.

Her capacity as an empathetic wordsmith inspired her to compose a poem on behalf of the mothers and sisters who would never know what fate had befallen their loved one:

Well Mothers I am here—here with your darling ones
Before me lie the narrow graves that hold your martyred sons
And sisters pale with weeping close clasp one another
Here lies the tribute wreath I've turned for that lost and noble
        brother

As a measure of Barton's contribution to the creation of the new cemetery, she was chosen to raise the American flag that would fly over the thousands of American graves. From Pericles delivering his funeral oration in the midst of the Peloponnesian War to Lincoln's eloquence at Gettysburg, a nation's treatment of the fallen is not just a testament to sacrifice but a declaration of what political principles a nation wishes to celebrate and perpetuate.

Barton's zeal to give names to unmarked graves and answers to brokenhearted families is a powerful reminder that happiness must be earned. Petty amusement and forgettable fun certainly have their rightful place in life, but genuine happiness is harder to achieve. That is what Barton has to teach us.

Modern Americans who wallow in their malaise or bemoan their station in life should study Barton's path to happiness and fulfillment. Happiness is more than a state of mind. It is more than wealth or possessions. It is a by-product of using one's individual liberty to connect to people, places, and causes bigger than oneself. As Barton wrote in her diary on the night of the cemetery's dedication, "Up and there it drooped as if in grief and sadness, till at length the sunlight streamed out and its beautiful folds filled—the men struck up the Star-Spangled Banner and I covered my face and wept."

CHAPTER 4

Thomas Jefferson

Don't Specialize, Be a Generalist

★

★

You know you have lived a life of towering significance when you write your own gravestone by cataloging your three greatest achievements and being a two-term American president fails to make the cut.

At the end of his life as he was signing his final will, Thomas Jefferson took the time to design his gravestone and write the epitaph that was to be engraved on it. As he explained, "On the faces of the Obelisk the following inscription, & not a word more." Unfortunately, the original granite obelisk became an object of temptation to Monticello sightseers who pocketed small chips of it as souvenirs. In 1882, Congress funded a replacement headstone featuring all capital letters, perfectly centered on twelve lines of granite, thunderous in its enumeration:

HERE WAS BURIED

THOMAS JEFFERSON

AUTHOR OF THE

DECLARATION

OF

AMERICAN INDEPENDENCE

OF THE

STATUTE OF VIRGINIA

FOR

RELIGIOUS FREEDOM

AND FATHER OF THE

UNIVERSITY OF VIRGINIA[1]

He explained that by the triad of achievements listed "as testimonials that I have lived, I wish most to be remembered."[2]

It is no surprise that visitors to Monticello wanted their own Jeffersonian talisman. Almost every prominent American politician, no matter their political affiliation or epoch, has claimed the imprimatur of Jefferson for their own personal aims and political agendas, from Andrew Jackson and Abraham Lincoln to Franklin Roosevelt and Barack Obama. And that is because Jefferson is perhaps the most eclectically accomplished American to have ever lived—there are so many versions and iterations of him in our national imagination that he can be simultaneously deified and denigrated, an object of both endless romanticism and effusive scorn.

There is Jefferson the man with perhaps the greatest résumé in the history of American politics: a revolutionary member of the Second Continental Congress where he wrote the soaring prose of the Declaration of Independence, an ambassador to France where he took over for Benjamin Franklin, a consequential governor of Virginia, the first secretary of state, the second vice president and third president.

There is Jefferson the quirky intellectual who was often more enthralled by science than by statecraft, who had a lifetime obsession with North American mammals, specifically the American mastodon, a cousin of the mammoth that he was convinced still roamed somewhere in the American West.[3] This is the president who had an affinity for mockingbirds and actually let his favorite bird, Dick, sit on his shoulder while he carried out the duties of the presidency.[4] He held pseudoscientific predilections as well, wholly convinced that soaking his feet in cold water every morning would promote good health, a habit he maintained for sixty years.

There is Jefferson the extraordinary friend and Jefferson the dogged enemy. The friendship between Jefferson and James Madison is the most consequential coupling in all of American history, spawning everything from the birth of political parties to the Virginia and Kentucky resolutions. The sometimes affectionate, sometimes thorny friendship between John Adams and Jefferson eventually led to the most interesting and lively epistolary exchange ever conducted by two former presidents. The enmity between Jefferson and Alexander Hamilton endures to this day as a dramatic narrative, its modern apotheosis being a series of hilarious rap battles in Lin-Manuel Miranda's hit musical *Hamilton*.

There is Jefferson the wordsmith whose superhuman capacity for lyrical expression made him the greatest spokesman of American idealism, coining phrases such as "Empire of Liberty," "pursuit of happiness," and "tree of liberty." His incorruptible commitment to the liberal ideals of education, free speech, and religious liberty are powerfully enshrined by chiseled quotes on the walls of the Jefferson Memorial in Washington, DC.

However, there is also Jefferson the man who spoke and wrote of New World freedom but whose lifestyle resembled an Old World aristocrat. Jefferson might be enshrined on Mount Rushmore, but rest assured, he was as human and broken as the rest of us.

The lights of his towering genius did not insulate him from the darkness of his temptations—temptations for political power, for sexual companionship, for the lifestyle afforded wealthy Virginia planters. After leaving Washington's cabinet, Jefferson suggested that the president had become senile and a clandestine monarchist, writing in a letter in 1796, "It would give you a fever were I to name to you the apostates who have gone over to these heresies, men who were Samsons in the field and Solomons in the council." Martha Washington described Jefferson's visit to Mount Vernon after Washington's death as the second-worst day of her life. Some historians have suggested that not only did Jefferson have a decades-long sexual relationship with his wife's half sister, Sally Hemings, but that the relationship began when Hemings was merely a teenage girl. He was perpetually in debt, especially toward the end of his life. He sold his personal library to Congress in 1815 in order to replace the library that had been destroyed by the British, but also because he was deeply mired in debt.

His contradictions were considerable—he championed the pastoral life but never actually did much farming with his own hands. He believed in the principle of congressional supremacy but unilaterally completed the Louisiana Purchase through executive fiat. He lyrically employed the phrase "All Men Are Created Equal" with great fanfare and rhetorical flourish while owning roughly six hundred human beings during his lifetime. He was not immune from heartache and all-consuming grief. Only two of his six children by his wife survived to adulthood. On his wife's deathbed he promised to never marry again; after her death he locked himself in his room for three weeks while pacing and weeping inconsolably. His friendships waxed and waned—at different points he had thoroughly alienated himself from George Washington and Abigail Adams, and had even attempted in his youth to seduce his best friend's wife.

So what about the "self-help" version of Jefferson? Can he make a useful contribution to our lives today given his titanic personal flaws? In order to learn from Jefferson, we have to pick one facet of a many-sided man. Being selective is necessary because his accomplishments can be just as unrelatable as his flaws.

What does this man—who had an encyclopedic knowledge of the ancient Greek and Roman worlds, whose grasp of the Western canon molded him into a supreme master of civilization, who imagined an America of plenitude built on the springs of agrarianism, who detested cities and lived most of his life among enslaved people—possibly have to offer the average well-meaning American today?

At a dinner honoring Nobel Prize winners of the Western Hemisphere in 1962, President Kennedy famously quipped, "I think this is the most extraordinary collection of talent, of human knowledge, that has ever been gathered together at the White House, with the possible exception of when Thomas Jefferson dined alone." Surely, this man is too unique, too sui generis, too separated by multiple centuries and boundless capacity to have anything meaningful to offer a modern seeker of guidance.

What Jefferson has to teach us lies in his very complexity—his variety. We live in a world in which powerful market forces constantly encourage us to devote our lives to extreme specialization. Jefferson modeled the opposite: a renaissance spirit of curiosity. He was a proud generalist, having chosen to be so. The poets and the saints have never encouraged us to become finely tuned parts in a great assembly line. Rather, they would have us embrace the multifarious wonders of life. A Jeffersonian life rejects an obsessive focus on any one thing. A Jeffersonian life perpetually rejects being siloed off into narrowly "productive" tracks. To be a generalist like Jefferson means cultivating multiple hobbies, even if you'll never be master of all of them. The effects on character, however, are profound. Building a habit of being *interested* in things means that you'll invariably be *interesting* to others.

Through it all, Jefferson was a supreme optimist about life, the human condition, and, most of all, the soaring possibilities of America.

He was an ardent believer in the possibility of moral improvement and intellectual enlightenment. He believed humans were imbued with the guiding lights of a rational mind and an innate moral sensibility.

Let's find out where these lights take us.

Lesson #1: Embrace the Spirit of the Renaissance

History teachers hoping to expose young minds to the rich intellectual personality or compelling moral imagination of the Italian Renaissance frequently turn to one of the greatest statements of the age from Giovanni Pico della Mirandola's immortal "Oration on the Dignity of Man": "We have made you neither of heavenly nor of earthly stuff, neither mortal nor immortal, so that with free choice and dignity, you may fashion yourself into whatever form you choose."

If ever there was a secular gospel extolling the mighty virtues of humanism, it is Pico della Mirandola's famous essay. His notion of a malleable inner nature is enthralling because it conceives of life as commandeered by individual agency, not cosmic predestination, a journey in which men and women are liberated from the capricious forces of the Fates and free to "fashion" themselves into "whatever form" they choose.

Thus, we are not captives of instinct or pawns of chance; instead, the spirit of the Renaissance teaches its followers not to wallow in static *being* but to endlessly strive toward *becoming*. Men and women are akin to clay, not steel, more than capable of guiding the rudders and raising the sails of their own adventures.

Jefferson was the walking embodiment of the Renaissance spirit, an Americanized version of Leonardo da Vinci whose eclectic interests continue to dazzle the modern student. As an 1874 biography of Jefferson famously noted, he "could calculate an eclipse, survey an estate, tie an artery, plan an edifice, try a cause, break a horse, dance a minuet, and play a violin."[5] His curiosity was infinite, his capacities and talents utterly astounding. In the 1997 Ken Burns documentary on Jefferson, the historian Andrew Burstein relates a story that humorously captures the essence of Jefferson's Renaissance ethos:

> There's an interesting story that takes place in the 1810s. There is a clergyman who stops at Ford's Tavern in Virginia, which is on the road between Monticello and Poplar Forest. And he encounters a man he terms a respectable stranger. And he engages in a conversation at some length with the stranger. First, they talk about mechanical operations, and he's certain that the man is an engineer of some sort. Then they move on to matters of agriculture and he thinks this is, in his words, a large farmer. Finally, they talk about religion, and he's certain that the man is a clergyman like himself. The hour gets late and they go to bed and the next morning, he arises and speaks with the innkeeper and asks for this stranger he has seen the night before. And he describes him and the innkeeper says, "Why, don't you know that was Thomas Jefferson?"

His assiduous capacity for deep study and endless reflection was the stuff of family lore, for it was said by his relatives that during his years as a student at William & Mary he routinely studied fifteen hours a day, often late into the evening.[6] His best friend in college, John Page, lamented that his bibliophile friend "could tear himself away from his dearest friends, to fly to his studies."[7] Even when he was on vacation, he spent most of his time reading books. As a child, Jefferson studied his Greek grammar book as other kids played around him. Years later, he famously wrote to Adams, "I cannot live without books."

But he wasn't one to quietly haunt the corners of libraries in isolation. He could play the violin with great virtuosity and skill, using his musical prowess to woo his future wife, Martha; she would play the harpsichord, Jefferson the violin, singing stanzas of songs together in perfect harmony. As a child, he practiced up to three hours a day and was proficient enough to play weekly concerts at the Governor's Palace during his years in Williamsburg.[8]

He believed in walking briskly, noting that he never knew a "great walker" who did not live a long and healthy life.[9] He was also a "consummate equestrian," usually riding in solitude for hours a day, no matter where he was in the world or the weather conditions—Monticello, Paris, or Washington, DC.[10] While Washington and Ulysses Grant were possibly the greatest riders of their respective eras, Jefferson was adept enough to evade British forces during the Revolutionary War.

He was a polyglot who could speak four languages—English, French, Italian, and Latin, the language of Cicero. He could read ancient Greek and modern Spanish, mastering Spanish in the course of just a few weeks as he crossed the Atlantic with only a copy of Don Quixote and a book of Spanish grammar.[11]

He harbored a deep and abiding love of mathematics that sprouted in his youth and lasted his entire life. As an older man, he fondly remembered that "mathematics was the passion of my life." He mastered the calculus of Newton's Principia Mathematica and the geometry of Euclid's Elements. When he was almost seventy years old and assisting his grandson with his own math studies, Jefferson continued to celebrate the satisfaction of mastering mathematics because "no uncertainties remain on the mind; all is demonstration and satisfaction."[12]

For Jefferson, rational thought was the ultimate ticket into the pantheon of an elevated existence, a plane of being where the noblest elements of life—truth, wisdom, beauty—were always to be found. It was said that on the door of Plato's Academy were engraved the words "Let no one ignorant of geometry enter." Like Plato, Jefferson believed objective reason untethered to subjective experience was the path to capturing the underlying order of the world and cosmos. Such activity of the mind was the apex of human activity.

Putting such knowledge to good use was one of Jefferson's passions.

He did so through his pursuit of architecture and his fondness for inventions. Jefferson's early drawings and designs for Monticello drew heavily on the work of the sixteenth-century Italian architect Andrea Palladio. He showed a "compulsiveness in mechanical effort and a fascination with numbers." His measurements were often carried out to four or five decimal places when carpenters had trouble meeting the instructions of a single inch.[13] "Almost single-handedly," notes historian Gordon Wood, "he became responsible for making America's public buildings resemble Roman temples."[14] With the assistance of his son-in-law, Jefferson developed an innovative plow designed to work on hillsides. Inspired by his years in France, he helped to design a machine for making macaroni.[15] As secretary of state, Jefferson invented a "wheel cipher" which was made from thirty-six cylindrical pieces of wood that would allow words to be scrambled and unscrambled as a way of protecting the integrity of diplomatic communications.[16]

Jefferson loved new advances and surges in technology. He relished scientific breakthroughs and would have been enamored by the never-ending innovations of the modern world. He was a member of the American Philosophical Society, founded in 1743 by Benjamin Franklin to "promote useful knowledge," serving as its president from 1797 to 1814.[17] From our perspective, Jefferson lived on the other side of a historic canyon separating him from the world-shattering breakthroughs of Darwinian evolution, Einstein's theory of relativity, and Mendelian inheritance, scientific revolutions that would have surely engrossed his hyperkinetic mind.

What would it look like to follow in the path of Jefferson today? How would one be a modern Jeffersonian apostle, to live as he lived and champion his habits of the mind and heart? For starters, it would obviously require a lot of reading and a vast palette of intellectual and artistic curiosity. It would require less screen time, less gazing at Netflix and Hulu, fewer anesthetized amusements, and a more robust commitment to the genuine study of consequential subjects. It would require a preternatural commitment to widening the cerebral circle of one's mental world. It would encourage us to acquire new skills, collect fresh capacities, and embrace the constant quest of trying to improve the world.

It would not be easy, but the treasures would be abundant. Our lives would be filled with the lush tapestry of an ever-expanding symphony of possibilities—Jefferson's was filled with wine and passion, books and friendship, math and poetry, achievement and tragedy. The best life rejoices in the glittering infinity of the human experience; it lurches in all directions, entertains any notion, questions any dogma, eats any food, talks to any person, or visits any location. It is a life that welcomes enormity and vastness, celebrates enchantment, levitates at the prospect of traveling to vistas of the unknown.

If there is a real frustration in living such a life, it is found in the begrudging reality of one's inherent limitations—of books unread and destinations untouched. For we are individual beings living but a single life, endowed with faulty and subjective faculties, forever foiled by a universe guarding its secrets all too well. We are creatures of our time and place, filled with unescapable biases and ever-fleeting capacities, often unaware that our particular lens will seem folly and provincial in just the blink of a historic eye. One life is simply too short to experience even a fraction of the world's splendors—the banquet of life is inexorably richer than we can possibly understand.

And yet, despite these real limitations, what Jefferson teaches us is that grandeur and wonderment abound for those who yearn to better themselves, who are never content with convention and see every day as an opportunity to enrich our inner fabric.

Lesson #2: Make Up with Your Friends

The friendship between John Adams and Thomas Jefferson ranks among the most consequential in American history—though not for the reasons you might think. Not because they brokered legislative compromises, negotiated historic treaties, or saved the union from imminent peril. No, it was significant because of how it fell apart and was put back together. It was a relationship forged in the crucible of great civilizational conflict. Eventually, it became a half-century friendship between two titans of the American Revolution, two ambassadors to European countries, two vice presidents, and, ultimately, two presidents.

Like so many American friendships today, it was made up of people who grew estranged as the frenzied politics of their time placed them in opposite and sometimes warring political orbits.

The importance of their friendship is best understood and revered because the form of their reconciliation was not just an exchange of daily events and arbitrary geriatric musings but was a series of profound and sober reflections on the deeper meaning of the America experiment—a correspondence totaling a hundred fifty-eight letters written during the final fourteen years of their lives. The Adams-Jefferson letters were a civic dialogue like no other, vividly capturing the competing strands of American idealism. The revival of their friendship endures as a model of nourishing political engagement, an archetypal American dialectic that touched on many of the same themes and conflicts that would animate American politics in the coming decades and centuries.

These two fathers of American freedom met at the Second Continental Congress. Their similarities and contrasts were obvious from the outset.

Adams was a Massachusetts lawyer, Jefferson was a Virginia planter. Adams was the older and more experienced political hand, shining brightest when standing before a courtroom or employing classical rhetorical skills in front of a convention; Jefferson was reserved, his charisma a bright candle in small gatherings. Adams considered debate and confrontation to be exalted elements of a constitutional universe devoted to political freedom and social pluralism. Jefferson demurred, avoiding conflict and personal controversy, perpetually positioning himself aloft of political squabbling, serenely cerebral, detached, and happy to play the role of the original American hierophant.

If Jefferson was the high priest of America's new civic religion, airily declaring that the birth of America represented a new chapter in the history of human progress, then Adams was the acerbic enforcer of the faith, insisting that freedom was the inevitable consequence not of American virtue but of a sturdy commitment to the rule of law. Adams's diary entries are fiery, laced with sharp opinions and raw emotive disclosures. Jefferson's diary was a sharp contrast, chronicling not the storms and sunshine within his soul but meteorological changes and purchases of wine and books.

Their contributions to the cause of independence reflected these differences.

Jefferson rarely spoke a word during the entire proceedings of the Continental Congress, to the point of being passive. Adams, on the other hand, is remembered in American civics classes today as the "Atlas of American Independence" because, as the New Jersey delegate Richard Stockton noted, "The man to whom the country is most indebted for the great measure of independency is Mr. John Adams of Boston . . . He it was who sustained the debate and by the force of his reasoning demonstrated not only the justice but the expediency of the measure."

Adams gave the speeches of the convention—"We are in the very midst of revolution, the most complete, unexpected, and remarkable of any in the history of the world"—but when it came time to write an official declaration of independence, to explain the reasons for rebellion by blending high-minded theory with real-world grievances, Adams judiciously turned to Jefferson. He offered three candid reasons why Jefferson was the better choice for the task: Jefferson was a Virginian, Adams was admittedly unpopular among some at the convention, and, most self-deprecating of all, Adams admitted, "You can write ten times better than I can." For the rest of his life, Adams second-guessed his willingness to ask his new friend to compose the Declaration, not grasping how central it would become in the framing of a new American identity. As he later wrote, "The Declaration of Independence I always considered as a theatrical show. Jefferson ran away with the stage effect of that . . . and all the glory of it."[18]

Without the spoken words of Adams and the written words of Jefferson, it is quite possible that American independence never would have happened. This is why Dr. Benjamin Rush, their mutual friend and the man responsible for the eventual renaissance of their friendship, would observe in a letter to Adams decades later, "I consider you and him, as the North and South poles of the American Revolution."

The warmth of their friendship blossomed during their time serving in Europe together—Jefferson as the American ambassador to France and Adams as the first American ambassador in the Court of St James's.

Jefferson visited London in March 1786. His two-month stay would be the tidemark of the Jefferson-Adams friendship as he not only deepened his bond with Adams but would become a quasi family member of the entire Adams clan. Jefferson bought corsets for Abigail and in return she arranged several dinner parties in his honor—his conversational elan expressed in a dazzling capacity to talk to anybody about almost anything. During a lull in their official duties, Jefferson and Adams took a six-day tour of English gardens, which included visiting the home and grave of William Shakespeare, the gardens of Alexander Pope, and the site of the first significant battle of the English Civil War.

Years later, Adams would reminisce about the intimacy of this time by noting that during their months together in London, his son John Quincy "appeared to be almost as much your boy as mine."[19] When the Adams family departed back to America, Abigail wrote to Jefferson, "a few lines to my much-esteemed friend, to thank him for all his kindness and friendship towards myself and family."[20]

What catalyzed the rupture between them? How did the deep intimacy of their time together in Philadelphia and London degenerate into a subtle hostility that would persist well into their retirement years?

The short answer is that the tumultuous political world of America in the 1790s and the climatic election of 1800 drove them apart.

They differed on the merits of the French Revolution. Jefferson glorified in the destruction of monarchical and aristocratic institutions he deemed as long-standing instruments of oppression. Adams could not back the spectacle of endless French bloodshed—the beheading of Louis XVI and Marie Antoinette, Robespierre's Reign of Terror, the radicalism of the Jacobins. Adams began to see his old friend less as a cheerfully besotted Francophile and more as a dangerously naïve radical. It was bad enough that Jefferson seemed unfazed by the violence of Shays' Rebellion. Now he seemed to hold a view of "the people" that curried chaos, a mythologized and poetic form of faith in the *demos* that willingly ignored the hard lessons of history.

Moreover, as a member of Washington's cabinet, Jefferson grew more hostile and agitated, even a bit duplicitous at times. He absolutely could not accept the policy program and machinations of Hamilton who, Jefferson believed, wanted to transform the American republic into a miniaturized version of Great Britain—private industry enmeshed with centralized banks, large standing armies, national policymaking that treated states as mere administrative units, and, worst of all, a locus of raw industrial power anchored in commercialized urban areas.

Jefferson and Adams's estrangement was a portrait of the country's politics in microcosm. By the time the election of 1800 arrived, the birth of political parties was well underway and the campaign between Adams and Jefferson featured its share of mudslinging. The Republicans led by Jefferson claimed that Adams was controlled by his wife and that he was a closet monarchist, too European in outlook and not truly American. The notorious pamphleteer and scandalmonger James Callender wrote that Adams was "a hideous hermaphroditical character which has neither the force and firmness of a man, nor the gentleness and sensibility of a woman."

Both men, of course, avoided directly attacking each other, with surrogates and partisan presses playing the role of political gladiators instead. Federalists claimed Jefferson would destroy Bibles, promote atheism, and ferry the anarchy of the French Revolution to American shores. After the election was over, Adams's midnight appointments, his choice of John Marshall as chief justice, and his absence during Jefferson's inauguration all served to further the breach between them.

All told, more than a decade of silence between the two men ensued from the morning Adams left the White House to begin his journey home and Jefferson arrived to begin his presidential term.

But then a peculiar magic of the subconscious intervened: Benjamin Rush had a dream. The dream occurred in 1809 and involved the "renewal of the friendship & intercourse" of the two former presidents.

Over the course of many years, Rush encouraged both men to take the first step.

Finally, on January 1, 1812, Adams took the initiative in the grand hope of reconciliation. The first letter was polite, with Adams writing about "two pieces of Homespun," which Jefferson awkwardly misinterpreted as an allusion to domestic manufacturing. Instead, Adams was referring to two volumes of John Quincy's work *Lectures on Rhetoric and Oratory* that Adams had mailed separately.

Their initial letters were a form of emotional irrigation, treading lightly on hardened soil, gently bringing each other up to date on issues related to health and daily routines. Jefferson claimed to have given up on politics "in exchange for Tacitus and Thucydides, for Newton and Euclid; and I find myself much the happier." The conciliatory tone of the early letters was indicative of a desire to avoid the possibility of a further rupture, both men prudently deciding to assess the state of the relationship before venturing on to more substantive but unstable ground.

But Adams possessed what the historian Joseph Ellis calls an "inveterate effusiveness."

"No matter how hard he tried, no matter how often he reminded himself to avoid controversy, no matter how frequently he vowed to provide posterity with a more serene, scrubbed-up image of himself as the classical hero, Adams found it impossible to behave like a proper patriarch."[21] Adams's deep need to engage—and even joust—on matters of supreme importance led to the most famous sentence of the entire fourteen-year exchange: "You and I, ought not to die, before We have explained ourselves to each other."

And explain they did—about old age, what they were reading, how they spent their time. While they certainly differed in disposition and temperament, the most persistent reason for the chasm between them was their disagreement on the fundamental makeup of human nature itself.

Jefferson was essentially an optimist, believing that common sense and conventional virtue were not the exclusive domains of the few or the exceedingly highborn. Popular sentiment could be properly harnessed for noble and just ends—the prerequisites for these ends were well known to purveyors of the Enlightenment: robust and accessible education, a culture broadly committed to responsible forms of individualism, and a moral framework oriented around self-reliance. Government's role should be limited, living space should be abundant, and common citizens should embark on a constant process of self-improvement. This was the heart of the Jeffersonian vision, an agrarian republic with a modest standing in the world.

The engine of America, its essential centerpiece, was not government or monarchy or control from any institution per se. It was freedom itself. Thus, the common man could be trusted to govern himself and, by extension, the nation. "I have great confidence," Jefferson wrote, "in the common sense of mankind, in general." Once liberated from a millennium of monarchical and ecclesiastic subjugation, Jefferson foretold, a free people would embrace rational thought, tempered action, and, most of all, a thoroughly democratic ethos. America would become a second, albeit secular, Eden. This was the true nature of American exceptionalism as understood by Jefferson.

But Adams was having none of it. As he wrote, "The Fundamental Article of my political creed is, that Despotism, or unenlightened Sovereignty, or absolute Power is the same in a Majority of a popular Assembly, an Aristocratical Counsel, and Oligarchical Junto and a single Emperor."[22] Unlike Jefferson, who found something mystical or even miraculous about the spirit of "the people," Adams believed this populist spirit could be just as unenlightened, just as corrupted, and just as dangerous as the spirit of a pharaoh, sultan, or king. His letters abounded with examples of popular excesses from ages past, fueled by a gauntlet of human extremism—religious massacres, the Crusades, or the French Revolution. Adams was skeptical about the promise of mankind's moral perfectibility, quite certain that human nature rests on a stable but low horizon of fallibility.

As Dumas Malone, Jefferson's most famous biographer, succinctly described the difference between the two men: "Nothing was more characteristic of Jefferson than his belief in the improvability of the human mind and the limitless progress of human knowledge. Adams, who prided himself on his realism, was considerably more skeptical."[23]

Their letters continued until the time of their deaths. There are few words, maybe none, that can adequately capture the magnitude of both men dying on the same day; that this day was on the fiftieth anniversary of the signing of the Declaration of Independence—July 4, 1826—is almost too much of a cosmic coincidence to fully process.

When one considers the coincidental timing of their deaths, it is tempting to evoke a specific word that was frequently used by our founders, a word that is almost completely absent from our modern vocabulary: providence. Perhaps it was providential that the last sentence Adams ever uttered mentioned his Virginia friend and fellow paladin of liberty, "Thomas Jefferson still survives."

Lesson #3: Take Religion Seriously—Even if You Aren't Religious

The letter Jefferson received in the spring of 1814 was long—more than eight thousand words—but its message was blunt: Jefferson's soul was in great peril.

The writer of the letter, Miles King, was a converted Methodist minister who had spent most of his life at sea, commanding a vessel and living a life of soft depravity and small hedonic pleasantries, being "much disposed to a luxurious life of debauch and intrigue . . . I lived a life of pleasure and gaity, with now and then a hair Breadth escape from death, either by shipwreck or other casualty."

He was writing to tell Jefferson that he had been dreaming of him lately, besieged with worry that the multiplicity of rumors surrounding Jefferson's religious views—that he was an atheist, a deist, an infidel—would prevent him from finding genuine salvation at the end of his life, that all his worldly deeds and triumphs would not matter in the realm of eternity. "Never rest until you feel it in the heart! Influencing all Your words and actions & regulating the thoughts of your heart!"[24]

Jefferson's response was extraordinary. Despite being constantly deluged with letters, he took the time to reply to King because he felt his heart was in the right place: "I believe it was written with kind intentions, and a personal concern for my future happiness."[25] Jefferson's eloquent reply touches on many of the themes and principles he spent a lifetime studying and considering. Indeed, to this day, with the possible exception of race, religion might be the most hotly contested facet of Jefferson's life.

The animating article of Jefferson's faith was a belief that reason is the only arbiter of ultimate truth. As he wrote in his reply, "for, dispute as long as we will on religious tenets, our reason at last must ultimately decide, as it is the only oracle which god has given us to determine between what really comes from him, & the phantasms of a disordered or deluded imagination."[26] Jefferson assumes a posture of rationalistic humility in his reply to King, reminding him that God did not imbue men and women with the mental and moral capacities to achieve anything approaching infallibility.

Because of our imperfect knowledge, an array of spiritual paths abound in human life, Jefferson argues, concluding the famous letter with the ecumenical hope of mutual salvation, that "there is not a quaker or a baptist, a presbyterian or an episcopalian, a catholic or a protestant in heaven: that, on entering that gate, we leave those badges of schism behind, and find ourselves united in those principles only in which god has united us all."

Jefferson spent much of his life concerned about these "badges of schism." Questions about God, Scripture, the life of Jesus, the possibility of an afterlife, and moral truth were never far from his mind. Indeed, in the final chapter of his life, Jefferson undertook a project that stayed out of the public's eye for almost a century, a mercurial intellectual venture in which he used a penknife and glue to re-create the life and teachings of Jesus, cutting out and removing all supernatural or miraculous events. In corresponding columns, he selectively edited the text of the Bible, entitling his work *The Life and Morals of Jesus of Nazareth Extracted*

Textually from the Gospels in Greek, Latin, French & English. Modern academics refer to his project as *The Jefferson Bible.*

When forced to describe his own religious beliefs, Jefferson referred to himself as a "sect by myself," zealously defending the notion that religion should strictly be between the individual and his God. As he wrote, "The legitimate powers of government extend to such acts only as are injurious to others . . . It does me no injury for my neighbor to say there are twenty gods, or no god. It neither picks my pocket nor breaks my leg." His Bible was a tribute to Enlightenment rationalism, an attempt to demystify the moral teachings of Jesus. Jefferson called himself "a real Christian," yet his heterodoxy was apparent in his skepticism toward the divinity of Christ, the concept of original sin, miracles, the holy trinity—even the resurrection had no mention in Jefferson's retelling of Jesus's life. To Jefferson, Christ's divinity was a phantom, a reformulated myth to serve the interests of those who corrupted the elevated morality of Jesus, a morality Jefferson labeled "the most perfect and sublime that has ever been taught by man."

He was a deist but waffled on the possibility of an afterlife or the existence of the immortal soul. One thing Jefferson never questioned, however, was the importance of taking the claims of religion seriously. He never doubted that such questions were worthy of muscular reflection, or that one's view of the metaphysical anchors the most defining convictions of life. As he wrote to his nephew Peter Carr in 1787, "Question with boldness even the existence of a god; because, if there be one, he must more approve the homage of reason, than that of blindfolded fear."

The problem today is not that Americans are either "fearful" or "blindfolded" about religious faith. The problem is that they are ignorant.

An ethic of staunch disbelief has tightened its grip on younger Americans. In 1972, a mere five percent of Americans classified themselves as religiously unaffiliated; by 2022, that number had risen to a jarring twenty-nine percent.[27] The percentage of Gen Z that identifies as atheists is double that of the general population.[28]

But being an atheist, an agnostic, or a skeptic should not condemn one to a state of abject ignorance about the teachings and history of the world's great religions. In the past few years, a disturbing reality in my high-school classes has become impossible to ignore: their profound ignorance of religion. Entire classrooms full of bright young Americans are often populated with students who have no idea that the first book of the Bible is Genesis, or who cannot identify the names Moses or Noah or Siddhartha Gautama. I tried explaining Theodore Roosevelt's concept of the "bully pulpit" to my political science students only to realize almost none of them had any idea what the word "pulpit" means. Even my students who identify as Catholic can rarely tell me the name of the pope.

But it's not just the kiddos. A recent survey by the Pew Research Center revealed that only one in five Americans knows that the teaching of salvation through faith alone is Protestantism, not Catholicism. Barely half know who delivered the Sermon on the Mount. Only fifteen percent could associate the Vedas with Hinduism. A slim eighteen percent could identify one of Buddhism's Four Noble Truths.[29]

Religion, whether or not one accepts the theology, the liturgy, or the dogma of any particular religion, has a lot to suggest about the penetrating and desperate stirrings of the human condition. Physical suffering? Spiritual despair? Existential dread? Epistemic confusion? All of them are mandatory stops in the voyage of life. None of us can escape them. There are no ramps to a detour, no signposts to speed by. The wisest among us are often overwhelmed, even annihilated, by the potency of mystery and the omnipresence of doubt. Most of us have experienced enough mountaintops and magic to sometimes suspect life is more than "a furtive arrangement of elementary particles."[30] On the other hand, as we age, suffering and torpor lead us also to occasionally question if there really is a deeper or more transcendent meaning buried within the fabric of time and eternity.

The opposite of faith is not disbelief, it's indifference. No one can say with certainty what resided within the soul of Jefferson—even he seemed to evolve as he aged, sometimes contradicting himself, providing posterity with enough conflicting material that his thousands of letters serve as vectors of ambiguity. If he were alive today, it is impossible to know what questions he would ask. But what is certain is that he would ask them.

For instance . . .

What do the brightest minds and most astute modern scholars say about the historic evidence of Christ's resurrection? Is there any compelling research or testimony that might give some veracity to the possibility of reincarnation? What does the modern surge of near-death experiences in the past half century suggest about the possibility of the soul surviving brain death? Where does consciousness come from? Is it an illusion? Is it a cosmic lottery ticket? Is it a cognitive transponder uniquely positioning human beings to crack the riddles of the universe? Why do patients being treated with psychedelics report mystical experiences in which the ultimate reality is one of cosmic interconnectedness, eerily similar to the Hindu conception of Brahman?

While a rich life may not require answers to these questions, a rich life also doesn't consist of passive incuriosity. We shouldn't question ourselves into nihilism. As G. K. Chesterton observed, "Reason is itself a matter of faith. It is an act of faith to assert that our thoughts have any relation to reality at all." But faith in reason will only enrich our lives. The one kernel of wisdom Jefferson considered beyond quibble or doubt is a hearty embrace of a rational Socratic spirit, a longing to explore the most important questions of life, a yearning to look up in wonderment and consider the possibilities that are offered by those who have come before. This is something to which we can all aspire.

CHAPTER 5

Arthur Ashe

Don't Let Other People Pick Your Fights

★

★

The 1975 Wimbledon final between Arthur Ashe and Jimmy Connors is not considered by anyone to be the greatest tennis match of all time.

That honor is often conferred to the 1980 Wimbledon final between John McEnroe and Bjorn Borg. For decades, American tennis fans watched a replay of the McEnroe–Borg classic during Wimbledon rain delays on NBC. In 2008, the five-set thriller between Roger Federer and Rafael Nadal, also played on the august lawns of the All England Lawn Tennis Club, finally replaced the earlier match in the minds of many tennis aficionados as the greatest tennis match of all time.

But Ashe's 1975 triumph is resonant for reasons that have nothing to do with epic tiebreakers or dazzling shotmaking. Wimbledon is the most prestigious tournament in the world. It exudes tradition, institutionalizes history, and acts as an athletic hermitage for fans of the game. After his victory, Ashe remarked, "When I walked on the court, I thought I was going to win. I felt it was my destiny."[1]

Destiny it may have been, but it wasn't simply passive fate that swept Ashe to become the first African American man to win Wimbledon. His defeat of Connors was a legendary upset grounded firmly in character, a character shaped by millions of choices spread over decades, building to one climatic moment. Ashe's public profile meant he felt constant pressure to performatively stand in line with movements large and small. He never let other people pick his fights. That made him a uniquely effective voice when he did finally choose to speak, but it also bequeathed to him a rock-solid sense of self.

Interestingly, his restraint wasn't due to detachment. It's instructive to see what Ashe himself had to say about the formation of his character. He minced no words in the opening lines of his bestselling memoir, *Days of Grace.* Instead of championing a stoic detachment from the searing gaze and judgment of his fellow citizen, he divulged a chronic inability to distance himself from the appraisals of others. In these words, he reveals his vital need to be respected as an indelible feature of his most basic, genuine self: "If one's reputation is a possession, then of all my possessions, my reputation means most to me. Nothing comes even close to it in importance . . . I can no more easily renounce my concern with what other people think of me than I can will myself to stop breathing."[2]

By the time Ashe died at the tragically young age of forty-nine, he had acquired a parade of possessions few can fathom, from Wimbledon and US Open championship trophies to a personal note from Martin

Luther King written just two months before his assassination. Ashe's eminence—and the reason why he was so beloved by the end of his life—transcended narrow silos of significance; he was more than merely a tennis champion, more than a quiet titan of civil rights, more than a fierce critic of South African apartheid and advocate for education and equal opportunity.

If a curious student endeavored to study the arc of Ashe's life by arbitrarily thumbing through pages of his biography, the episodic richness one would encounter is vast. A reader might stumble upon Ashe getting sued by Connors in the early 1970s or observe him on the verge of punching McEnroe in the 1980s. Turn a few pages earlier and one might learn that he played tennis with Bobby Kennedy in the days before he was killed, or that he was spared a tour in Vietnam because his younger brother went in his place, or that Kareem Abdul-Jabbar once referred to him as "Arthur Ass." Fast-forward and witness the extraordinary moment, decades later, during Nelson Mandela's first trip to New York after his release from prison; when learning Ashe was in the audience of a town hall event, Mandela immediately sought him out, saying "Come here!" before affectionately embracing Ashe with the heartfelt words, "Oh, my brother."

Go back to the beginning of his life, and a reader would learn he lost his mother at the age of six. Go to the end of his life and learn he died when his daughter was only five.

Ashe did not crave the shallow accolades afforded to those who are merely celebrities. He knew that a good reputation is rooted in something finer than momentary acclaim. It is one thing to be celebrated, Ashe understood, but something else to be worthy of the celebration. Many people yearn to be honored, but he wanted to be honorable, so he actually behaved honorably.

The author of the most exhaustive and authoritative biography of Ashe, the celebrated historian Raymond Arsenault, spent the better part of a decade researching and writing about Ashe, and dramatically concluded by the end of the project, "Of all the historical characters I have studied during my long scholarly career, he comes the closest to being an exemplary role model. He wasn't perfect, as the chapters following will demonstrate, and he, like everyone else, was a flesh-and-blood human being limited by flaws and eccentricities. Yet, through a lifetime of challenges large and small, he came remarkably close to living up to his professed ideals."[3]

From a historian's perspective, Ashe is a fascinating subject—both socially and psychologically—because of his gradual and sometimes painful turn toward activism, which took a variety of forms, from pioneering American awareness about South African apartheid to getting arrested in front of the White House while protesting the immigration policy toward Haiti, just six months before his death.

But Ashe should be considered more than a historic subject. He was a humanitarian in the truest, most consequential sense of the word. The longer he lived, the more humane he became, continually broadening his capacity to work for justice and opportunity for fellow human beings, no matter where they were born in the world, no matter their skin color, no matter the disease coursing through their veins. "Circles," the famous essay by Ralph Waldo Emerson, encapsulates the political and moral sojourn of Ashe. Emerson writes, "The life of man is a self-evolving circle, which, from a ring imperceptibly small, rushes on all sides outwards to new and larger circles, and that without end."

Ashe's circles of significance widened as he learned and lived. The pensive UCLA student who was hesitant to speak out on the racial atrocities taking place in the American South eventually became an activist who traveled the world and had the largest tennis stadium in the world named after him. Like the expanding universe itself, he voyaged to causes and issues far removed from the Richmond, Virginia, tennis courts where his journey began. When one carefully studies Ashe, it becomes powerfully apparent that tennis was only the inner, "imperceptibly small" ring of his being.

The forty-nine years he lived are richly filled with life lessons worthy of consideration.

Ashe's choices—when to be silent, when to speak, and most importantly, when to act—offer an important guide for those of us learning how to manage our public selves in the online age of self-appointed expertise and ersatz activism. His most important lesson: Never let others pick your fights for you. You'll find your own voice at a moment of your choosing. Speaking from ignorance and inordinate haste helps no one.

This certainly doesn't mean fleeing conflict or averting our eyes from the sorrows and injustices we are certain to encounter in this world. Ashe learned over time how and when to handle confrontation, especially when a potent and high principle is at stake. He discovered the power of self-confidence and individual belief, even in the face of past failures and personal doubt. By the end of his life, the man who proclaimed, "I want to be the Jackie Robinson of tennis," yearned for a reputation that had little to do with tennis and everything to do with the noble aspiration of forging a more humane and just world. The words of his father— "What people think of you, Arthur Junior, your reputation, is all that counts"—were a guiding credo.

Few Americans can compare to the elephantine stature and reputation he enjoys in the hearts and minds of his fellow citizens. Let's find out why.

Lesson #1: Don't Fear Necessary Confrontation

The English language is rich with metaphors for demonstrating oppositional characteristics: fire and ice, black and white, north and south, oil and vinegar, day and night. But if tennis could offer its own submission, it would be "Ashe and McEnroe."

Ashe was collegial and urbane, the embodiment of grace, elegant in both body and mind. He spoke in a soft, mellifluous voice, the cadence of his language unremarkable but warm. On the court, he was inerrantly respectful of his opponents, the chair umpire, and the spectators. Even when he won major championships, his celebratory gestures were symbolically grand in their understatement. If his emotions were inwardly volcanic, he never outwardly erupted. Championship trophies were lost by a losing score, yes, but honor could also be lost by failing to live up to a particular standard of sportsmanship.

The on-court shenanigans of McEnroe, by contrast, are the stuff of legend. As beautiful and sublime as he was with a tennis racket, especially at the net, his titanic tantrums and frenzied outbursts of purified rage are the primary sources of his fame. Nicknamed "Superbrat," his most famous outburst at Wimbledon in 1981—"You cannot be serious!"—pales in comparison to some of his more colorful eruptions. In Stockholm, he hit a ball into the crowd after receiving a point penalty for verbally abusing the umpire, then proceeded to swing his racket at cups filled with water next to his chair. He was disqualified from the Australian Open in 1990 for a variety of infractions. Connors grew so tired of McEnroe's antics in a 1982 match that he walked onto McEnroe's side of the net and aggressively pointed his index finger a few inches from his eyes "like a father telling off his child."[4]

These two Americans, occupying opposite poles of decorum, became forever entangled when Ashe was offered his dream job of becoming captain of the Davis Cup team almost immediately after his retirement. The previous coach, Tony Trabert, himself a Grand Slam champion, was utterly disenchanted by the atrocious behavior of the new generation of American tennis players.

The incoming president of the United States Tennis Association warned Ashe of the effect the team had had on the previous coach. "The behavior of the players. McEnroe. Gerulaitis. Peter Fleming. They are driving him nuts."[5]

When Ashe replied that he didn't know it was that bad, the incoming president doubled down on his warning, "You don't know the half of it." Trabert echoed the sentiment by telling Ashe, "I'm happy for you, Arthur . . . You would have been my first choice, too. But good luck to you with some of these guys. It's just not the way we were brought up."[6]

It didn't take Ashe long to find out exactly what they were talking about. In his first year as coach, he encountered the quandary of

wondering just how involved to be in the active coaching of his players. He knew tennis inside out, was a three-time Grand Slam singles
champion, twice reached the number-two ranking in the world, and won
five Davis Cups as a player. He would eventually win two Davis Cup
Championships as captain with a sterling win percentage of .812. But in
the early days of his captaincy, it was unclear what tact he should take
with his temperamental star players.

At one point, McEnroe's doubles partner explicitly told Ashe, "We
don't need advice or coaching."[7]

Each man fundamentally misunderstood the other.

To McEnroe, Ashe was passive and unsupportive, hiding behind the
fuzzy imprimatur of mawkish concepts like honor and sportsmanship.
In his own mind, McEnroe was in the midst of battle, fighting for his
country, yet his captain sat quietly on the bench, admonishing his players
with his silence. To Ashe, McEnroe hated authority, refusing to show up
on time, to uphold traditions of respectability, to be coached. Ashe was
the opposite of Machiavellian, forever believing the ends do not justify
the means, believing the way a man approaches a goal is sometimes as
important as the goal itself. What good is winning the Davis Cup, he
asked, if he and his players dishonored their nation in the process?

The principle that winning is not always the most important outcome an athlete should strive for was put to the ultimate test during his
first year as coach, dramatically juxtaposing the diplomatic aura of Ashe
with the volatile behavior of McEnroe.

In the semifinal round of Ashe's first campaign for the Davis Cup in
1981, McEnroe and his partner, Peter Fleming, insulted everyone around
them during their doubles match—officials, players, spectators—while
uttering an endless stream of profanities. Ashe could not support or
cheerlead such audacious behavior from his players and tried his best
to maintain a basic level of respectability, which McEnroe resented and
rebelled against. When Ashe told them how disgraceful their behavior
was, they were utterly unapologetic.

But the real climatic moment occurred a few months later during the final round in Cincinnati. In the midst of a tense doubles match against the Argentinean team of Guillermo Vilas and Jose Luis Clerc, Ashe had to come between McEnroe and the Argentineans. He told McEnroe, "John, get to the line and serve! Now!"[8] McEnroe complied but on the next changeover got into a verbal tussle with Clerc and Ashe had to warn him again, "This is a disgrace. You cannot continue like this. You are playing for the United States. Remember that!" McEnroe seemed to respond to Ashe's admonishment before Clerc provoked him again with McEnroe taking the bait.

"Go fuck yourself," McEnroe yelled.

Ashe was immediately out of his chair. What transpired next was unprecedented in the life of Arthur Ashe. As he recounted these extraordinary moments years later: "I was stunned. I stormed onto the court, and John and I exchanged some bitter words for a few seconds. This time I thought I might punch John. I have never punched anyone in my life, but I was truly on the brink of hitting him. I had never been so angry in my life. I couldn't trust myself not to strangle him."[9]

Although the Americans went on to win the match that day and were close to winning the Davis Cup, Ashe knew a higher principle was at stake. His next step was astonishing but emblematic of his devotion to the integrity of the game and his nation. He took the unprecedented step of calling the president of the United States Tennis Association early the next morning and threatening to "forfeit the match if McEnroe acts anything like that again."

When Ashe warned McEnroe what would happen if he persisted in his behavior, McEnroe simply asked, "Is that all?"

McEnroe kept his emotions in check and triumphed in a particularly gutsy match. Ashe's treatment of McEnroe demonstrates an important and essential principle: Don't fear confrontation when it's necessary to promote, protect, and defend a cherished ideal. Confrontation was never Ashe's preferred modus operandi, never his stylistic signature or favored tactic. But as he aged, he became more accepting and comfortable with the harsh reality that a smiling face and disarming demeanor wouldn't be enough to successfully promote his hopes and standards. In the case of confronting McEnroe's boorish behavior, the principle of representing one's nation with unflinching honor and unbounded integrity trumped Ashe's desire to hoist the Davis Cup trophy.

Years later, both men came to have a deep and genuine affection for each other. At the grand opening of Arthur Ashe Stadium in 1997, McEnroe eloquently and emotionally honored the memory of his Davis Cup captain. "We may not have always seen eye to eye," he observed, "but we always set our sights on the same thing: a championship that brought us pride as a national team." He went on to describe Ashe as "a fully realized human being" and "a man who embodied the best that tennis and sports in general can provide."[10]

Ashe's later perception of McEnroe's riddling behavior is utterly fascinating, almost Freudian in its implications. Far from being disgusted with McEnroe's vulgar and violent displays, a decade removed from almost punching him, Ashe's reflections seemed to ripen in a way that enhanced his admiration for McEnroe. McEnroe was a great teammate. His outbursts were never malicious. He was never cocky or hurt team morale. Quite the opposite. He was filled with an irrepressible marrow for excellence. Ashe came to regard McEnroe as a proxy for the pent-up, repressed rage he was never allowed to express in his own life. "I suspect now," he wrote, "that McEnroe and I were not so far apart, after all. Far from seeing John as alien, I think I may have known him, probably without being fully aware of my feelings, as a reflection of an intimate part of myself."[11]

As he aged, the saccharine version of Ashe was replaced on occasion with a more confident and combative Ashe. As he was giving a speech at Howard University following one of his visits to South Africa, two students started yelling at him, "Uncle Tom! Uncle Tom! Arthur Ashe is an Uncle Tom and a traitor!" In the past, Ashe never responded in a way that demeaned a questioner. But this time the stakes were too high and he embraced the moment. He hit back at the smug students . . . hard.

"Why don't you tell everybody in this hall tonight why, if you are so brave and militant, you are hiding away in school in the United States and not confronting apartheid in South Africa, which is your homeland?" Then he needled the students on the essence of their misplaced sanctimoniousness: "What do you expect to achieve when you give in to passion and invective and surrender the high moral ground that alone can bring you victory?"[12]

He even stood up to the conceit of Jesse Jackson, one of the most famous activists of his time. At a party given by an Atlanta Hawks basketball player in the 1970s, Jackson took a dig at Ashe's manner of activism, commenting, "The problem with you Arthur is that you're not arrogant enough." Ashe acerbically replied, "You're right Jesse, I'm not arrogant. But I don't think that my lack of arrogance lessens my effectiveness one bit."[13]

Ashe was right. It didn't lessen his effectiveness. His ability to successfully navigate the taxing terrain of the political landscape of the 1960s and '70s with both grace and fortitude is a testament to the banquet of virtues within his soul. Ashe was tough but kind, eloquent and substantive, athletic and cerebral, a man whose assets were so bountiful that he would surely be celebrated no matter where and when he appeared in human history.

But to our enduring good fortune he is our American hero. Our American icon. Our fellow citizen who can inspire and guide each of us to live better, reach higher, and scale the apex of mountains in our own lives.

Lesson #2: Everyone Has Their Own Way of Changing the World

Toward the end of his life, Ashe lamented the political passivity of his earlier years, poignantly stating in his memoir, "There were times when I asked myself whether I was being principled or simply a coward."[14] Even more dramatically, he observed, "While blood was running freely in the streets of Birmingham, Memphis, and Biloxi, I had been playing tennis. Dressed in immaculate white, I was elegantly stroking tennis balls on perfectly paved courts in California and New York and Europe. Meanwhile, across the South, young men and women of my age were enduring pain and suffering so that blacks would be free of our American brand of apartheid."[15]

But it's important to remember that we all have our own path to finding our voice. Ashe's may have been all the more effective because he did it in his own way and in his own time. Understanding why he made the choices he did requires looking at his past.

Ashe lost his mother when she was only twenty-eight years old. He was too young and too frightened to attend her funeral. The only parent left in his life, Arthur Ashe Sr., firmly believed in the importance of respect and authority. As his younger brother, Johnnie, later remembered, "Daddy was a strict disciplinarian . . . first day, no matter what school we went to, he would tell the principals 'This is my boy. If he does anything wrong, at any time, you discipline him here. Give me a call and I'm going to discipline him at home.'"[16]

Perhaps this explains why Ashe was never the loudest person in a room—never obnoxious, never boorish, never overbearing. As a tennis player, under no circumstance did he ever curse at or berate an umpire, never broke his racket in the tempest of inconsolable rage, never dishonored his name, his nation, or the sport itself. As an advocate for various civil rights causes, he was cerebral and soft-spoken, believing that measured persuasion and negotiation would catalyze the march for progress far more effectively than outrage or fists held up in the air. Militantly scolding white America, he feared, would yield little progress while possibly inviting a throng of regressive responses.

Ashe had other good reasons to be a hesitant personality in his early years. He grew up in Richmond, Virginia, filled with vivid memories of the tragic fate of Emmett Till, acutely aware that Blacks occupied an exceedingly vulnerable nook in the Jim Crow South. Ashe could remember the trappings of segregation: "I can clearly recall the white line on the floor of the bus . . . and I understood that I was required to stay behind it."[17] The discipline his father worked so hard to cultivate in his sons existed "to protect them." One of Ashe's early tennis mentors, Dr. Robert Johnson, known as "the godfather of Black tennis," insisted that all of his players adhere to a strict code of conduct beyond reproach, almost to the point of subservience, so as not to give anyone an excuse to disqualify them from any of the tournaments they were participating in.[18]

Ashe left the South as a senior in high school to spend his final year in St. Louis, Missouri, before heading to the progressive mecca of UCLA. He was far removed from the blood and strife that erupted in the South throughout the 1960s, a wave of social upheaval largely in response to the federal laws and legal directives coming from the nation's capital. Quite simply, in his early years his focus was tennis, and political activism was seen as a distraction. Other athletes and habitués of activism were frequently frustrated with Ashe's early reticence. But tennis is a famously lonely sport—dogmatically individualistic in the way it is played and rewarded. There are no teammates. No coaches on the court. No home field. Ashe's entire ecosystem was populated by white Americans. At every club and in every tournament, no one looked like him.

Given his background and the everyday reality of his life, his reticence to speak loudly or embrace outrage or fury made perfect sense. In the early days of his career, he resented the pressure from fellow African American athletes to become more vocal on issues related to race. He once asked, "What do black athletes, most of whom are not politically inclined, have to offer? Speak out if you've got something to say, otherwise say nothing."[19]

However, in 1968, one of the most consequential and violent years in American history, Ashe was forced to radically reevaluate his role in the racial machinations of his own nation.

"Getting better" or "making progress" were no longer reliable escape valves in the aftermath of 1968. As Ashe recalled in an interview, "It was just a very difficult time being Black in 1968 with everything that happened that year." Being a "light touch" activist no longer held the same appeal after the assassination of Martin Luther King. Ashe was driving across the George Washington Bridge into Manhattan when he heard the news; he was so horrified and upset he eventually pulled over to the side of the road where he witnessed other African Americans doing the same thing. "I was very angry," he recalled, "and felt slightly helpless. Things would be different now."[20]

Ashe was devastated again just two months later when Robert Kennedy was shot after winning the California primary. Although Kennedy was wealthy, Ivy League educated, and the closest thing to royalty in America, he was deeply admired by Ashe, who was put off by Lyndon Johnson's "folksy Southern twang" and harbored no love for Hubert Humphrey. Kennedy was genuine in his rhetoric and convictions, a form of authenticity Ashe felt he was uniquely qualified to assess: "You believed in Bobby Kennedy. You know if you're Black growing up in the South you have an extra set of antennas. You have a third eye and you can spot a phony most of the time. Bobby Kennedy was not phony."[21] Ashe admired King from afar, but he knew Kennedy personally. In fact, he spent time with Kennedy in Sacramento the day before his assassination.

Following the unrest of 1968, Ashe took a decidedly different tone. A metamorphosis was taking place within him. An essential element of his character was now oriented toward speaking out against the injustices surrounding him. Tennis would no longer be enough. Ashe the tennis player would become indistinguishable, even indissoluble, from Ashe the advocate for political justice. While he would always practice the virtues of tolerance, peace, and compassion, he became increasingly vocal about issues of inequality.

If Ashe felt remorse for the inaction of the first half of his life, he more than made up for it in the second half, starting in 1968. The first order of business was to utilize his greatest strength: playing tennis. Winning the US Open would be a colossal achievement for any player, no matter the year or circumstance. But for Ashe to win in 1968 as the first African American man to hoist the trophy, in the midst of America's annus horribilis and in the wake of devastating assassinations and bicoastal rioting, would brim with resonance and national meaning. Ashe admitted that he felt "a sense of urgency" during this time. After losing a match in July, he would not lose another match for more than two months, stringing together twenty-six straight victories, culminating in winning the US Open, as an amateur no less.[22]

In a sign of hope and possible progress, the crowd thunderously cheered Ashe's victory and the breaking of the color barrier in men's tennis. It was also the only time his father walked onto a tennis court to embrace and congratulate his son. Half a world away, in Vietnam, his younger brother wept.

It was also the year when Ashe became "emotionally involved" in the cause that would define his activism for the next two decades: apartheid in South Africa.[23] If he was late to the American Civil Rights Movement, as his critics often observed, no one could deny his early advocacy in raising American awareness about the evils of South Africa's racial caste system.

But his approach to raising awareness and evoking change was mired in controversy.

Ashe consistently favored active engagement with the South African regime. While many preferred ostracism and isolation, he wanted to "change South Africa primarily through increased contact and dialogue with the outside world."[24] Ashe noted that a strategy of rigid isolation didn't work in China and Cuba and that he was imbued with unique qualifications to facilitate this dialogue. As he observed in *Off the Court*, "I feel I have some credibility in talking about South Africa. I was brought up under a similar situation, having lived in the segregated South."[25]

For years he petitioned the South African government for a visa in order to play the South African Open. He was rejected on numerous occasions, despite assistance from President Nixon. Finally, in 1973, he was granted a visa, though on the paperwork it insultingly described Ashe as an "honorary white." While he lost to Connors in the final of the South African Open, he gained firsthand experiences as a pilgrim to the epicenter of apartheid that fortified his commitment to the cause of ending South African oppression. He visited South Africa numerous

times throughout the 1970s, admitting that "from the early 1970s I consciously made South Africa the focus of my political energies inside and
outside the United States."[26]

He witnessed signs that read WHITES ONLY at tennis courts,
learned about the diabolical effectiveness of the criminal justice system,
came into frequent contact with angry South Africans who viewed him
as a guileless pawn of a repressive regime, inadvertently legitimizing the
very government he came to confront.[27] He also met "dedicated apolo-
gists for apartheid" and, conversely, "liberal whites" who condemned the
very system supporting their privilege. But of all the people he met on
his travels, it was a fourteen-year-old South African whose words moved
Ashe the most. This particular boy followed Ashe around Johannesburg's
famous Ellis Park where the South African Open was played. Ashe finally asked the boy why he was following him. The youngster answered:
"You are the first truly free black man I have ever seen."[28]

Ashe once observed about the nature of heroism, "True heroism is
remarkably sober, very undramatic. It is not the urge to surpass all others
at whatever cost, but the urge to serve others at whatever cost." For the
next decade, he was a model of inspired diligence, advocating for policies
aimed at exerting persistent pressure on the South African regime. He
favored sanctions against South Africa, and intervened to stop a highly lucrative exhibition match between McEnroe and Borg because it was set to
be played in Bophuthatswana, a phony and internationally unrecognized
state controlled by South Africa. He took care to always make a distinction
between South African players and the South African regime, opposing
the banning of individual players from tournaments. He became heavily
involved in the apartheid-fighting group TransAfrica and was even arrested outside the South African embassy in 1985.

But always—always—he believed in the power of persuasion over
violence. As he noted, "I am with Thoreau, Gandhi, and Martin Luther
King, Jr."[29] To his critics, Ashe was too cautious, too timid, and often
too late. To others, he unnecessarily politicized sports and interjected
controversy when it was wholly unnecessary. What Ashe understood,

what all Americans should understand, is that when it comes to making any kind of positive impact on the world around us, there is no correct road map, no master key, no Bible, *I Ching*, or divine oracle. Ashe was not Muhammad Ali, Jackie Robinson, or Kareem Abdul-Jabbar. He was always and forever his own man. He chose his own causes, his own voice, and did so in his own time. We can certainly take inspiration and guidance from others; Ashe certainly did. But as long as we march in the direction of progress, in pursuit of a principle chosen of our own volition, we should always take pride in the uniqueness of our own journey.

Lesson #3: Confidence Comes from a Million Choices

Looking back on the day of Ashe's greatest victory, there was absolutely no reason to believe he would—or even *could*—defeat Connors. Modern tennis fans have enjoyed a spree of extraordinary tennis for almost two decades as the three greatest Grand Slam champions—Roger Federer, Rafael Nadal, and Novak Djokovic—have ended up playing in the same era. Sports fans often forget that Connors, especially in the early and middle 1970s, was an unadulterated force of nature. His blue-collar doggedness, his deific determination, not to mention his flat backhand that took the ball on the rise, made him a player with powers never seen before on a tennis court. The legendary tennis commentator and broadcaster Bud Collins labeled him the "Brash Basher of Belleville."

What was Ashe up against in the 1975 Wimbledon final?

Connors was only twenty-three and the number-one ranked player in the world. The year before he had won three of the four Grand Slam tournaments while winning ninety-six percent of his matches.[30] The esteemed sportswriter Frank Deford wrote a famous column about Connors in 1978, brusquely observing, "Conqueror was what he was, too, because Connors did not merely win. He assaulted the opposition, laid waste to it, often mocked it, as well, simply by the force of his presence."[31] Coming into his final match again Ashe, Connors had not lost a single set.

Ashe and Connors ended up playing seven times, with a number of the matches being lopsided victories for Connors, such as the two South Africa Open finals Ashe had desperately wanted to win. The intensity of their rivalry spilled off the court. Ashe was a traditionalist, Connors a proud contrarian. Connors refused to join the player's union. Ashe was fiercely patriotic and revered the Davis Cup. Connors's hesitation to play for his country prompted Ashe to label Connors "unpatriotic." In response, Connors initiated a $5 million libel lawsuit against Ashe, which he eventually withdrew. In a subtle jab of one-upmanship, Ashe wore his Davis Cup jacket onto the court for the warm-up session before the match.

All told, Ashe beat Connors a grand total of one time in his playing career.

However, this sole victory is a testament to one of the most important lessons Ashe has to offer: Individual belief always precedes grand achievement. No one ever achieved anything of substance or reached a mountaintop without first believing it could be done. As Ashe explained, "If you are confident, you can do anything."

However, there is an important corollary to Ashe's sentiment about confidence. As he also observed, "One important key to success is self-confidence. An important key to self-confidence is preparation."[32] The first part of that preparation was for Ashe to analyze himself. He knew his greatest asset was not a booming serve or a fierce forehand but his powerful intellect. He would have to outthink, out-strategize, execute a novel scheme of attack if he stood any chance of becoming the first African American man to win Wimbledon. (It didn't hurt, of course, that Connors had aggravated a foot injury in a previous match.) Thus, the night before his match with Connors, Ashe convened a diverse council of some of the greatest tennis minds of his time who also happened to be his friends. Their advice was brutal: Trying to outduel Connors with brawn instead of brains was a fool's errand. If David wanted to defeat Goliath on the grass of Wimbledon, he would have to fundamentally change the way he played. He would have to chip the ball. Keep it in the middle of the court. Take away the angles Connors loved to hit. Hit a lot of lobs. Don't engage in power tennis. Make Connors come to the net. As one of Ashe's friends commented, "Chip the ball. Don't hit over. Chip it. You want to make him hit up all the time . . . Don't hit the ball hard. No pace. No pace."[33]

Ashe decided to employ a tactic seldom used at the time: underspin. While topspin elevates a tennis ball once it hits the ground, underspin prevents a ball from bouncing. If Connors was known for anything, it was for taking the ball early, on the rise. Ashe's approach was to simply deprive Connors of his greatest assets. Ashe also decided to do something fairly unorthodox: Instead of going to bed early the night before the most important match of his life, he went out with his friends for a late-night dinner and some blackjack at the Playboy Club, of all places.

The next day, Ashe could soulfully sense he was walking on the path of his destiny and knocking on the door of his greatest triumph. Years later he remembered, "I had the strangest feeling that I just could not lose."[34] His feelings were more than fanciful hopes. His strategy immediately bore fruit. Connors had not lost a single set the entire tournament, but Ashe quickly defeated him 6–1 in the opening set. A befuddled and disoriented Connors failed to adjust in the second set, unbelievably losing it by the same 6–1 score. After two sets in a Grand Slam final the extraordinary Connors had only won two games. But Connors is not known as the most intense tennis player of all time by accident. He recovered to make the match competitive, winning a close third set 7–5.

Tennis is a sport that is an amalgam of boxing and chess, both brutal and cerebral. At the beginning of the fourth set, many in Ashe's box worried he would abandon the strategy that had worked the first two sets, that he would revert to his typical power game, that he couldn't make it to the finish line. And yet, Ashe understood that confidence is not simply a vision of a hopeful outcome but also a tool for how to get there. With great patience and pertinacity, Ashe persisted in his strategy, winning a close final set 6–4 to secure the finest moment of his tennis career.

No matter how much energy Ashe devoted to American and

international affairs, he always understood that the better he played, the bigger his megaphone for the issues he cared about. Before there was Venus and Serena Williams, there was Arthur Ashe. For the rest of his life, he demonstrated a keen ability to successfully catapult himself into different arenas because of his inner resolve and steely sense of confidence.

Ashe retired from tennis following a heart attack at the age of thirty-six. But his portfolio of activities and causes only seemed to accelerate in his post-tennis life. He became the successful captain of the Davis Cup team. He was a prolific writer, penning columns for *Time* and the *Washington Post*. He always enjoyed his commentator duties at HBO. He sat on the boards of companies like Aetna Insurance Company. Many of the philanthropic contributions of his lifetime endured long after his death, such as the National Junior Tennis and Learning network, Association of Tennis Professionals, and Safe Passage Foundation, among many others.[35] He never stopped doing tennis clinics for young people, and even when he was diagnosed with AIDS kept up a busy schedule. In fact, Ashe's primary reason for not disclosing his status to the public for so long was because he desperately wanted to keep up the pace of the eclectic life he had created in his post-tennis years. It is easy to forget that in the late 1980s and early 1990s AIDS was rarely associated with "a buttoned-down, well-educated, heterosexual man."[36] Trying to beat an inquisitive media to the punch, he didn't make the revelation by choice, and yet the manner of the announcement, presented with a dignified and calm demeanor while explaining that he probably caught the disease from a blood transfusion, amplified and accelerated efforts to demystify AIDS to the American public. His elegance and grace made it easier for the public to support public health initiatives to fight the disease that ultimately took his life. His reputation as a reluctant activist made him, albeit tragically, the perfect spokesperson for a disease often mired in public misunderstanding.

Ashe was even confident that he could face down the moment of death with deep dignity and an almost mystical sense of divine purpose.

"I do not brood on the prospect of dying soon. I am not afraid of death. Perhaps fear of death will come to haunt me when the moment of death is closer. On the other hand, perhaps I will be even less fearful, more calm and at peace."[37] Greatness is not a chance, not a whimsical by-product akin to winning a lottery ticket, not a state of being accidentally stumbled upon by denizens of an unfair world. No, greatness is only won by those with the confidence of self-belief, who know they have climbed mountains and traversed valleys in preparation for defining moments, who have faith that their lives are meant for certain ends and specific moments, who know that one day vindication will call upon the vanquished.

CHAPTER 6

Abraham Lincoln

Read for Pleasure and Purpose

★

★

There are episodes scattered throughout the American story that pulsate with grandeur, moments that seem to reveal a sincere national purpose, ticks of time unironically suggesting that America is fated to play a significant role in the history of human affairs. In these moments, even the crank, the curmudgeon, or the cynic might give an unstinting pause to honor what is unique and special about America.

Events such as the deaths of Thomas Jefferson and John Adams on the same day, July 4, 1826, the fiftieth anniversary of the signing of the Declaration of Independence. Moments like Martin Luther King Jr. uncannily declaring before his followers the night before his assassination that "I've been to the mountaintop" and have "seen the Promised Land," soulfully sensing, perhaps, that "I may not get there with you." Instances like the night House Speaker Tip O'Neill knelt at the foot of President Reagan's hospital bed following an assassination attempt and begged God to spare his life, reciting Psalm 23.

Four years after Abraham Lincoln insisted to his fellow Americans that the "mystical chords of memory" could "swell the chorus of the union" if he could but appeal to "the better angels" of their nature, something genuinely astonishing transpired as he stood on the east steps of the Capitol to deliver a speech that would one day be considered the greatest inaugural address of all time. After almost four years of the Civil War and endless sectional strife, Lincoln rose to speak on the occasion of his second inauguration.

In the hours leading up to the speech, the weather was utterly foul, a miserable mélange of "drenching rain," "drizzling," and "a heavy gale."

Yet, as if on cue from the gods, when Lincoln rose to deliver his remarks, the clouds dramatically parted and the sun burst forth, functioning as a type of divinely sanctioned meteorological spotlight. Chief Justice Salmon P. Chase seemed to sense the providential gravity of the moment, remembering "the beautiful Sun Shine which just at the time the oath was taken dispersed the clouds that had previously darkened the sky . . ."[1]

If Lincoln was, as he appeared in that moment, a cosmically consequential actor in the eternal drama between light and darkness, between benevolence and evil, and ultimately between freedom and bondage, he would not have been surprised. Of any American in our rich history, no one had a deeper and more penetrating sense that he was fated and framed for a life of deep historic consequence. He was summoned by that great and irresistible force that sometimes whispers in the ears of those whose names thunder loudly in the pages of history books. Famed Lincoln biographer David Herbert Donald observed, "From his earlier days Lincoln had a sense that his destiny was controlled by some larger force, some Higher Power." Lincoln's admiration for Shakespeare was evident by his repeated recitation of Hamlet's words: "There's a divinity that moulds our ends, Rough-hew them how we will."[2]

Yet his sense of calling was not the same as complacent entitlement. Rather, his calling drove him to worry that he would never achieve his great task. He frequently fretted about his own insignificance, opining, "Oh, how hard [it is] to die and not be able to leave the world any better for one's little life in it."[3] During the winter of 1841, Lincoln suffered one of the worst bouts of depression of his entire life, so potent that his friends suspected he was suicidal, removing all trace of knives and razors from his room. His best friend, Joshua Speed, warned him that his despair could become fatal, to which Lincoln replied death would be acceptable, except for the fact that he had done nothing "to make any human being remember that he had lived."[4]

He suffered potent and excruciating losses throughout his life—his baby brother Thomas, his sister Sarah, his mother, a youthful fiancée, and most agonizing of all, the death of his son, Willie, while serving as president. For weeks after Willie's burial, Lincoln would "shut himself in a room so that he could weep alone."[5] His marriage, while loving and loyal, was never an easy one. He often evinced a fatalistic Greek spirit that would have been recognizable to the likes of Aeschylus, Sophocles, and Euripides.

He thought little to nothing of his childhood, asserting that it was "folly to attempt to make anything out of my early life," pithily summarizing his childhood as "The short and simple annals of the poor." From an early age, Lincoln embraced that most quintessential of American sentiments: The shape and intensity of our dreams should not be determined by the circumstances of our beginnings.

Lincoln's greatness was not achieved by working harder than his peers, though he did work tremendously hard, nor was it simply the result of lucky genius. His latent talent sprang into life because of his insight into the nature of learning. Lincoln understood that we learn not to fit ourselves for narrow, practical jobs, like cogs in a great machine, but in order to ready our souls for the destiny in store for us. His belief can be demonstrated throughout his life, but perhaps its most simple expression was in his habit of reading for pleasure, and ultimately, greater purpose. Lincoln knew that learning always enriches us, and that we don't have to draw a direct line from knowledge to application to make learning "worthwhile."

This man, whose childhood gave no suggestion of the greatness to come, suffered the most famous assassination in American history. The first words uttered on his death were an amalgamation of Greek tragedy laced with Shakespearean pathos: "Now he belongs to the ages!" If Lincoln "belongs to the ages," then that must mean he also belongs to our age, an age of deep and pronounced civic cynicism, an age of profound personal bewilderment and anxiety, an age in which the American soul is in perpetual flux, enmired in the mindless trappings of digital malaise and cancerous commercialism. Lincoln found a way to forge a remarkable soul in times that were even more divided than ours.

In an age of such personal and national dissension, it is imperative to ask one of the greatest Americans to have ever lived—maybe the single greatest—what advice he has for a nation in the midst of a civilizational identity crisis.

But if he truly did experience such a sense of destiny—seemingly confirmed at every turn by "chance," "history," or "Providence"—what could we possibly do to become more like him? "Be born with a great destiny" seems unlikely to put gusts of wind in our sails when we feel a potent lack of agency in our lives. However, what's interesting about Lincoln is that his overwhelming sense of destiny never caused him to be complacent or blithe. He took nothing for granted when it came to success. And when it came to the dark side of the destiny coin, his regular black moods and intuitions of doom, he looked for healthy coping mechanisms. He structured his life with routine, humorous stories, a sort of magpie love of learning, prioritizing ideals over personal ambition, and through immersing himself in the lives of those who'd lived before him. His habits and perseverance showed hope in the future, as his study and reflection found wisdom and motivation from the past.

While the self-help version of Lincoln may not be the subject of historical studies or bestseller lists, he is the version we desperately need today, for he teaches us that while ambitions can orient and structure a single human life, it is only the ideals we embrace that imbue it with higher or transcendent meaning.

Lesson #1: Learning Is a Form of Hope

Sometimes the legends we hear about American heroes are true.

Lincoln really did endure a childhood filled with constant sorrow and pounding poverty. His father was both illiterate and uneducated. His mother died when he was only nine years old. He and his older sister were paternally abandoned for long stretches of time until a new stepmother, Sarah, eventually made life more bearable for the two young Lincolns. The log cabin myth is no myth at all—a replica can be visited today in LaRue County, Kentucky.[6]

Life on the frontier was more brutal than bucolic, eternally taxing and perpetually full of toil. One thing it was not full of was educational opportunity. The academic background of America's earliest political leaders often reads like a laundry list of Ivy League and elite universities: both John Adams and John Quincy Adams attended Harvard. James Madison was educated at Princeton. Alexander Hamilton went to King's College, which eventually became Columbia University. Thomas Jefferson and James Monroe both attended William & Mary. While George Washington never attended a university, he also didn't come from squalor and was thoroughly patrician in his stature and stock.

Looking at this hardscrabble youth, the first thought to occur would probably not be "this boy needs to learn about the law." Certainly, the adults in his life didn't think so. When asked what practical tasks Lincoln was good at as a boy, his cousin said, "Well, not much of any kind but dreaming, but he did help me split a lot of rails when we made a clearing twelve miles west of here." (The slim expertise was spun by a canny politician friend into an image of Lincoln "the rail-splitter." Lincoln was annoyed by the "stage trick," but it was too late, the legend was printed.)[7]

Lincoln's early education was erratic, at best. It was clear from a young age that he possessed unusual intellectual qualities. He was gifted with an extraordinary memory, mastering difficult material faster than any of his peers. He was almost certainly aware of being the smartest person in any room he entered. These natural capacities, however, were never interpreted by Lincoln as a guarantee of success nor as an invitation to show off his cerebral breadth. Instead, he understood that his gifts were merely embers of a potential intellectual fire, a fire that would grow bright enough for him to become an authentic autodidact, a maker of his own mind, and, ultimately, the architect of his own life.

Lincoln was born into a world in which nothing was ever given, absolutely everything had to be earned. Any success he enjoyed unfurled itself at a crawling pace, and only as a consequence of endless scratching, continual clawing, and boundless grit. It was a life of scarcity coupled with backbreaking industry.

His powerful journey of self-learning was motivated, therefore, not by observing his circumstances and needs but by following a dream of what life could be. He shows us how such learning can be a form of hope, of imagining a world that isn't yet but that could be.

Lincoln made a simple but momentous discovery at a young age: The best learning is self-learning because it proceeds not from fearful obligation but from liberty and love. Self-willed learning anchored in joy bolsters natural capacity, awakening a symphony of aptitudes that would otherwise lie dormant. He revered books because they widened and enriched his world, adding splendor and color to the possibilities of his own life. Aristotle's observation in *Politics*, "It is evident, then, that there is a certain kind of education that children must be given not because it is useful or necessary but because it is noble and suitable for a free person," lends credence to the notion that human beings must be framed for freedom, that the raw material of the human psyche is more akin to clay than analogous to marble.[8] Our ability to mold the "clay" of ourselves depends tremendously on our imagination for what is possible. Lincoln's imagination and yearning for knowledge were titanic.

As a young man, he read the Bible and *Aesop's Fables* so frequently that he could recite long passages for the rest of his life.[9] He acquired a deep love of Shakespeare, so much so that Lincoln and a man he boarded with, Jack Kelso, "used to sit on the bank of the river and quote Shakespeare back and forth at each other."[10] The essence of classical learning—contact with great minds from long ago coupled with a hearty engagement with books that have endured the test of time—provided a young Lincoln with a glimpse of what is finest and best in the human condition.

Lincoln's devotion to this type of learning is powerfully demonstrated by a famous episode about a book he borrowed as a young man. The book, *The Life of George Washington* by Parson Weems, was owned by a wealthy neighbor who lived sixteen miles from Lincoln's home. While modern historians don't hold Weems's book in particularly high regard—it is Weems who is responsible for the wholly fictionalized account of Washington cutting down his father's cherry tree—the book made a powerful impression on young Lincoln.[11] He absorbed the essential truth of Washington's high moral character, his reverence for service, and his deep devotion to the experiment of the infant republic. The problem was that the book was accidently ruined in a rainstorm. Lincoln confessed to his neighbor and offered to work off the value of the book. His unforgiving neighbor responded by telling Lincoln he owed him two full days of work, which Lincoln spent cutting the tops from corn. It was a small price to pay for the inspiration it provided for the rest of his life.

As Lincoln grew older and used his foundation of learning to catapult himself into a new world of letters, his efforts had a much more obvious application. While he often exuded a poet's sensibilities with words and phrases, he also learned for intensely practical reasons.

When he decided to run for the Illinois legislature his friend and

teacher William Mentor Graham convinced him that he would never succeed unless he could powerfully master the rules of grammar. Lincoln
focused his considerable intelligence on Samuel Kirkham's *English
Grammar*. Graham later commented, "I have taught in my life four or
six thousand people as School Master and no one ever surpassed him in
rapidly quickly & well acquiring the rudiments & rules of English grammar."[12] He learned the complex concepts of geometry and trigonometry
in order to become a deputy surveyor.[13] Lincoln didn't attend law school
but instead methodically read law books one at a time and studied previous legal cases. As Doris Kearns Goodwin notes in her book *Leadership
in Turbulent Times*, "After finishing each book, he would hike the twenty
miles from New Salem to Springfield to secure another loaner."[14]

As he aged, Lincoln transcended the tedium of intense, practical
learning and returned to his youthful love of learning for the joy of it.

In his younger days, he recognized that to be a surveyor required
knowledge of geometry, that a freshman assemblyman needed to know
the rules of the legislature, and that a lawyer must know the law. But an
older and wiser Lincoln discovered a richer dimension of self-learning, a
dimension having more to do with spiritual enlargement than acquiring
the necessary knowledge to obtain a job. The lifestyle afforded a lawyer
riding on the legal circuit left Lincoln with a considerable amount of time
to indulge his promiscuous love of learning. He used his time at night
after everyone else had gone to sleep to deeply immerse himself in a rich
syllabus of subjects and studies. He engaged the humanities: philosophy, literature, drama, and poetry. He read up on math and science. He
famously mastered the six books of Euclid and is the only president to
hold a patent for a device "buoying vessels over shoals."

Lincoln revered his studies because he possessed an unquenchable
curiosity about life and the broader world. But beneath the reading and
mental exercises, the late-night reflections and intellectual striving, lay
something raw and unspoken. It can be intriguing to wonder whether
those who achieve greatness knew, or at least had a vague inkling, of what
they would become. None of us feel like we can know the future, but in

retrospect, it often seems to fall into place with a certain inevitability—choice leads to choice leads to choice. Lincoln seemed born with a dream of greatness, even if he wasn't certain of the details. What made him different from all of the men whose dreams ended up in the dustbin of history was choosing to believe in a benign future, over and over again.

Choosing to learn—not for practical or utilitarian reasons—is an implicit act of faith that knowledge is good, that the future will provide opportunities to use it. In retrospect, the fruits of such hidden labor can seem like destiny or Providence. Lincoln, late in life, seemed more inclined than ever to attribute the sweep of history—and his own role within it—to God's purposes, calling himself "an instrument of Providence." But earlier, in less fraught moments, he still made hundreds of small decisions to push against his persistent melancholy and persevere. Upon hearing that his son's friend, a young man whose father had recently died, had failed his entrance exams to Harvard, Lincoln penned an impassioned letter of encouragement, writing at one point that "I know not how to aid you, save in the assurance of one of mature age, and much severe experience, that you can not fail, if you resolutely determine, that you will not." The mystery of his perseverance lies somewhere in the space between that choice to persevere and that conviction that Providence was trustworthy. Perhaps one could not exist without the other.

Seen in this light, our sixteenth president wasn't just learning and reading for pleasure. He wasn't just sharpening a mental blade to become a legal logician for juries and judges. No, he was *preparing* himself for a historic destiny he sensed he would one day fulfill. He was *readying* his mind and soul for a great trial that lay sprawled somewhere in his future. To absorb the Gospels of the Bible, to commit to memory the plays of Shakespeare, to steep in the seraphic poetry of the Scottish writer Robert Burns, is to prepare a man's soul for something that is far more than merely technical, something that will demand a human possess a rhapsodic medley of intellectual, moral, and leadership qualities that appear on the world stage only sparingly in history.

Lincoln may not have realized it, but as he voraciously read and mentally labored, he was preparing to be the president of the United States in the midst of a bloody and protracted Civil War. He may not have realized he would be the man destined to free the enslaved men, women, and children of the American South, or that he would preside over the ratification of the Thirteenth Amendment. He could never have imagined that future generations of Americans would one day regard him as the greatest American to have ever lived, and that, of all the abundant blessings of our history, having this extraordinary self-taught man at the helm of the nation in the midst of our greatest constitutional crisis would be the greatest blessing of all.

This is not to mythologize or canonize a flesh-and-blood man. But Lincoln was unique. His intuition was strong—uncannily so. In the same way that he seemed to have a vague but powerful intuition of his own destined significance, he saw his own death coming. Ward Hill Lamon, Lincoln's friend and biographer, later reported a conversation he had with the president three days before his death about a dream Lincoln had of being assassinated. In the dream, Lincoln observes a corpse lying in state in the East Room of the White House. When he notices a soldier standing guard he asks, "Who is dead in the White House." The soldier responded, "The president. He was killed by an assassin."[15]

Lincoln didn't live to preside over Reconstruction or celebrate the ratification of the Fourteenth Amendment, which constitutionalized his beloved Declaration of Independence with its sunny promises of "equal protection" and "due process" for all. But what he did live to accomplish powerfully demonstrates why learning should be forever intertwined in all of our lives.

Lesson #2: The Cause Is More Important Than the Man

If schoolchildren are asked what they associate with the name "Abraham Lincoln," a patchwork of famous events, high-profile speeches, and memorable phrases are probable answers: the Civil War, the Gettysburg

Address, the Emancipation Proclamation, the Lincoln-Douglas debates, the first and second inaugural speeches, maybe even "log cabin" or "top hat."

What is almost never mentioned or known is Lincoln's failed bid to become the senator from Illinois in January 1855.

This failed attempt is now considered a trivial blip in an otherwise magisterial biography, a small letdown endured by Lincoln before winning the ultimate prize just a few years later in 1860. But this specific failure isn't so small. It should be magnified and widely remembered, for it reveals one of the central lessons of Lincoln's life: Ambitions are personal, local, and fleeting, whereas ideals unite a human being to a deeper and richer sense of purpose. Durable happiness requires a commitment to a higher principle than one's momentary objectives or fleeting fantasies. Lincoln's ability to take the long view was another expression of his hope and equanimity, despite the rockiness of his personal life and political times.

The story behind Lincoln's failed bid in 1855, and the righteous rationale for it, are worthy of remembrance—even veneration—by Americans today.

A slim antislavery majority composed of two different parties, mainly Whigs and a few antislavery Democrats, had been elected to the Illinois legislature in 1855. In the days before the Seventeenth Amendment, senators were not directly elected by the voters but chosen by state legislatures instead. On the first ballot all of the Whigs, of course, voted for Lincoln, totaling forty-five votes, six short of the fifty-one needed to secure victory. The other antislavery candidate, Lyman Trumbull, received a mere five votes, all from fellow Democrats who were vehemently opposed to voting for a Whig. Pro-Trumbull antislavery voters absolutely refused to budge. Lincoln eventually reached forty-seven votes, excruciatingly close to a majority.

Round after round of voting produced no winner. After nine taxing rounds, Lincoln did something utterly remarkable: He chose principle above pride. He directed his floor manager to tell his supporters to vote for Trumbull, the only other antislavery candidate. The men who had stood with Lincoln faithfully carried out his instructions, but they were furious; some were sobbing, some were perplexed, and some were frankly resentful. One of his allies claimed "he would never have approved of the five being in control of the forty-seven men."

Lincoln, though, spoke above the apoplectic din, eloquently explaining "the cause" is "preferred to men."

Lincoln was, of course, deeply demoralized by the setback, swearing afterward that he would never run for public office again. Americans are so accustomed to remembering Lincoln as a towering moral and political figure that it is easy to forget at the time of his 1855 Senate defeat he had served but a single unremarkable term in the House of Representatives. Despite the bitter disappointment, he was gracious in defeat, affably attending Trumbull's victory celebration, though Mary Lincoln steadfastly refused to speak to Trumbull's wife, a woman who had formerly been a close and intimate friend.[16] Moreover, he harbored no ill will toward Trumbull or the Democrats who had stubbornly withheld their votes from him. In fact, two of them eventually "became wheel horses in his later political campaigns."[17]

Lincoln's predicament in 1855 resembled the fate of fictional baseball player Dr. Archibald "Moonlight" Graham, the iconic character from the classic movie *Field of Dreams*, of whom it is said: "Fifty years ago, for five minutes you came within . . . y-you came this close. It would KILL some men to get so close to their dream and not touch it. God, they'd consider it a tragedy."[18] But Lincoln never regretted his decision of handing the Senate seat to Trumbull. And he certainly didn't consider it "a tragedy." Lincoln's obligation was never to himself but to a higher moral principle; he deeply understood that fidelity to a cause sometimes requires sacrificing personal glory.

"The cause," as Lincoln described it, was akin to the Roman god Janus, a deity capable of projecting two unique faces.

One face of "the cause" was famously articulated years later by Lincoln in the Gettysburg Address. The meaning of Gettysburg, and the moral epicenter of the Civil War itself, lay in testing for all time the "proposition that all men are created equal," and proclaiming the responsibility to make this proposition more than an intellectual claim, more than high-sounding words grandly written on parchment, more than a geometric theorem proven correct by the dictates of Euclidean logic. For a nation to be truly just and for its politics to be properly oriented, this proposition must be tightly stitched into its conscience, forever an unambiguous object of its will.

The founding generation Lincoln cherished deserves eternal credit for articulating and enshrining Jefferson's "abstract truth" into the founding documents of the nation, for fertilizing the cause of human liberty for posterity, and for establishing the first liberal democratic republic in human history. But they came up short. Despite all that the fathers of American freedom achieved, and despite all that they did, the abstract truth cementing and anchoring American civilization—"We hold these truths to be self-evident, that all men are created equal"—remained a mere abstraction as long as the evils of slavery were allowed to persist within the American republic. Or, put another way, if the founding ideal and organizing principle of the American polity are truly rooted in "the Laws of Nature and Nature's God," then those laws must be obeyed. If they aren't then the soul of the nation will become utterly despoiled of its righteousness.

Thus, electing an antislavery candidate in 1855 who correctly understood what was at stake was absolutely paramount, trumping all personal ambitions Lincoln might have harbored for himself.

But what about the second face of "the cause"?

The second face of Lincoln's cause had even broader historic and global implications than the American Civil War. This other cause is not a central focus of debate in our time, but that's only because its rightness is taken for granted. Lincoln did not have that luxury. He recognized that the repercussions of Vicksburg, Antietam, and Fort Donelson would echo in Europe, Asia, and beyond. There was an essential question about human nature and political life that Lincoln wanted to answer, a question of colossal historic significance: Do human beings have a genuine capacity for self-government in pursuit of justice?

Lincoln answered the question once and for all by harnessing the might of the Union Army, by keeping the Union intact, and by laying the groundwork for the Thirteenth, Fourteenth, and Fifteenth Amendments.

Royal eyes were certainly observing the turmoil of American sectionalism. The stakes for these rulers—kings and queens, sultans and czars, emperors and kaisers—were much higher than revolution and regicide. If the American republic could survive and eventually flourish, if constitutional self-government was proven to serve the aims and aspirations of human freedom and genuine justice for all, then the autocratic sovereigns of the world would know their days might well be numbered.

The future of America, then, was the future of the world. The cause of the North was the cause of all mankind. What Lincoln was working to establish, in perpetuity, was "the form of government that is best for mankind, everywhere and always."[19] As he wrote in his special message to Congress on July 4, 1861, "this issue [of rebellion and secession] embraces more than the fate of these United States. It presents to the whole family of man, the question, whether of a constitutional republic, or a democracy—a government of the people, by the same people—can, or cannot, maintain its territorial integrity, against its own domestic foes."[20] Thus, the crucible of the American Civil War demanded there be no armistice, no premature cease-fire, no hollow settlements. The war must be won, the Union must endure, and the cause of human freedom must triumph above all.

Such an outcome would alter the trajectory of all of human history.

While Lincoln revered the founders and was certainly a passionate defender of Enlightenment principles, he was a man of a wholly different era, more romantic in nature and fatalistic in temperament. Unlike Jefferson, he wasn't merely interested in disembodied Newtonian truth but yearned for personal, inward meaning as well. He found this meaning by promoting ideals over ambitions and the cause over the self; it was never in question that Lincoln would rather promote the abolitionist ideal than attain the venerable post of a US senator. Perhaps he had read the words of Alexis de Tocqueville, who wrote of America three decades earlier, "The greatness of America lies not in being more enlightened than any nation, but rather in her ability to repair her faults."

Lesson #3: Study the Past to Forge a Better Future

The passage of the Kansas-Nebraska Act of 1854 stirred the mighty energies and ambitions of Lincoln. Historians agree that the Act, which repealed the Missouri Compromise, created new territories and allowed for popular sovereignty, was infinitely complex, and yet for Lincoln, his objections to its passage centered on a straightforward question: Did it violate the original intention of the founders for individual states to now decide for themselves (popular sovereignty) if they wished to be a free or slave state?

Lincoln knew this controversy was the most important and momentous contest of ideas since the ratification debates of the late 1780s; the destiny and meaning of the American polity itself was at stake. To win the argument, Lincoln did what he had done his entire life: He dedicated himself to the task at hand. He did his homework. He did something utterly staggering. He went back into the record of the American founding and achieved a depth of understanding and nuance that empowered him to triumph over his most ardent opponents.

In truth, Lincoln had learned from a young age that putting in long hours and doing the necessary homework were fundamental ingredients in any rise to prominence. "Work, work, work is the main thing," he observed in 1860.[21]

And work he did.

As an up-and-coming attorney, Lincoln wowed his clients and other attorneys with a superhuman, almost godlike capacity to put in long hours. He would draft all of his legal opinions himself and was said to have written an entire forty-three page "answer to the plaintiffs' bill of complaints" in a single sitting.[22] In an era in which pixilated screens have severely depressed attention spans and American schools have precipitously lowered academic standards, it is worth remembering that success like Lincoln's was built on the back of a prodigious work ethic.

He brought this ethic to bear on the debate engrossing the nation in the years leading up to the Civil War. In countless speeches and debates, Lincoln marshalled forth the necessary arguments that would become the vehicle for the eventual abolishment of slavery in America. His objections to the Kansas-Nebraska Act had been noted as far back as his famed Peoria Address in 1854, "the plain, unmistakable spirit of that age, towards slavery," he observed, "was hostility to the principle, and toleration, only by necessity."[23] Even then, the historian Doris Kearns Goodwin notes, people wondered when Lincoln had the time to do so much homework to master the issue of slavery so completely. "The answer," she writes, "lay in the long period of work, creative introspection, research, and grinding thought."[24]

The most dazzling display of his understanding, a genuine master class in rhetorical statecraft, occurred on February 27, 1860, at an event that would come to be known as the Cooper Union Address. The speech was part of a series featuring different national speakers, Lincoln not particularly prominent among them. He was virtually unknown in the East at the time and almost nobody in the media or the party apparatus considered him a serious contender for the Republican nomination later that year. The extraordinary success of the Cooper Union Address would change their perceptions of Lincoln, and, by extension, the fate of the nation forever.

To prepare for the speech, "he hit the books."[25] Between court appearances, he spent countless hours in the Illinois State House library. He conducted granular research by reading deeply about the earliest national debates regarding the power of the congress to legislate on the issue of slavery—the Constitutional Convention, the Northwest Ordinance, and the different ratification debates among the states. Instead of making broad declarations about the framers or founding fathers, he meticulously looked at the individual voting records of the thirty-nine men who signed the Constitution to discern how they each voted on issues related to slavery and legislative power. Again and again, he emphasized that they had a firm understanding of the issue at hand, "even better than we do now."

Lincoln's voice was firm and his delivery powerful. For only the second time in his career, he used a manuscript for a major address. His research was richly detailed and his argument eloquently expressed. He demonstrated that of the twenty-three signers who had a chance to register an opinion about the federal authority over slavery, twenty-one voted to prevent the spread of enslavement into new territories. Of the sixteen that were left, Lincoln's exhaustive research suggested that fifteen left "significant hints" they opposed slavery. To reinforce that the founding generation stood on the side of the Republican Party, Lincoln's party, he evoked the name of George Washington eight times and the name of Thomas Jefferson twice.[26] Lincoln's reverence for the founding generation was vital and present in many of his previous addresses—in Peoria, in Lewistown, and in his famous Lyceum Address in 1838. But nothing compares to the scholarly virtuosity of his Cooper Union Address.

Lincoln's tour de force was met with immediate and resounding approval. The audience in New York erupted in applause. Newspapers across the country reprinted his address for public consumption. Lincoln had successfully catapulted himself to the top tier of Republican Party presidential candidates. His consistent ability to do his homework and master a subject at a depth that others were unwilling or unable to match exemplifies an important aspect of the relationship between knowledge and power. Power, for Lincoln, had to be more than raw force; it had to be principled, rooted in something beyond brute will or naked ambition.

Thus, Lincoln's lesson to "work, work, work," to study the past to improve the future, can be far more than just a narrow, rudimentary directive for life. It can, and should, become a specific commandment about the high principle of meaningful American citizenship.

The best rhetorical flourishes in his career tended to appeal to notions of a binding civic spirit. He was often concerned with finding an all-powerful national cohesive to counter the toxic regionalism engulfing the politics of his time, a concern that should certainly echo in American ears today. "The mystic chords of memory" and his belief that each generation must "return to the fountain whose waters spring close by the blood of the Revolution" are not just fanfares of oratory. Lincoln believed each American generation required renewal, a renewal that was only possible through shared memory of a common history.

Thus, to study American history, to do our homework as citizens, is to renew the nation and revivify America.

The passage of time, however, presented specific pitfalls for the American republic, pitfalls that are glaringly obvious today. Hamilton and Madison both believed the passage of time would promote and swell the legend of the American founding. Posterity would naturally grow more reverential. The fathers of American liberty, they believed, would be broadly and loudly venerated by future Americans.

Lincoln, however, was far less sanguine, believing that "time induces forgetfulness, indifference, and eventually irreverence for laws, ideals, and other values that arise from human struggle."[27] There is no question that as it relates to the American body politic of the present day, Lincoln's anxieties about democratic decay and historic amnesia were well-founded. No one teaching high-school or college civics today could possibly side with Hamilton and Madison over Lincoln.

One need only observe the swagger of college students tearing down statues or the haughty iconoclasm of young Americans eager to rename, remove, and reinterpret the personalities of American history. Whereas eighty-three percent of the Silent Generation feels warmly about the Fourth of July, only sixty-one percent of Gen Z feels the same level of affection. When it comes to Veterans Day and Memorial Day, holidays celebrating the sacrifices of previous generations, the gap is even more pronounced, with ninety-three percent of the oldest age group finding these holidays personally significant as opposed to only fifty percent of

Gen Zers. Only fifty-nine percent of Millennials consider the ratification of the Constitution to be significant compared to eighty-five percent of Baby Boomers.[28]

Clearly, the "mystic chords of memory" have been forgotten and the waters of the revolution have receded.

The British thinker Alfred North Whitehead observed there are only two moments in Western civilization when political leaders in the midst of revolution behaved as well as could be expected: the Rome of Caesar Augustus and the American Revolution.[29] Why this is the case, and how a robust study of our own founding can reanimate the stale waters of toxic political discourse, is the real lesson Lincoln accords to us today.

But we, too, will have to do our homework.

CHAPTER 7

Ben Nighthorse Campbell

Don't Worry About the Best, Worry About *Your* Best

★

★

The life of Ben Nighthorse Campbell defies conventional descriptions. Even the most imaginative scribbler of prose would be hard-pressed to produce the right words or manufacture enough clever phrases to adequately capture the fierce originality of his journey.

He was utterly unique.

While his achievements are certainly unprecedented, what makes

Campbell such a forceful and appealing source of inspiration for con-
temporary Americans is that his life could only have been lived in the
United States of America. And yet, he is more than an icon of the Native
American community or a symbol of American striving and grit. He is
extraordinary in his normalcy, eloquent yet plainspoken, making him
both comprehensible and accessible.

As one of his Senate colleagues humorously described him when
Campbell retired in 2004, "Ben Nighthorse Campbell is a unique, proud
leader of heritage. He is a man of principle. I look at Ben Nighthorse
Campbell as one who runs on his own gear ratio. He is a character with
character, whom I will certainly miss." Another senator remarked, "I
have always considered Ben to be larger than life, someone you would
read about in a novel about the Senate rather than someone actually
serving in the Senate."[1]

Like Lincoln, he suffered through a daunting childhood mired in
tragedies evoking the first act of a Dickens novel. His mother, Mary, was
a Portuguese immigrant who endured decades of tuberculosis, living
and working in a sanatorium for approximately twenty-two years, where
she met Ben's father, Albert, an alcoholic whose affliction was so intense
that his mother was forced to place Ben and his sister in a Sacramento
orphanage. As an adult, Ben could still remember a cruel nun who once
threw him into a pigpen as punishment for having dirty hands.[2]

Albert would disappear for long periods, the days sometimes stretching into months. Ben and his sister would go looking for him, once
witnessing a barroom brawl in which their father got stabbed in the
head with an ice pick.[3] Violence and hunger were occasional visitors to
the Campbell home. In response to Albert slapping her, Mary once took
a frying pan and coldcocked him. For the rest of his life, Ben could remember a meal in which his mother had but a single can of peas to eat,
splitting the peas between her two children and drinking whatever juice
was left.[4]

This child, who knew next to nothing about his Native American roots until later in life, who spent time in jail as a teenager for siphoning gas out of a car, and who dropped out of high school, would go on to be inducted into the National Native American Hall of Fame in 2021 after a life of eclectic and soaring achievements.[5]

He would carry the American flag during the closing ceremonies of the 1964 Summer Olympics in Tokyo. Decades later he would be a co–grand marshal in the 1992 Rose Parade with a direct descendant of Christopher Columbus, and dressed in traditional Native American regalia would ride a horse during Bill Clinton's inaugural parade. Today, visitors can swim, fish, and water ski in Lake Nighthorse located in La Plata County, Colorado.

He is famous for serving twenty-two years in public office and for his powerful advocacy on behalf of Native Americans, sponsoring or cosponsoring fifty-four bills related to Native American issues that eventually became law. But Campbell—the politician—is merely scratching the surface. In every colorful chapter of his life, he reached summits of achievement that, on their own, would have supplied enough glory for one normal lifetime.

Whatever he did, he did well and with powerful aplomb. He participated in the Olympics in judo and was instrumental in popularizing the sport back home in America. As a teacher, he was respected, influential, and deeply kind to his students. He trained champion quarter horses. When he became an artist and jewelry maker, he won some of the most prestigious prizes in the country and was commercially successful. When he ran for public office, he refused to cut his ponytail, insisted on dressing like a Westerner, and proudly rode a motorcycle. He is famous for speaking his mind and for his unflinching authenticity, neither courting controversy nor shying away from it if an important cause or principle was at stake. He has never been accused by anyone of phoniness. Richard Lamm, the former governor of Colorado, once exclaimed, "He's such a unique individual. My God! He just sings depth and commitment."[6]

He sometimes could come across as gruff or rough around the edges, projecting unrepentant authenticity. When the Rose Parade organizers asked him to be a co–grand marshal with a descendant of Columbus, he agreed as a gesture of inclusion and reconciliation. He also decided to ride a horse, and when a heckler yelled, "Why aren't you walking like your ancestors did?," Campbell quickly retorted, "Fuck you!"[7]

"No one had ridden a horse as grand marshal since 1938. Not Roy Rogers, not John Wayne, and I found out why," he said, with trademark candor. The horse was absolutely petrified when confronted with 150,000 spectators.

> I was riding an Indian saddle with very little padding and I could feel my horse's heart pounding through my legs and I think he could hear my heart pounding through a part of my anatomy. I just patted his head and reminded him that I had raised him and fed him and he must have decided that it wouldn't look good to see an esteemed member of Congress flat on his back on a manhole cover.[8]

During his college years, he once broke a drunken football player's arm at a party by tossing him off a second-floor balcony. To a fellow citizen who didn't like Campbell's negative opining about voters who are single-issue or uninvolved, he acerbically replied, "I have a right to express my opinion on the state of our society just as you have a right to. I did not give up that right to speak out when I was elected to office. I'm sorry if you think all politicians should say only soothing things. I don't operate that way, and will not. If the truth hurts, I'm sorry. Isn't democracy great?"[9]

His approach to public service was always practical but principled. He cherished the notion of the citizen-legislator, resisting politics as a career, a way of life, or the epicenter of his existence. He never stayed in a single office for more than a few terms, and when he found his political party had strayed too far from his core beliefs, he bravely decided to switch from the Democratic to the Republican Party, to the great ire of many friends and supporters. Yet when he retired, many of his former Democratic colleagues professed a deep and abiding affection for Campbell, with longtime Connecticut senator Chris Dodd admitting, "Despite that change, we have continued our strong friendship over the years."[10]

Campbell knew that his life could serve as a powerful inspiration to others. He admitted as much when trying to recruit his eventual biographer, the Smithsonian curator emeritus Herman Viola: "I started at the bottom and look where I am today . . . I want every kid in America to know that this great country will give them the opportunity to make something of themselves, if they are willing to work for it."[11]

Campbell scraped and battled for every judo win, for every election and legislative victory, and on every piece of jewelry he produced and sold. Undergirding each of his lessons is a universal and timeless truth: A life that lacks genuine dimensions of sacrifice can never inject its will into the world. His life is a true demonstration of how free societies create great men and women. He took the opportunities before him and lived a life of extraordinary adventure, industry, and innovation. Through it all, he was driven by a powerful desire for excellence and a belief in the principle that he didn't have to be *the* best but he had to reach his own limit, to be *his* best.

Presidents, athletes, and historic names from previous centuries can sometimes seem encased in a sheen of remoteness, often foggy to modern eyes. Fortunately, Campbell is one of us, a man of our time and our world. His virtues are not anchored on the peaks of mountains that can be seen but seldom visited. He wants to take our hand. He invites us to walk in his shoes. He yearns to enliven our hopes and warm our ambitions through the furnace of his own colossal achievements.

Let's see where he takes us.

Lesson #1: You Don't Have to Be the Best, Just the Best You Can Be

Decades after Campbell competed in his final competition, he wondered aloud about the enduring value of his years chasing judo glory: "When I ache everywhere in the morning, when everything hurts, I think of the enormous energy I expended and the torturous training I endured, and I wish I had done golf or tennis, something with a professional counterpart that I could have enjoyed for many more years and that would not have been so harmful to my body and that would have enabled me to provide for my family."

He broke his nose nine times, had two of his teeth knocked out, and was perpetually bruised for years. Not only did these injuries do damage during his judo years but they continued to inflict serious doses of suffering later in life—"I've got every kind of 'itis' now—bursitis, arthritis, tendinitis. Calcium in my joints, all that stuff . . . I sometimes reflect: 'Did I do the right thing?'"[12]

His ascendent dream was to medal at the first Olympics where judo was recognized as a sport, the 1964 Tokyo Summer Games. Sadly, the years of training, sacrifice, and agony in pursuit of this particular dream didn't translate into a transcendent moment of joy on a podium or medal stand. Instead, he suffered a tear of an internal ligament in his right knee while training for the Olympics and didn't have time to fully heal. The knee completely collapsed midway through his second match of the games.

This isn't to suggest that he wasn't successful. He won six Pacific Coast titles and three national championships. But in the end, for Campbell, judo was never about trophies, medals, and championships. It was about much more. In fact, as his biographer powerfully noted, "The key to Ben Campbell's success is the sport of judo. Judo gave his life purpose, it channeled his aggressions, and it taught him self-discipline."

What defining life lesson did judo impart to Campbell?

In his own words: "I have never felt that I had to be the best, but I have always felt I should be the best I could be." To be blunt, few people have ever endured the blinding agony of Campbell's path toward being the best that he could be. It is a journey filled with multiple divorces, endless physical torment, and the highest level of personal disappointment. But at its root is a lesson everyone can understand—the steadfast belief that life is a gift, that talent must be nurtured more than discovered, and that potentiality must be nourished by the waters of sacrifice.

In return for his suffering, he acquired the most precious knowledge anyone can ever obtain—the gift of self-knowledge. Without it, Campbell would never have tasted the splendors of so many different forms of achievement. Judo imbued him, and many others from the judo world, with inordinate inner strength and resolve. As he explained, "The mechanical skill of throwing some guy on the floor may not help you feed your family, but judo teaches you to persevere, to never give up."[13]

His initiation into the world of judo was not a particularly auspicious moment. While working at a fruit-packing plant he decided to pick on the wrong coworker—a young, somewhat diminutive Japanese man who made the claim of being a judo expert. No matter what Campbell did he always seemed to end up on the floor, despite the difference in their statures. It shocked and fascinated him. As he remembered, "That this little shit could do something like that surprised the hell out of me, but I couldn't get a hold of him. I couldn't do anything to him. He made a believer out of me, a convert for life."[14]

At the time of Campbell's brutal but amusing introduction to judo, few people in America knew much about the sport. There were no local organizations or national leagues on par with some of the more famous American sports, like football or basketball. His coworker invited Campbell to learn at his own modest judo club. Around this time, he decided to drop out of school and join the US Air Force, eventually and fortuitously ending up in South Korea as a military policeman. After meeting a Korean doctor who was also a judo instructor, Campbell began intensively training five hours a day, six days a week.

By the time he left the service, he was hooked.

He enrolled at San Jose State University, which had one of the first judo programs in the country, as far back as 1946. While officially a police major, by this time his real passion and focus was judo. His coach, Yosh Uchida, himself a legend in the world of judo, remembered that Campbell was simply "indifferent" to pain, responded to losses with an even more ferocious work ethic, and was greedy for tips on how to get better.[15]

He always seemed to embrace a challenge, seeking out superior athletes in pursuit of improvement. One of his more eccentric habits was to plaster the pictures of these competitors on his wall or in his locker. He would yell out, "I will beat you." Other times he would exclaim, "I'll get you, you son of a bitch. Wait and see."[16]

His devotion to judo only increased after college. In the years following his graduation, he would get up early in the morning to train. After work, he would go to a Buddhist temple annex in downtown San Jose to put in even more time. His judo ambitions trumped everything else—his job, his marriage, his house and car, even his life insurance policy. All of it would be sacrificed when he made the most daring and audacious decision of his life: He resolved to move to Japan and enroll in Meiji University in order to deepen his commitment to judo. It was a decision that set him on a path of monumental suffering, a path that would even kill some of his classmates.

His decision was influenced by the fact that the 1964 Olympics were set to take place in Tokyo and would be the first Olympics featuring judo. The Meiji team was "world renowned," and Campbell would credit the training for his 1961, 1962, and 1963 US National Titles.[17] As Campbell remembered years later, "The training I had done in the United States was kid stuff compared to what I went through the next four years. It was by far the hardest, most disciplined, most painful thing I ever did. I mean, God, you hurt all the time."[18]

What was so brutal? The expectations. Students' legs were expected to be black and blue from their ankles to their knees. They were expected to have blisters, calluses, and cuts all over their bodies. The workouts were so taxing and intensive that Campbell regularly lost ten pounds in a single session, utterly drenched in sweat. When a student was thrown down during a match another student would kick him in the head or the stomach, or he would be beaten with a bamboo stick. The Meiji program simply did not acknowledge injuries and suffering. In fact, during

Campbell's time at Meiji, three teammates died—two broke their necks and another ruptured his aorta.

The results speak for themselves. In Campbell's time in Japan, he competed in fifty matches and lost only two of them. The high point of his career was winning the gold medal in the open division of the Pan American Games in 1963. After a disappointing Olympics he returned to the United States with a new goal in mind: to popularize judo in his homeland. It was a goal he had harbored for a long time. He became a founding member of the United States Judo Association. He helped coach the national team and assisted a number of collegiate gold medalists with innovative training methods and unique drills. He was instrumental in turning his home city of Sacramento into the judo capital of the nation. While Campbell's utter devotion to judo cost him his first two marriages, it also led to his third life-defining marriage to Linda, whom he met while giving judo classes.

America is not filled with rich promises of specific outcomes or guarantees of grandeur. American citizenship is not a shield from misfortune or failure. What fueled the fire of Campbell's intensive patriotism was the belief that no one needs to be the best, the richest, or the smartest to find a good and noble American life. But being the best that you can be requires a certain approach to life and a specific disposition about the many verities of noble struggle. Campbell would tell modern Americans to embrace their difficulties and proudly display the bruises and scars of life. Upward paths are never bereft of danger.

But that doesn't mean we shouldn't attempt to rise.

Lesson #2: Life Is Better as an Adventure

In Campbell's first campaign for the House of Representatives, one of his most politically astute advisers made a savvy decision that also revealed Campbell's uncanny ability to embrace new adventures.

His campaign chose to portray him as a "Renaissance Man" by highlighting the fact that he had walked an exceptionally diverse array of paths. If the function of a representative in a legislature is to represent as many different interests and perspectives as possible, then Campbell's multilayered life would serve him well as a member of the House of Representatives. In essence, "the idea was to get the voters to identify with Ben as one of them, and this was easy to do because of his wide experience—semi-orphan, high school dropout, Korean war veteran, small businessman, Olympic athlete, artist, truck driver, teacher, rancher, and admired state legislator."[19]

Of all the clever aphorisms or folksy expressions Campbell was adept at spinning, the one that best captures his spirit of continual self-renewal and adventure is "Be a winner or a loser, but don't be a spectator." He was never a spectator; he was a compulsive and eclectic doer, exemplifying the notion that the best life is one that is unafraid of new challenges and fresh adventures. The lesson that people should vigorously seek rejuvenation and resist the habitual plodding of adult-hood was demonstrated by two unique threads in Campbell's journey: The first was an awareness of his Native American identity, what he called "a detribalized Indian awakening to my heritage," and the second was his unquenchable desire to embrace new challenges and forms of competition, which continued into old age.

Campbell's father, Albert, came of age in the United States at a time when one's Native American identity was often shrouded in secrecy and shame, cloaked in penetrating feelings of disgrace. Albert closely guarded the family secret, never knowing about the specifics of where and when he was born. Information was scarce and Albert was never especially forthcoming on this issue of his background. Ben once asked his father why he left the reservation. His father simply replied that he was "tired of being hungry" all the time.

Around the time of his marriage to Linda, Campbell's curiosity about his heritage became more intense. He started asking questions. This interest coincided with a broader change in the political culture about Native identity. The Red Power movement of the 1960s was led by young Native Americans and aimed, among other things, to push back against notions of racial shame, supplanting indignity with a powerful sense of pride and increasing calls for Native American self-determinism.

Campbell had no idea how closely he was related to legendary members of the Native American community, specifically the Northern Cheyenne tribe, nor was he aware that his relatives had actually taken part in some of the most famous—or infamous—battles in American history.

He was never able to discover a perfect historic record, but in the late 1960s he met Alec Black Horse, who confirmed that Campbell was a member of the famed Black Horse family of the Cheyenne tribe. Not only was Black Horse his great-grandfather but he was a famous warrior who fought alongside Crazy Horse at the battle of the Little Bighorn and helped the Cheyenne flee to Montana to avoid imprisonment.[20] The name Nighthorse was given to Campbell during a name-giving ceremony on the Northern Cheyenne reservation; its intention was to reflect his great-grandfather's roots.

In the wake of a powerful 1976 commemoration of the battle of the Little Bighorn, Campbell became completely committed to the Cheyenne people, their culture and customs, as well as their challenges and concerns. As much as he loved judo, by the time he reached middle age it was his affiliation and connection to the Cheyenne people which became the most vital and soulful connection of his life. He formed deep friendships with the Cheyenne people, he listened to and played their music, and eventually he came to serve as a member of the Council of Forty-four Chiefs.

In addition to searching out and confirming his Native roots, after his judo years he was never afraid to pursue new interests, cultivate fresh loves, and explore wholly different paths of life. Consequently, Campbell's life seemed to constantly unfurl in new, distinct, and unpredictable chapters—he dabbled in teaching and police work, and got into the horse business and trained some of the best quarter horses in the world. Each chapter ushered in new challenges and, in typical Campbell fashion, new triumphs and emblems of success.

However, if someone were to ask Campbell to describe himself using one word, to distill his soul with one adjective alone, there is a decent chance that single word would be *artist*.

His artform was the creation of unique jewelry. In fact, to an entire subculture of Americans interested in collecting Native American art and jewelry, Campbell is known as "Ben Nighthorse."[21]

The designs on his jewelry are created to "reflect the mosaic patterns of his life, combining symbolism and techniques borrowed from Japan and Europe as well as his Native American origins." What made his early jewelry truly distinctive was its blending of cultures and styles. It turns out his years spent in Japan were good for more than just judo. In his spare time, which was admittedly sparse, he visited Japanese craftsmen, specifically sword makers, to observe their methods. He learned to adapt a Japanese process used for constructing sword blades called *mokume* to make Native American designs. Years later, Campbell observed, "I may not have been the first American to do this but I am the first American Indian."[22]

The result was jewelry featuring an evocative fantasia of different colors and metals.

Campbell experimented and perfected his craft as he spent almost half a decade teaching jewelry-making classes, primarily to Native American students, some of whom went on to become successful jewelers themselves. But as he observed, "my father taught me how to use a few tools, but design cannot be taught."[23]

Like all talented artists, Campbell had strong opinions about the creative process, arguing that the key to true art is maintaining a certain level of imaginative spontaneity. Even after he became a national politician with endless professional commitments, he insisted on maintaining a creative space and time in his life for the design and creation of jewelry.

What started out as a hobby soon blossomed into a business, becoming quite lucrative. Campbell's jewelry started to be entered in juried shows, such as the California State Fair where a piece he created won first place out of thirty-five hundred entries.[24] In 1979 numerous pictures of his jewelry were also prominently featured in the well-known art-and-travel magazine *Arizona Highways*, which significantly boosted his sales at jewelry shows and helped to burnish his reputation as a designer of the highest quality.

Other markers of success began to appear.

He designed a ring specifically for an appearance on the famed QVC network with extraordinary results. The national television exposure bore significant commercial fruit as he sold fifteen hundred rings in a mere seven minutes. Celebrities began purchasing some of his jewelry. But the zenith of his career came when the Franklin Mint in Philadelphia requested a handcrafted gold pendant to be reproduced and sold. The pendant was named "Pendant of the Winding Water" by the Franklin Mint, a name Campbell was not especially fond of. The results, however, were spectacular—the pendants sold out and grossed $2.7 million.[25]

After retiring from politics in 2004, Campbell changed directions yet again, becoming a policy adviser at a law firm in Washington, DC, before starting his own consultancy business in 2012, Ben Nighthorse Consultants, where he assists his clients in navigating the federal legislative process.[26]

Campbell had a talent for adventure and was acutely alive to the rich panorama of possibilities just beyond his field of momentary vision. And unlike the average citizen who finds success stubbornly fleeting or hauntingly elusive, he always seemed to triumph, even if his victories extracted heavy emotional and physical tolls. More impressive and rare is that he never seemed intimidated by the specter of grand opportunity or wobbled in the face of intimidating odds. The gusts of life's misfortunes—poverty, injury, abandonment—never stunted his sense of agency or deadened his impowering perspective.

In short, it might be logical to conclude that Campbell is beyond duplication or even emulation. But this would be wrong.

Seeking adventure does not have to be as dramatic for everyone as it was for Campbell. We don't have to travel to new countries to pursue gold medals or run for public office in long-shot campaigns. New chapters of life don't necessarily require new spouses, new careers, or a stop on the road to Damascus. Reinvention can be small and achievable. Or, if we dream big, these new chapters can be grand and dramatic.

But whatever form adventure takes, it requires a steadfast belief that life can be enlarged and enriched. It asks us to have faith that everyone can become palatially souled, radically hopeful, and exuberant in the belief that tomorrow can be more interesting than today.

Lesson #3: Don't Let Politics Dominate Your Life

More than a decade after Campbell left office in 2004, PBS conducted a wide-ranging interview with him to explore the various chapters and achievements of his life, during which he voiced a sentiment that is rarely heard from prominent politicians these days, and yet it powerfully reveals the wisdom of his unique approach to politics.

In the interview he revealed an intense, almost haunting, life regret: In his quest for political success, he missed out on vital years of his children's lives.[27]

Throughout his twenty-two years of public service, Campbell consistently held to the conviction that public service should be a temporary post, a transitory station of one's journey, never a career destination or a position of permanence. Such wisdom isn't just good for the soul; it is essential for American democracy.

Career politicians who pine for perpetual warrants of power, who impede the natural rotation of the nation's political offices, ultimately tarnish the nobility of public service. As Campbell once commented, "I'm sure that there have been others like me who don't look at Congress as a place where the sun rises and sets, but not in my lifetime. I think a real problem on the Hill is that people get addicted to the lifestyle."[28]

In his late sixties, he started to experience health issues. He underwent treatment for prostate cancer and during his second Senate term in 2004 had to be hospitalized for chest pains. He quickly decided he didn't want to die in the Senate, clinging to power and the vestiges of senatorial prestige.[29]

Although Campbell has only been out of public life for about two decades, his approach to politics, service, and civic life seems tragically passé. And yet, in an era in which national politics in all three branches have come to be dominated by the elderly, resulting in what is sometimes called a "gerontocracy," Campbell's ideas about service and political identity are refreshing. And not just because one generation should never be allowed to hold a perpetual grip on the nation's affairs.

Many of the everyday connections that once defined ordinary life for common Americans—strong familial bonds, robust religious commitments, rich varieties of friendship, community kinship and service—are simply not as present in the lives of modern citizens. That doesn't mean they aren't forming connections. They certainly are. But they are doing so in a way that is fraying the delicate social fabric of the nation. Instead of God, family, and country, Americans increasingly center political attachments and cement ideological commitments to the epicenter of their identities.

This is why parents don't want their children dating or marrying people from a different political party. It is why ideology is increasingly listed as a personal characteristic on X (formerly Twitter) and other social media biographies. It's why so many people move to different states, which perpetuates division even further, concentrating the red and the blue voices of America, making them seem even more foreign and fringe to one another.

The consequence is a nation in the grips of potent tribalism, endlessly seething with political polarization and malignant rhetoric. Seven in ten Americans now believe that American democracy is "imperiled."[30] Whereas Americans once defined themselves through a rich spectrum of personal and moral commitments—the elements of identity forever enumerated on gravestones or heroically celebrated in eulogies—they increasingly do so through political affiliation and specific forms of media consumption. Frequently offended. Eternally outraged. Spasms of apocalyptic alarmism polluting our news feed and demanding our attention. In such a world, cynicism sells. Rage is triumphant. Paranoia refracts the daily news into mindless dollops of conspiracy.

Enter Ben Nighthorse Campbell, who knew a better way. He understood that political life has its inherent limitations—it is a world of competing interests, clashing claims of power, and an endless maelstrom of conflict. It can be a brutal dungeon of pessimism or an elevated space of idealism. This world is essential in the democratic order of a constitutional republic. But what Campbell understood so well is that it is not necessarily the place to find deeper meaning or purpose. Euphoria and enchantment, when they are found, are encountered on mountaintops and in the embrace of those we love. It is never experienced watching cable news or participating in congressional committee hearings.

Governing institutions should be practical places that solve problems and hopefully inch closer to justice. They govern, but they are not meant to nourish. This is why Campbell found political life to be personally taxing. He was often away from his home for long periods of time, missed family events, and took a serious financial hit when he decided to enter public life.

This isn't to suggest that he lacked institutional pride or that he didn't sometimes wax poetic about membership in an institution as significant as the US Congress. As he stood on the verge of retirement he conceded, "I have to tell you, on each moonlit night, particularly in the wintertime after a fresh snow, as I view the dome of this great building as the first or last thing I do in my workday, I am just thrilled that I was here for a while and it was a part of my life."[31]

Campbell never defined his own political identity through the lens of opposition. The famous quip—"Tell me who your enemy is, and I will tell you who you are"—would be utter jabberwocky to Campbell. He didn't have political "enemies," he had policies he simply disagreed with. This is why he focused on practical issues like the use of public lands, water projects, Native American living conditions, education, and the safety of law enforcement officers. He was quietly one of the most effective legislators of his generation. A colleague once observed of him, "He has passed a lot of legislation. A lot of people are not aware of that. Many of his bills have become law. In many cases, he is a quiet legislator. He is effective and he gets things done."[32]

Many of these "things" are not blips of inconsequential law akin to renaming post office buildings or slipping pork barrel projects into omnibus bills. His achievements are not accidental—they are derived from a proper understanding of how politics is to be conducted in a representative democracy characterized by multiple layers of pluralism. We should pay close and meaningful attention to the type of person who is able to make our institutions function properly.

Campbell knew how and when to listen to his constituents. In his first campaign for the Colorado legislature—a campaign in which he was told by a party patron, "I think you have two chances . . . you have little and you have none"—he embraced the retail side of politics by "obtaining maps of every community in his four-county district and then systematically" walking through every street.[33] He went on to defeat a popular incumbent.

But just as important, he also knew when to stand on principle and push back against the excesses of constituent demands. At a town hall meeting, a stubborn constituent kept demanding Campbell respond to the same question over and over again. Finally, Campbell snapped, "You know, I hate it when people feel that because you're an elected official, they somehow own you. Do you realize that my salary costs every man, woman, and child in this country about one-half of one cent each year?" Campbell then took out a penny, flipped it to the man, and said, "Here's your refund!"

His manner would have been wholly familiar to the likes of James Madison or Sam Rayburn or John Kennedy. It was Kennedy who famously wrote in *Profiles in Courage*, "This may mean that we must on occasion lead, inform, correct and sometimes even ignore constituent opinion, if we are to exercise fully that judgment for which we were elected."

Speeches make the spirit soar, and Campbell was a fluid and con-
vivial orator, but consensus and coalition-building are how one moves
legislation in a republic as large and diverse as ours. His ability not
only to listen but also to lead explains why he was so good at politics.
He understood the institutional mechanics of the American legislative
branch and the specific grammar of governance it promulgated—a
legislator who wishes to be successful cannot often pass legislation
and be a cable news provocateur and social media flamethrower at the
same time.

He was always comfortable in both political camps, describing himself as socially liberal but "as fiscally conservative as any rock-ribbed
Republican. I had been too poor as a youngster to give away someone
else's money."[34] It comes as no surprise that a relatively constant feature
of his political career was the Republican Party trying to recruit him to
its side, an effort that eventually bore fruit during his first Senate term.

Having always considered himself to be a moderate who made friends
on both sides of the party aisle, he was a consistent thorn in the side of
both parties. He supported a Balanced Budget Amendment, one of the
central tenets of Republican Party orthodoxy in the mid-1990s, and was
disheartened to see Democratic Party efforts to kill the amendment.[35]
His switch to the GOP angered a lot of people, both in Washington and
back home in Colorado, given that he had won election to the Senate
by using a lot of the financial and organizational infrastructure of the
Democratic Party. The voters weren't especially upset with him, however,
as he was reelected in 1998, this time as a Republican.

Because his politics didn't define him, he never forgot who he was
or where he came from. His clothes. His ponytail. His motorcycles. His
charisma. He brought all of it to the House of Representatives and then
to the Senate. The motorcycle even came in handy at times. When the
new king of Jordan visited the Senate, he asked to go for a ride. Campbell
also thought it was wise policy for the Capitol Police to buy American and
exchange their Japanese-produced motorcycles for Harley-Davidsons,
which they did and continue to do.[36] When a homeless man attacked

Senator Strom Thurmond, Campbell grabbed the attacker and managed to handcuff him.[37]

His approach to politics was both bipartisan and practical. His popularity never cloaked itself in messianic messaging or ideological idioms. He wanted to solve problems, even if some of those problems were difficult to address or deeply rooted in the muddied land of historic controversy.

With a great deal of assistance from Senator Daniel Inouye, he was instrumental in the creation of the National Museum of the American Indian, which opened in 2004. As an addendum to the creation of the museum, Campbell worked to ensure that the Smithsonian, which had been holding roughly twelve to eighteen thousand items of Native American remains in storage, were returned to the appropriate tribal communities.

In 1998, he sponsored a bill to establish a Sand Creek Massacre National Historic Site.[38] The Sand Creek Massacre is one of the most vivid and grisly massacres of Native Americans in our history. On November 29, 1864, almost seven hundred army soldiers killed more than two hundred thirty Cheyenne and Arapaho in an assault lasting seven hours. By killing thirteen Cheyenne peace chiefs, the massacre severely disrupted governance of the tribes for generations.[39]

But the most controversial measure sponsored by Campbell was his effort to rename the Custer Battlefield National Monument in Montana as the Little Bighorn Battlefield National Monument, and authorizing the construction of a memorial to Native Americans who died during the battle.[40] Others had tried for decades to officially install a plaque representing the perspective of the Native American side, yet had failed. As Campbell eloquently observed about the power of national symbols, "Symbolism is important. The American flag is important to millions of people; so is the Statue of Liberty. The monument we're going to build over there is going to be the Indian Statue of Liberty."[41]

If Americans wonder why so many of their political institutions appear to be broken, maybe they need to take a close look in the mirror.

In our unquenchable zest to own political adversaries or elect people who are consummate fighters, we have distorted what political leaders are actually supposed to do with their time and misunderstood how they are supposed to behave. They aren't elected simply to give speeches or engineer viral moments for a niche audience of activists and cable news hosts. They are, in fact, supposed to be national custodians of integrity and honor who spend their days in pursuit of the common good while representing their constituents.

Would Campbell, or anybody like him, even want to run for elected office today? Would his enormous and vital talents for telling the truth, making friends from both parties, and solving difficult problems be considered a virtue in today's political climate?

I think we know the answer to these questions, which begs a final one: What does that say about us?

CHAPTER 8

Ruth Bader Ginsburg

Prioritize Relationships

History books will remember Ruth Bader Ginsburg as a titan in the civil rights movement for American women. While she is rightly adulated for her oracular words and deeds concerning women's equality, both on and off the court, her life lessons go far beyond the political and legal realms.

More than one hundred justices have sat on the Supreme Court in American history, and none of them have come close to Ginsburg's prominence in pop culture.

Young Americans who are not known for being well-informed court watchers heartily embraced the celebrity of Ginsburg. Millennials often took to calling her "the Notorious RBG." They bought T-shirts and bobbleheads featuring her likeness. My oldest daughter purchased multiple biographies. Hollywood made films about her life. Netflix streamed movies about her achievements. She was mentioned on late-night television by the likes of Stephen Colbert and *Saturday Night Live*.

Cameras were rolling, in fact, when President Trump was told by a gaggle of reporters about Ginsburg's death. He had just finished a political rally in Bemidji, Minnesota, when a reporter asked about her passing. Even though the distant music playing from the rally gave the scene a surreal quality—the booming rhythm of "Y.M.C.A." gave way to the piano intro of "Tiny Dancer" as the president approached the press—his spontaneous and generous response was sober and touching, reflecting the way many Americans felt about Ginsburg, even those who often disagreed with her progressive constitutional judgments.

President Trump seemed genuinely stunned. "She just died? Wow. I didn't know that. You are telling me now for the first time. She led an amazing life. What else can you say? Whether you agreed or not, she was an amazing woman who led an amazing life. I am actually sad to hear that. I am sad to hear that."[1]

Ruth Bader Ginsburg's life is richly embroidered with powerful lessons for our time, especially for young people who frequently lack the meaningful connections of ages past. Ginsburg did not achieve her acclaim or scale the peaks of jurisprudential prominence by choosing her career over her family. She did not become a liberal icon by eschewing the friendship of conservatives on the court. She did not empower women by denigrating men.

It is taken as a given that no one can "have it all" these days, that the encompassing commitments of the modern workplace require a certain level of sacrifice in the home, that one's hobbies or passions must take a back seat in the hierarchy of life if one is to have even a passive touch of soaring professional success. There is a fascinating duality about Ginsburg that imbues her with a dynamic modern authority, one perfectly suited to offering timeless lessons to Americans who are often lacking in substantive life attachments: While she was certainly a woman with liberal social and political preferences, in her private life she radiated conservative values and cherished the traditional relationships and institutions that conserve the building blocks of a flourishing and free society.

The commitments of life that are life-affirming and soul-defining—to family, to friendship, to country—were modeled by Ginsburg in a humane and lively manner that always seemed to bring her genuine and authentic joy. Sadly, this joy is absent in the lives of enormous cross-sections of the American public today. In polls that ask if a respondent is "completely satisfied" with life, of the four categories identified by ideology and gender—liberal men, liberal women, conservative men, conservative women—it is the subgroup that certainly adulate Ginsburg the loudest, liberal women, who scored the lowest by a large margin, with only fifteen percent answering in the affirmative.[2]

There is no doubt that Ginsburg was a liberal woman. There is also no doubt that she was a fully realized, fabulously successful, enormously committed American who found colossal reservoirs of delight in her life. It would be helpful to discover just where, exactly, these delights came from, and why they grew larger as she aged.

In short, Americans who agree with her interpretation of the equal protection clause and the First Amendment should also listen to her when it comes to family, friendship, and patriotism. She knows what she is talking about.

LA Times writer Libby Hill has insightfully noted, "It feels as though by lionizing Ginsburg, we miss the most beautiful thing about her. She faces the same challenges, the same workouts, the same frustrations as anyone, yet still manages to do good things. You can live like Ruth Bader Ginsburg. You just have to stop rapping about her long enough to go out and do good."

Lesson #1: Put Your Family First

Ginsburg's daughter, Jane, always knew she wanted her mother to be a justice on the Supreme Court. This thunderbolt of maternal faith was humorously revealed by Ruth the day she was nominated to the court on June 14, 1993, in the White House Rose Garden. "In her high school yearbook," Ruth explained, "on her graduation in 1973, the listing for Jane Ginsburg under 'ambition' was 'to see her mother appointed to the Supreme Court.' The next line read, 'If necessary, Jane will appoint her.' Jane is so pleased, Mr. President, that you did it instead. And her brother, James, is, too."

This story would not have come as a surprise to anyone familiar with the legendary bond of the Ginsburg family. Thirty-four years earlier when Ginsburg received her diploma from Columbia Law School as the number-one ranked student of the graduating class, a four-year-old Jane yelled out, "That's my mommy." As the Ginsburg biographer Jane Sherron De Hart aptly described the occasion, "For her part, Ginsburg treasured both of her loves—the intense pleasures of family and her boundless passion for the law."[3]

While modern graduate students often approach their studies with a singular focus and zeal, believing excellence only occurs when life is untethered to anything beyond one's own narrow, single-minded ambitions, Ginsburg argued that her success was "in large measure because of baby Jane."

It is a unique and, sadly, thoroughly unconventional way to look at the power and benefit of having a family.

"I attended class," she recalled, "and studied diligently until four in the afternoon; the next hours were Jane's time, spent at the park, playing silly games or singing funny songs, reading picture books and A. A. Milne poems, and bathing and feeding her. After Jane's bedtime,

I returned to the law books with renewed will. Each part of my life provided respite from the other and gave me a sense of proportion that classmates trained only on law studies lacked."[4]

Ginsburg's stem-to-stern devotion to her family never wavered, even as she aged and achieved iconic status beyond the legal world. One of her law clerks, Ryan Park, who later became the solicitor general of North Carolina, wrote a moving essay for *The Atlantic* in January 2015 appropriately titled "What Ruth Bader Ginsburg Taught Me About Being a Stay-at-Home Dad."

Park was inspired by Ginsburg's ability to take familial ideals and translate them into an everyday reality, even in the face of tragedy. As a young couple, she and her husband, Martin (Marty), were forced to confront a testicular cancer diagnosis. Marty was attending Harvard Law School at the time. Her response to his cancer can only be described as Herculean—while nursing her husband back from the abyss of possible death and taking care of their baby, she somehow found the time to help him keep up with his coursework and assist him in writing law school papers.

During these early years of her marriage, Ginsburg was more than a tower of strength—she was the embodiment of mental and emotional fortitude. Having already lost her mother and sister to diseases, she buried herself in work to avoid the possibility of mentally considering the loss of her husband. She often worked all night, feverishly, as though prodigiousness alone could prevent her life from capsizing. Marty recovered and her life became more manageable.

The marriage of Marty and Ruth Ginsburg vividly demonstrates the extraordinary power afforded to couples who view each other as equals. As Dahlia Lithwick points out in *The Atlantic*, "Yet this romance for the ages—which it certainly proved to be—was also a business partnership almost unrivaled in feminist history. They both went to law school, they both worked, they had a daughter and a son, and they tried their first big gender-equality lawsuit together."

To a fascinating and profound extent, their marriage is a demonstration of the power of gender equality: When both parents see themselves as the sometimes breadwinner, sometimes caretaker, but always a supporter of the other, the potential for all members of the family, children included, is greater than the sum of its individual parts.[5]

Years later, Marty would return the favor by going the extra mile to help his wife realize her dream of ascending to a seat on the Supreme Court. His efforts during the nomination process reveal a marital dynamic in which he was part cheerleader, part strategist, but always a supportive and loving husband first.

President Clinton's first Supreme Court nominee had the potential to be the first justice appointed by a Democrat since Thurgood Marshall was nominated by Lyndon Johnson in 1967. The journey toward an eventual nomination was a long and seemingly endless one, what the journalist Brit Hume famously described as having "a certain zigzag quality."

Clinton, always eager for more input from a diverse chorus of voices, was tempted at various times to nominate a number of different people, including New York governor Mario Cuomo and Senate majority leader George J. Mitchell.

Ginsburg's objections to *Roe v. Wade* were a critical roadblock. Shockingly, she wasn't even on the original list of suggestions sent by feminist groups to the White House. Marty flew into action. He had meetings with women's groups. He talked to the press. He got thirty-four letters of support from different legal academics who expressed their distress that Ginsburg's gentle criticisms of *Roe* were being used as ammunition for opposing her nomination. He strategically forced the hand of women's groups to come out and publicly announce they would not oppose his wife's nomination. Much of this he did without Ruth's knowledge.

Later in life, Ruth bluntly admitted, "I have had more than a little bit of luck in life, but nothing equals in magnitude my marriage to Martin D. Ginsburg . . . I betray no secret in reporting that, without him, I would not have gained a seat on the Supreme Court."[6]

Years later, even as he neared death in June 2010, Marty—Ruth's "biggest booster"—remained forever proud of his wife. When Ruth went to the hospital one final time to bring him home, she spotted a yellow pad in the drawer next to his bed with a handwritten note from her husband:

> *My dearest Ruth—You are the only person I have loved in my life, setting aside, a bit, parents and kids, and their kids. And I have admired and loved you almost since the day we first met at Cornell some 56 years ago. What a treat it has been to watch you progress to the very top of the legal world.*

Young, ambitious Americans who see their lives in sad binary terms, of having to choose between professional ambitions and personal relationships, would do well to study the power of intertwined ambition and unyielding marital commitment. Indeed, despite the fact that her husband died on a Sunday of metastatic cancer, she attended the final session of the court's term the next day in order to announce her majority opinion in a case that held that a public law school could not bar gay students.[7]

In an act of almost Herculean strength and loyalty, in the weeks and months that followed, she honored every speaking arrangement that had been made prior to Marty's death. As if that were not enough, she also honored every single one of her late husband's speaking commitments.

The Ginsburgs spent a lifetime honoring each other, believing in each other, ultimately growing old together. There is a deep and underappreciated joy in traveling the difficult waters in life "oar to oar," knowing that life is better when it is built on a foundation of complete and unconditional love.

Of course, marriage is not for everyone. And having children is not for everyone.

History, after all, is scattered with scientists, philosophers, poets, and painters who either resisted marriage or were very bad at it— Socrates's treatment of Xanthippe by modern standards was nothing to brag about and Picasso's private life was an endless labyrinth of conflicts and disputes.

What Ginsburg shows us about life beyond the courtroom, however, is that one of the central tenets of a meaningful and joyful life is active participation in the creation and life of one's family. In her circumstance, she would argue that her family life was not only *not* an impediment to her dreams but was central to eventually realizing them.

This lesson is especially vital and resonant in an era in which family life is in decline and rates of loneliness are surging. The traditional adult aspiration of marriage is in free fall. The biological desire to reproduce is also quickly becoming more of an antiquated hope. Scholars have certainly offered a variety of fascinating hypotheses for this collapse of marital desire, from a suffocating Millennial and Gen Z devotion to unabashed individualism to increasing housing and education costs.

But the phenomenon is real. From 1970 to 2018, the median age for a first marriage for women increased from twenty-one to twenty-eight. For men it rose from twenty-three to thirty.[8] The percentage of Americans who have never married increased almost fourfold, from nine to thirty-five percent.[9] Or to phrase the problem another way, "in nearly three decades, the number of Americans between the ages of 25 and 54 who are married dropped from over two-thirds to roughly half. Four in 10 (38 percent) of this age group are now living 'unpartnered.'"[10] A record number of forty-year-olds have never been married, particularly among the working class and African Americans.[11]

And yet, across five decades of research and surveys, it is clear that married Americans tend to be happier, and not just during the honeymoon phase but in later life as well. For those who fret about divorce, the divorce rate is actually lower today than it has been since the late 1960s.[12]

What Marty and Ruth Ginsburg understood was that family life is a noble aim and a joyful aspiration. The "Gospel of Me" and the "Church of I" might not be as appealing as popular culture suggests. The tropes and headlines portraying parenthood as abject misery are utterly false— eighty percent of parents enjoy parenting and eighty-seven percent see it as central to their sense of identity.[13] The profiles chronicling the perpetual bachelorhood of Leonardo DiCaprio and other Hollywood stars gives the wrong impression of the bacchanalian lifestyle.

It might work for DiCaprio, but most of us yearn for the permanence of love and commitment.

The comic George Carlin once said, "Trying to be happy by accumulating possessions is like trying to satisfy hunger by taping sandwiches all over your body." Americans like Ginsburg who truly flourish, who reach professional summits while still in possession of immutable moral fiber, rarely do so by taping pleasantries and amusements to themselves. They do so by digging deep into the soil of life, no matter how hard or frozen it may be at times, knowing the richest treasures often await those who put their families first.

One of the most famous psychological studies in recent history, the Grant Study, tracked two hundred sixty-eight Harvard students over the course of seventy years to investigate what factors, habits, attitudes, and behaviors tended to lead to fulfillment. A summary of the study confirms what Ginsburg knew to be true: The most meaningful elements of life require intimate connections, usually in the form of powerful friendships and positive family relationships. To summarize the seventy-plus years of research, "If they could be boiled down to a single revelation, it would be that the secret to a happy life is relationships, relationships, relationships."[4]

Not great wealth. Not lustrous career success. Not unblemished beauty.

Relationships, relationships, relationships.

Lesson #2: Have Friends Who Vote Differently

If someone asked Ruth Bader Ginsburg and Antonin Scalia if they agreed on the meaning of a variety of constitutional clauses—the Establishment Clause, the Equal Protection Clause, the Commerce Clause—it is likely they would admit to far more disagreement than consensus. But the differences wouldn't stop there. If you read their legal opinions, Scalia's resonated with vigor and pugnaciousness, a cantankerous but humorous arch conservatism often ringing out from the pages. Ginsburg, the endlessly lionized liberal, wrote cogent, understated prose.

Nonetheless, the authentic vitality of the friendship between these two colossi of the Supreme Court is a powerful lesson to Americans about how they ought to approach their political disagreements today. It is heartening to note that their friendship is one of the more famous dynamics of the modern court, detailed in numerous articles and essays—there is even an operatic edition of their unique friendship: *Scalia/Ginsburg: A (Gentle) Parody of Operatic Proportions.*

Why is there so much interest in the friendship of two judges from opposite sides of the ideological spectrum with such divergent backgrounds and dispositions? The answer lies in a deep-seated suspicion that they understood something we modern Americans have forgotten; chiefly, that authentic, soul-nourishing friendship has little to do with politics and everything to do with common loves and mutual interests. It is why they could disagree on the meaning of the Second Amendment but still vacation in India together, or spend New Year's Eve in the company of each other's families, or, of course, attend the opera side by side.

The day after Marty passed away the Supreme Court was in session. Ginsburg was able to contain her tears. Scalia could not.

Tragically, this Ginsburg-Scalia approach to friendship in which Americans are able to easily compartmentalize the political and the personal is not just increasingly rare—it's tragically unfathomable. A gnawing and sinister sense that large segments of the country are fundamentally motivated by bad intentions and seismic disdain for one another has become a permanent fixture of modern politics. We frequently employ a host of fancy terms to denote a potent and apocalyptic fear of one another—terms like "Orwellian" or "Potemkin" or "dystopian."

The Ginsburg-Scalia approach to friendship between political foes redirects the suspicious ray of frustration away from one's rivals and points it directly into one's own psychological mirror. Maybe, just maybe, our American brethren understand something we do not. Maybe they have unique experiences that have led them to specific convictions we are not privy to. Maybe we are seen as ignorant or rash or myopic in their eyes. Instead of assuming a defensive posture of certitude and judgment,

Americans would be better off assuming they simply don't quite understand one another, that their differences are epistemic and experiential, not existential and spiritual, and that the proper response to this chasm of misunderstanding is not venom or rage, but genuine effort to humanize the perspective one so ardently disagrees with.

In short, their approach to political disagreement has the potential to either change our minds for the better or reaffirm our most cherished convictions.

As Ginsburg recalled, "I disagreed with most of what he said, but he said it in such a charming, amusing way. And if truth be told, if I had my choice of dissenters when I was writing for the court, it would be Justice Scalia, because he was so smart, and he would home in on all the soft spots, and then I could fix up my majority opinion."[15]

It should come as no surprise that both of these towering intellects and personalities were capable of cultivating such a deep and abiding friendship. As judges, they were forced to work in an arena of argumentation and persuasion. They operated in the realm of facts, not bumper stickers, sound bites, and platitudes aplenty. Innuendo, clichés, and paranoia held no sway. They could joust, argue, and engage without the accompanying toxicity of personal animosity.

This is why Ginsburg made a special point in her later years to celebrate the collegiality of the court. In a pre-COVID world, she noted whenever the court was in session the day began with each justice shaking the hands of the others—thirty-six handshakes in all. The justices lunch together most days. They occasionally host legal and judicial events, such as taking turns introducing speakers at the Supreme Court Historical Society's biannual lecture series. As Ginsburg observed, "All of us appreciate that the institution we serve is far more important than the particular individuals who compose the court's bench at any given time."[16]

When Ginsburg spoke at Scalia's memorial service in 2016, she recalled with fondness that when President Clinton was in the midst of deciding who to nominate to the court, someone asked Scalia, "If you were stranded on a desert island with your new Court colleague, who would you prefer, Larry Tribe or Mario Cuomo?" He swiftly answered, "Ruth Bader Ginsburg."[17]

Both Ginsburg and Scalia understood that political ideologies, judging philosophies, and constitutional interpretation should never poison the deep well of friendship that exists when it is predicated on personal qualities, shared values, and common loves. As Scalia once observed, "I attack ideas. I don't attack people. Some very good people have some very bad ideas. And if you can't separate the two, you gotta get another day job. You don't want to be a judge. At least not a judge on a multi-member panel."[18]

After Scalia passed away, his son Eugene noted the instructive vitality of the Ginsburg-Scalia friendship for the rest of the country. In an interview with CNN, he eloquently observed, "Whenever you have two such important, accomplished people who have a rich friendship like that, there's something to be learned from it."[19]

The eldest Scalia son understood that "their ability to engage on ideas and yet respect one another's abilities and maintain a friendship is an instructive lesson. And I think they would both heartily agree that we want to have people on two sides of an issue to explain what the right answer is."

Ginsburg and Scalia, two titans of American jurisprudence whose opinions will be studied by American law students for centuries to come, fundamentally understood that friendship is a form of affection rooted in earth that is far more fruitful than the dirt thrown by modern political gladiators on television and social media. They understood that friendship is one of the transcendent pleasures of human beings. And most of all, they understood that America is a big enough place for it to include the both of them.

American history is ripe with examples of men and women who understood what so many of us have forgotten in modern times.

Ronald Reagan's greatest legislative foe, Speaker of the House Tip O'Neill, prayed at his bedside on the night he was almost assassinated. Bill Clinton ended what is arguably the greatest political career in modern times, that of George H. W. Bush, and yet both men developed a deep, resonate, and genuine affection for each other as they grew into elder statesmen.

Senator John McCain never became president because he was defeated twice—in the Republican primaries by George W. Bush in 2000 and in the general election by Barack Obama in 2008—and yet these rivals came to celebrate his life of service in moving eulogies at his funeral.

President George W. Bush and First Lady Michelle Obama genuinely enjoy each other's company.

Former Speaker of the House John Boehner appeared in a hilarious video with President Obama during the 2016 White House Correspondents' Association dinner and later admitted he enjoyed Obama's company more than he could admit to his base at the time.

There is an assumption in all of these relationships that what unites Americans is always stronger than what divides them.

Vituperative partisanship makes the most sinister of assumptions: that one's political beliefs are a barometer of one's inner character. In such a view, the wrong political beliefs render a person unworthy of friendship or romance. Americans who champion personal ideology above any element of personality, or who hold it as paramount to the traits of kindness and high integrity, have created a dynamic that deadens the soul. For example, dating apps now report that their users increasingly use political criteria in order to find romantic matches; this doesn't bode well for the future of marriage or friendship as the sexes are migrating in opposite directions, with young American men moving right and their female counterparts shifting even more left.[20]

When we refuse to befriend our fellow citizens and coworkers, when we reject the love of others simply because they possess a different point of view, we are inadvertently arguing that ideology is now synonymous with virtue or grotesqueness, that it signals not political preferences but one's worthiness of affection. Polls and surveys have revealed, for instance, that almost half of all voters acknowledge judging other people based on their politics and almost one in five admit friendships have been adversely affected in recent years.[21]

But friendship can take a rich variety of forms. It can surprise us, especially if we are willing to take politics out of the equation. Plato and Aristotle disagreed on the nature of ultimate reality. Groucho Marx and T. S. Eliot came from entirely different social orbits. Friendship is one of the highest and most sublime pleasures, perhaps even greater than erotic or romantic love. As Cicero once wrote, "The reward of friendship is friendship itself." Americans who withhold their hand of friendship out of a misguided and remote fidelity to ideological reflexes do so at their own peril. Ginsburg took the hand of friendship from those with whom she disagreed, and her life was better and richer for it. Perhaps in an era of potent American loneliness and frequent despair, we should do the same.

Lesson #3: Love Your Nation Enough to Make It Better

Ruth Bader Ginsburg's version of patriotism does not require the making of political enemies. Quite the opposite, her form of patriotism insists upon intensive fidelity to a variety of the American Creed that is becoming tragically passé.

Ginsburg never engaged in the heated rhetoric of ideological screeds nor did she ever participate in the souring cosplay of a modern progressive gladiator attempting to slay well-meaning conservatives.

Decades later it is utterly fascinating to remember that at the time of her nomination to the court women's groups were deeply suspicious of Ginsburg. They were not ardent Ginsburg champions in any meaning sense. The reason centered on her genuine objections to the legal reasoning behind *Roe v. Wade*. In a speech she famously observed, "*Roe v. Wade* sparked public opposition and academic criticism, in part, I believe, because the court ventured too far in the change it ordered and presented an incomplete justification for its actions." Furthermore, when asked by the ACLU to litigate a defense of *Roe*, she declined the opportunity.

President Clinton asked the beloved senator of New York at the time,

Daniel Patrick Moynihan, to suggest a woman as a potential nominee for the court vacancy. When Moynihan said "Ginsburg," Clinton was quick to point out, "The women are against her."

However, the tide eventually turned.

Ginsburg was a perfect practitioner of civility. But beyond simple political gentility, her patriotism was anchored by an unshakable faith in a particular form of political universalism, a principled belief that American political values ought to be enjoyed by all citizen regardless of the accident of one's birth, that magnifying our principles and extending our creed is the very definition of a "more perfect union." Patriotism transcends labels. It doesn't dabble in short-term political calculus. It is one-half conviction, one-half commitment. And no one was more committed to the principle of legal equality for all.

Before becoming a federal judge, she was the head of the ACLU's Women's Rights Project where she argued a total of six cases before the Supreme Court. In four of those cases her client was a man. She shrewdly advocated on behalf of these men to make a broader and quintessential American argument—that "gender lines in the law are bad for everyone: bad for women, bad for men, and bad for children."

In the mid-2020s such a sentiment is anything but radical. In fact, it is even a little bit prosaic and banal compared to the political tornadoes of fourth-wave feminism. But there is a word for this assumption of banality: *progress.*

Ginsburg authored an important legal brief in the landmark case *Reed v. Reed*, which helped convince the Supreme Court for the first time that discrimination on the basis of gender was antithetical to the equal protection clause of the Fourteenth Amendment. In her brief, she powerfully argued that laws propagating gender discrimination or differential treatment without regard to the capacities of the individual were worthy of a strict scrutiny standard from the courts. She would know. Despite her extraordinary academic record at Columbia Law School, she couldn't obtain employment from any New York City law firms when she graduated.

Her argument was not that identical treatment for men and women had to be universally proscribed at all times and in all circumstances but that subordination merely as a matter of tradition or antiquated stereotypes violated the Fourteenth Amendment's fundamental commitment to equality for all American citizens.

Ginsburg professionally came of age in the 1960s and '70s as women were beginning to challenge the long-held orthodoxy that men worked and women stayed home with the children. Thus, long-standing discriminations in the law could no longer be interpreted as self-evident markers of gender differences but instead as pernicious subordinations unworthy of America's constitutional guarantee of equal protection.

Indeed, in a 1973 article published in the *American Bar Association Journal*, she noted that several laws still existed that were worthy of the "scrap heap," including an "Arizona law [that] stipulates that the governor, secretary of state, and treasurer must be male. In Ohio only men may serve as arbitrators in county court proceedings. In Wisconsin barbers are licensed to cut men's hair and women's hair, but cosmeticians may attend to women only."[22]

Legal equality was a fight, and no one was a better fighter than Ginsburg.

Numerous states adopted their own equal rights amendments. Congress passed Title VII of the Civil Rights Act of 1964, Title IX of the Higher Education Act of 1972, and the Equal Pay Act. And while the Equal Rights Amendment did not pass on a national level (fifteen states failed to ratify it by the 1982 deadline), it did confirm that the national commitment to robust equality had substantively changed to include gender.

In many ways, Ginsburg is the Jeffersonian torchbearer of her era. The Yale law professor Akhil Reed Amar has eloquently argued that the equal protection clause of the Fourteenth Amendment is the constitutionalization of the Declaration of Independence. At the heart of America's founding document is the Enlightenment notion that justice is not an arbitrary construct of power, not a whimsical pawn of culture or happenstance, but is grounded in a ubiquitous force known as natural law—a system of rules rooted in human nature that applies to everyone, at all times, always and forever. The rights enshrined in the Declaration are as universal and objective in the political realm as Newton's laws of motion are in the physical.

As Amar notes, "Lincoln's Republicans re-glossed the Declaration and incorporated their gloss into the very text of the Fourteenth Amendment: Precisely because 'all men are created equal,' all persons born in America would be legally equal—and thus equally citizens—at birth, and no government could heap legal disabilities upon a person simply because of his or her birth status."[23]

Our rights are "inalienable" because we cannot get rid of them, even if we wanted to, for they are not grounded in the accidental character- istics of an individual's unique biology but in a common and shared nature. We are guided and bound by natural law because we are human beings. Our rights, in fact, exist prior to the establishment of govern- ment. The philosophes and enthusiasts of the Enlightenment did not invent the rights we celebrate on July 4th and that were enumerated in the Declaration of Independence. They were there all along.

Echoes of the Enlightenment were heard on June 26, 1996, during Ginsburg's bench announcement regarding the landmark court case *United States v. Virginia*, more commonly known as the VMI decision. In voting to strike down state-sanctioned single-sex education, Ginsburg explained that, "Under this exacting standard, reliance on overbroad generalizations, typically male or typically female 'tendencies,' estimates about the way most women (or men) are, will not suffice to deny opportu- nity to women whose talent and capacity place them outside the average description."[24]

This contribution of Ginsburg's should inspire every American— young and old, liberal and conservative, rich and poor—because it was aimed not at altering natural law but at following it more closely, which led us to include women. Ginsburg's patriotism is elegantly thoughtful not because she lacks partisan bluster or the vitriolic toxins that occupy so many of our public places. Her patriotism is elegant because it extends our principles, it animates the words on our founding documents, it reminds Americans that constitutional promises require constant vigilance and care.

The Americans who end up in our history books, whom we celebrate and admire through the ages, are not deceived into believing that their country is free from embarrassing historical blotches or glaring modern blemishes. In one of the most powerful statements about the arc of American history, President Clinton argued in his first inaugural speech, "There is nothing wrong with America that cannot be cured with what is right in America."

There is a cynical corollary to Clinton's dictum that seems to hold great appeal to a large and pessimistic block of the public these days: There is nothing right with America that is not negated by what was once wrong with America.

Instead, consider the words Judge Ginsburg spoke in April 2018 at a naturalization ceremony:

> At the start, it is true, the union very much needed perfection. The original Constitution permitted slavery and severely limited who counted among "We the people." When the nation was new, only white property-owning men had the right to vote, the most basic right of citizenship. But over the course of our history, people left out at the start—people held in human bondage, Native Americans, and women came to be embraced as full citizens.[25]

Patriotism is not a sentiment built on claims of a nation's perfection. Idealism rarely conjoins perfectly with reality. To be patriotic is not to deny injustices, inconsistencies, or areas in need of activism. Quite the opposite, Ruth Bader Ginsburg demonstrates that patriotism is believing in one's country so much, and so effusively, that it spurs passionate commitment to it.

CHAPTER 9

James Madison

Do What Others Are Unwilling to Do

★

★

Father of the American Constitution.
Formulator of American federalism.
Collaborator of *The Federalist Papers*.
De facto doula of the Bill of Rights.
Fourth president of the United States.

And yet . . . there is no significant monument in Washington, DC, celebrating the titanic contributions of James Madison to the American experiment of self-government. No American temple featuring quotes chiseled in marble, no miniaturized version of his home, no statue strategically placed on the National Mall, no allusion to membership in the American Mount Olympus.

When listing the famous homes and estates of former presidents, Madison's home, Montpelier, rarely garners the same adulation or tourist affection as George Washington's Mount Vernon, Thomas Jefferson's Monticello, or Andrew Jackson's Hermitage. While Americans, especially schoolchildren yearning for a day off in the middle of February, are well acquainted with the twin birthdays of Lincoln and Washington, tragically few know of Madison's March 16 birthday.

Madison's main totem of celebration in the nation's capital is the third of three buildings constituting the Library of Congress. The James Madison Memorial Building opened in 1980, a full forty-one years after the second building in the Library of Congress, the John Adams Building, was opened, and seventy-nine years after the magisterial original library, named after Thomas Jefferson.

Madison isn't molded onto Mount Rushmore nor is he headlined on Broadway every evening. He is ignominiously ranked in the middle of the pack by presidential historians, and unlike Washington and Franklin who are forever loved and celebrated, or Adams and Hamilton who have both enjoyed a modern renaissance in the past two decades due to sympathetic and bestselling historians, Madison's place in the pantheon of American titans is decidedly underwhelming.

And perhaps this is for good reason.

To awaken and vivify Madison's life lessons we have to listen closely—for he lacked the physical stature of Washington, the celebrity of Franklin, the force of personality of Hamilton, and the political charisma of his best friend, Jefferson.

By all accounts, Madison, or "Jemmy" as his friends knew him, was not a towering figure in any sense of the word. Instead, he stood at a measly five feet four, which wins him the notorious distinction of being the shortest president in American history. Depending on which historian one consults, he weighed anywhere between just over a hundred to a hundred twenty pounds, so squat in fact that his stouter wife, Dolley, was purported during dinner parties to have given him piggyback rides to the grand amusement of White House guests.

He made absolutely no impression on strangers during dinner parties, except guests frequently mistook his shyness for standoffishness. He was unfairly pilloried as uninteresting or glum, described by a fellow Virginian as "a gloomy, stiff creature, they say is clever in Congress, but out of it there is nothing engaging or bearable in his manners."[1] Madison persistently dressed in macabre black and his one constant was an awareness of a weak physical constitution that made him susceptible to sudden and severe illnesses.

He frequently predicted an early death yet outlived all of his contemporaries, dying at the advanced age of eighty-five. A mysterious ailment would suddenly strike him in times of stress and strain—after prolonged study at Princeton, in the midst of the Virginia ratification debate, and even during the presidency itself.

While Madison was hesitant to label his disease epilepsy, a penchant for hypochondria and stomach discomfort prevented him from ever embarking on voyages across the Atlantic for fear of triggering pronounced sickness. Indeed, William Bradford, his friend from Princeton, wrote to his friend, "I believe you hurt your constitution while here, by too close application to study."[2]

Given these traits, perhaps his failure and disappointments with women should come as no surprise. His ineptitude with the opposite sex lasted until he was forty years old and led to occasional heartbreak. In the spring of 1783, Madison fell in love with a fifteen-year-old named Kitty Floyd whose family occupied the same Philadelphia boardinghouse. Eventually, she abandoned him for a man closer to her age.[3]

More than a decade later, Madison, now past forty and still as vertically challenged as ever, fell in love with the widow of a Quaker lawyer. With the unlikely assistance of Aaron Burr, a fellow Princeton alumnus, who acted as an epistolary cupid for the eventual couple, Madison ultimately won the heart of Dolley Payne Todd.

But don't be fooled. Madison might have been small in stature, but he was imminently large in life—a stentorian example of how to live a full life consistent with one's ambitions and talents. He possessed ambition without vanity, brilliance untethered to ego, and kindness unmoored from calculation. Madison possessed all the virtues necessary for greatness without the common accompanying vices that lead to a concomitant fall from grace.

As Americans, we should follow his inspiring example.

Lesson #1: Try to Be the Most Prepared Person in the Room

Perhaps it is dull, lacking in both dramatic flair and flamboyant bombast, but if Americans want to understand how Madison was able to achieve so much, the central reason is because he worked harder, studied more, and was always willing to put in more hours of concentrated labor than others.

"Determine never to be idle. No person will have occasion of the want of time, who never loses any. It is wonderful how much may be done, *if we are always doing*." While this sentiment was expressed by Jefferson in a letter to his eldest daughter, Patsy, it was Jefferson's best friend, Madison, who best embodies its spirit, more than even the writer of the letter himself. While others may have had lustrous oratorical power in a crowd (Patrick Henry), exceptional bravado at a social gathering (Jefferson), or advantageous physical attributes (Washington), rarely did Madison ever enter an arena of competition or debate in which he was not the most supremely prepared combatant.

Indeed, it is not hyperbole to suggest some of the most consequential gatherings in American history were steered to their eventual outcome by the grand power of Madison's work ethic. In the aftermath of the disappointing Annapolis Convention, which only served to galvanize the need for a future meeting with a broader scope and more attendees, Madison readied himself for the Constitutional Convention of 1787 on numerous fronts.

Beyond the revolutionary political ideas or the historic constitutional schemes that were to come, merely getting Washington to attend was perhaps the greatest boon of all. Madison coaxed, flattered, and convinced "the indispensable man" to come to Philadelphia for a simple reason: Washington's mere presence bestowed the gathering with trusted authority and infused it with popular credibility. Madison's masterstroke was to understand that Washington's attendance at the Philadelphia convention was the equivalent of ensuring that a teenager's party had a trustworthy chaperone. When other parents know nothing untoward is going to occur, they are more open to their children attending the gathering. In this instance, Washington was the chaperone, the states were the parents, and the convention was the party.

Even then, in typical Madisonian fashion, he had a backup plan—with Benjamin Franklin waiting in the wings—in case Washington refused or couldn't preside over the convention.[4]

Beyond imbuing the gathering with legitimacy, the task before Madison was titanic in extremis. His undertaking was to harness the lyrical truths of the Declaration of Independence and institutionalize them into a coherent system of government. That government must yoke the fractured states into a solidified union, simultaneously protect the individual liberty of citizens, and finally position states into orbits of power sufficiently sovereign, without being independent per se. In short, he needed to marry political poetry to constitutional prose.

History was not on Madison's side in this endeavor and he knew it.

Democracies always seemed to succumb to chaos, uniquely susceptible as they are to the empty oratory of demagogues. Indeed, democracy is decried far more frequently in *The Federalist Papers* than monarchy is. The case against monarchy had already been made and settled definitively for Americans by the revolution. Monarchy in post-revolution America was understandably synonymous with tyranny. Crowns, churches, and titles of nobility were the domain of European subjects, not newfangled American citizens. However, the case *against* nationwide democracy was strong across human history. Republics, it was thought by all the greatest minds of the time, must be both small and homogeneous, otherwise they became nothing but rule by mob. Natural law insisted that government serve and protect the rights of the people, but leading thinkers perceived that "the people" and the mischief of the mob were often indistinguishable from each other.

The problem Madison attempted to solve before arriving in Philadelphia in May 1787—finding a way to create the first large-scale liberal democratic republic in human history—would certainly require an arsenal of talents befitting all of the Greek muses combined. Moreover, it required a different form of godliness—the ability to work and prepare like no other. As the Madison biographer David O. Stewart observed of this time, "For the next two months, Madison stayed at Montpelier to do what he always did: prepare."[5]

For more than two centuries, historians have marveled at the prodigiousness of Madison's efforts during the spring of 1787 in preparation for the Philadelphia convention. He was simultaneously studying ancient and modern history, critiquing the deep weaknesses of the current American confederacy, while formulating original theories of constitutionalism that would eventually embody themselves in a uniquely American brand of governance.

At Madison's request, Jefferson, then serving as the American diplomat to France, sent across the Atlantic two trunks of books from Paris that provided Madison a hearty syllabus that would make his knowledge of ancient and modern confederacies nothing short of encyclopedic.

His detailed analysis of the Amphictyonic League, the Achaean Confederacy, as well as the Dutch and German confederacies, empowered him to arrive at a stark realization about confederate arrangements: They were almost always transitory in nature, precursors to large-scale feuds and bloody disagreements, fueled by a narrow statecraft that usually ended in calamity.[6]

The solution to this problem was to shift the continuum of sovereignty away from the parochial and small-minded state capitals, toward a more nationalistic, unitary locus of power. Madison's time in the Virginia legislature reinforced his belief that local and state leaders were narrowly focused on their own provincial concerns, more prone to squabbling and quarreling than demonstrating any real capacity for enlightened, deliberative leadership. Local majorities could not be trusted to produce wise policy nor could they be trusted to protect the interests or voices of minority sentiment.[7]

Much of Madison's preparation that spring was geared toward avoiding the bellicosity, belligerence, and bloodshed of a thousand years of European history in which neighboring nations of roughly coequal size constantly found excuses to go to war with one another. Madison's voracious efforts leading up to the Philadelphia convention required that he embody the Janus-like ideal of possessing two faces at once—policy wonk and philosopher, statesman and social scientist, historian and hard-nosed realist.

If America wanted to avoid the fate of Europe, then a genuine proposal for nationhood, a focus on *unum* and not *pluribus*, was the solution. Madison saw the Philadelphia convention as an extraordinary historic opportunity, the kind of opportunity brimming with political fertility that appears only sparingly in human history. He wanted to make the most of it.

Madison arrived in Philadelphia a week early, held frequent conversations with fellow nationalists who were equally committed to bringing thirteen quasi-nations into a common union. But most important, he arrived with what came to be known as the Virginia Plan.

No one else had put in the time, the thought, or the effort to solve the problems posed by the Articles of Confederation; and while these confederate problems were not unique to the American confederacy, there was still a pressing urgency to reconcile American notions of natural rights, popular sovereignty, and the social contract to a system of government that would be palatable to the American people. Ultimately, the Virginia Plan was a stark constitutional counterpoint to the structure of the Articles of Confederation and reflected Madison's keen concern about the inherent dangers and instability of confederate arrangements.

His commitment to reorienting political power and fidelity away from the states and toward a national framework could be discerned through the features of the plan he brought to Philadelphia, so unitary in tone and structure that it quickly became apparent he was not attempting to make itemized, patchwork improvements to the articles but was embarking, in fact, on an ingenious project of new wholesale nation creation.

His plan created a bicameral legislature in which both chambers were based on the populations of the states, three different and overlapping branches, and, most jarring to the states-rights delegates, the power of the federal government to veto individual state laws.

Madison's supreme powers of preparation allowed him to immediately set the agenda in Philadelphia by using his plan as a starting point for their ongoing deliberations. Of course, three months of arguments, compromises, and changes left Madison feeling dejected and utterly disappointed as the finished product of the convention did not entirely settle the question of where ultimate political power stood.

The delegates rejected his plan for the federal government to have veto power over the states. Furthermore, the Connecticut Compromise dictated the Senate be a check for the small states against the large as each state was to have two representatives, no matter its population size, a feature disturbingly reminiscent of the legislature under the Articles of Confederation. Lastly, there were loud complaints at the end of the convention about the lack of a Bill of Rights.

When Madison left Philadelphia in September 1787, he never would have imagined that he would one day be known as the "Father of the Constitution."

Lesson #2: Be Willing to Change Your Mind

One of the most unfortunate trends in modern politics is the blood sport involved in forcing leaders to change a position, recant a previous statement, or extract an admission of having made a mistake. While some cast this as a form of weakness or a vulnerability, much of Madison's legacy stems from the fact that he was always willing to change his mind.

Specifically, besides being the Father of the Constitution, he also deserves credit for both the birthing process and the finished product of what has come to be known as the Bill of Rights. Ironically, he started off firmly opposed to having a Bill of Rights. The story of his conversion is a fascinating one and contains a vital lesson about the power of being able to adjust one's thinking as facts and circumstances change.

One of the more interesting episodes of the Constitutional Convention involves the waning days of the gathering, on September 12, 1787. After almost four months of deliberation in Philadelphia in the heat and humidity—with the windows closed to safeguard complete secrecy—the delegates were utterly exhausted, approaching the limit of human endurance, eagerly awaiting a return to their homes and families.

George Mason rose to address the convention and complained about the lack of a Bill of Rights and even suggested they could finish the task in a single day. He had already achieved fame for penning the Virginia Bill of Rights and was now refusing to sign the proposed constitution because of this deficiency. Anyone who has ever been in a long meeting eagerly awaiting its conclusion knows what happens when a single person prolongs the gathering—eyerolls, deep sighs, and general annoyance.

The delegates later offered philosophical and elaborate reasons for omitting a Bill of Rights, yet the real reason was rooted in a universal desire to get home.[8] The motion was defeated.

Madison was resolute in his belief that a Bill of Rights was wholly unnecessary, even arguing that it might be dangerous and labeled it a "parchment barrier." This put him in a rare position of disagreeing with fellow Virginian and best friend Thomas Jefferson, who wrote from Paris that "a bill of rights is what the people are entitled to against every government on earth."

By contrast, Madison argued that a Bill of Rights had very little to do with the mandate of the delegates at the Constitutional Convention. Their task in Philadelphia, as Madison saw it, was to create new institutions of government, to enumerate what powers these institutions possessed, to decide how these institutions worked together, to explain how one is elected or appointed to these institutions, and hope that the constitutional framework achieves the ultimate goal of justice.

Writing down rights is a completely different task, he protested, one rooted more in philosophical rumination than constitutional design. The task of the delegates in Philadelphia was not to produce loud proclamations of liberty but to offer to the states a plan whose constitutional architecture and institutional mechanics provided for the steady administration of political power in a limited but just fashion. The aim of the Philadelphia convention was to blend statecraft with high political idealism, to concurrently protect individual liberty and provide for the general welfare.

Nothing else was necessary. Madison believed a system of complex majority rule undergirded by robust checks and balances with clearly enumerated and defined powers provided sufficient protection of basic rights. As he wrote in *Federalist Paper* No. 45, "The powers delegated by the proposed Constitution to the federal government are few and defined. Those which are to remain in the State governments are numerous and indefinite."

Moreover, not only were high-minded statements of individual rights wholly unnecessary and redundant, given the robust protections provided by state constitutions, but a statement of rights at the federal level was potentially dangerous. By deciding to codify into constitutional text some rights and not others, the omission of certain rights could be interpreted by future Americans as a tacit acknowledgment that some rights can be denied. Article 1, section 9 listed the denied powers to Congress. Article 1, section 10 listed the denied powers to the states. This, Madison believed, should be enough of a safeguard against the specter of tyrannical power.

But Madison was wrong.

As time went on, he softened his reticence toward a Bill of Rights, understanding as the state-by-state ratification process progressed that this was the strongest objection lodged by the Anti-Federalists. By eventually acquiescing to the demands for a Bill of Rights, the strategically astute Madison realized he was now blunting the primary argument against his beloved Constitution and preventing his greatest fear from coming true: a second Constitutional Convention, which he knew would undermine the first.

With a promise that the new Congress would immediately begin the process of amending the Philadelphia document, the Federalists carried the day in pivotal but close ratification contests in Virginia and New York.

But before Madison could spearhead the amendment process in Congress, he had to actually get himself elected to Congress. And standing in his way was no political slouch, his friend and sometimes competitor, James Monroe.

The thrust of Madison's argument during his campaign against Monroe was that adding amendments before ratification was a dangerous prospect, one that could undermine the entire constitutional experiment. But once ratified, new amendments could serve "the double purpose of satisfying the minds of well-meaning opponents, and of providing additional guards in favor of liberty."[9]

All told, Madison defeated Monroe 1,308 votes to 972.

While the Constitution was clearly a collaborative document, the Bill of Rights was more of a virtuoso Madisonian performance. As the preeminent historian Joseph Ellis observed, "There is no question that Madison was the 'Father of the Bill of Rights.' He wrote the first draft single-handedly, ushered it through the House, and negotiated with leaders in the Senate as they reduced the seventeen amendments proposed by the House to twelve."[10]

Once in Congress, Madison set to work fulfilling the promises he made during his campaign against Monroe. He had received more than two hundred amendment recommendations from the states.[11] He eventually submitted nineteen amendments and seventeen were agreed to by the House of Representatives. The Senate only passed twelve of them,

notably rejecting one of Madison's most important amendment propos-
als, which would have limited state power to curtail rights of speech, conscience, and jury trial. Among all the founders, Madison alone seemed to
be ahead of his time in understanding that the real menace to individual
liberty would not come from the federal government but from state governments, a bloody reality that culminated in the Civil War and would
eventually be remedied by the Fourteenth Amendment.

It could be argued that Madison's ability to change his mind, to pivot
when essential in service of a larger political idea—chiefly, the American
union itself—put the embryonic nation on a more stable footing. By giving the Anti-Federalists a victory, it blunted their most powerful argument, won their loyalty for the new government, and, most of all, created
a common notion of what it actually means to be an American.

By joining thirteen separate notions of identity under a common
constitutional umbrella, it imbued the infant republic with a genuine
national voice and character. While the preamble sets forth a soaring
ideal—that we may become one "people"—it is the Bill of Rights that
actually captures the democratic energy of a new nation struggling to
define itself.

The presence of a Bill of Rights puts into motion the dynamic saga
of the American legend. While the United States is anchored by founding texts and documents that graft durable flesh onto a novel national
identity, the chain to this anchor possesses enough slack in the form of
an amendment process for each generation to redefine what it means to
be American. This aptitude to revere the past but not be unduly bound
to it is the essence of the American character, a character made possible
because of Madison's ability to change his mind.

What Madison teaches us is that assuming a posture of humility
and embracing a willingness to reconsider previous biases and opinions
isn't just a positive attribute of statesmen and politicians. It turns out to
be one of the most important traits for living a happy and well-adjusted
life. As Arthur Brooks, the host of the podcast *How to Build a Happy Life*,
has noted, "Rethinking your opinions—and changing your views when

your facts are proved wrong or someone makes a better argument—can make your life better. It can make you more successful, less anxious, and happier."[12]

But don't just take Brooks's word for it.

Edmund Burke observed that the world is so infinitely complex, so full of mystery and infinite oddities, and at the same time our capacity for understanding it so slight, that the appropriate response to most significant questions is "epistemic humility." Kant argued we can never truly know "things-in-themselves," as knowledge is always contingently obtained through the filter of our own experiences and systems of cognition. Socrates powerfully exclaimed, "wisdom begins in wonder." As Brooks also points out, Saint Augustine gave a student three pieces of advice, "The first part is humility; the second, humility; the third, humility: and this I would continue to repeat as often as you might ask direction."[13]

Sad is the citizen who clings to the same battery of beliefs at fifty that he or she did at eighteen. Those who approach life with a posture of powerful humility, who experience life as an infinite pasture of unfathomed possibilities, find themselves enriched and ripened by a startling development: Life stops being defensive. It stops being a slog of embittered apologetics. It ceases to be a daily grind of showing the world just how right and smart you are. As a wizened Franklin once observed, "The older I grow the more apt I am to doubt my own judgment, and to pay more respect to the judgment of others."

The power of embracing a disposition of wonderment and awe over certitude and dogmatism wouldn't just make us more pleasant to be around as friends, spouses, and coworkers. It would almost certainly cultivate a change in our political culture by fostering genuine dialogue aimed at mutual understanding.

Lesson #3: Be Generous—Don't Worry About Who Gets the Credit

On countless occasions throughout his extraordinary but underappreciated career, Madison was willing to put in the hours and endure the

grind of hard mental labor, but when the moment to step forth into the
spotlight arrived, to bask in adulation or acclaim, he would often defer
to others. He never worried about who got the credit; he was results-
oriented without being a Machiavel or a deceiver.

After months of preparing the Virginia Plan as a blueprint or starting
point for the Constitutional Convention, when the time came to present
his plan, he allowed the governor of Virginia, Edmund Randolph, to present it instead.

This act of deference is especially commendable when one takes the
time to truly consider the historic depths of Madison's achievement. The
Greek thinker Polybius is famous for his observation that each form of
government possesses internal contradictions that result in a particular
form of political failure: Monarchies descend into tyranny, democracies
have a penchant for chaos, and aristocracies succumb to the excesses
born of indulgence and easy wealth. In short, as Polybius notes, "each
constitution has a vice engendered in it and inseparable from it."

The solution is a "mixed constitution" that combines elements of
all three. The Greeks were especially aware of historic cycles of decay—
kyklos—that seem to play out time and time again in the tragic theater
of human affairs. Madison's colossal achievement was to institutionally
arrange a government in which elements of all three forms of government could act as ballasts against one another, preventing decay and pre-
serving the liberty of each citizen. Thus, the House of Representatives
played the democratic role of giving voice to "the people," the Senate
reflected the aristocratic voice as senators were appointed by state legislatures, and the president's unitary nature carried our traditional monarchical responsibilities such as defending the nation and enforcing
legislative laws and judicial writs.

It is both fascinating and disappointing to note that history remem-
bers this blueprint as either the Randolph Plan or the Virginia Plan, but
no one ever gives it the moniker it truly deserves, the Madison Plan. A
fascinating sidenote about Randolph: He was one of three people who
decided not to sign the Constitution, and in the most famous painting of

the convention, Howard Chandler Christy's 1940 masterpiece, Randolph is nowhere to be seen.[14]

Madison's self-abnegation continued at later conventions. As much attention and focus as American civics classes give to the Constitutional Convention, or at least *used* to give, a strong case could be made that the state ratification conventions were even more vital in forging the nation's future.

If the Constitutional Convention was a collaboration of creation, the ratification conventions were pure democratic dogfighting. These were the venues where a new form of political power took shape in the aftermath of the convention, a debut of power that would flow from consent not decree, majoritarianism not monarchy. It was the opening salvo of a new era of Western civilization in which authority would be radically reformulated, flowing from the bottom up, not the top down. The men who spent their summer in Philadelphia had absolutely no power or sway once the question of ratification was brought before the different assemblies of the various states. If the states decided to hoist the constitutional yoke upon themselves, it would be the consequence of their own democratic acquiescence alone.

At stake in these gatherings was the very question of self-government's feasibility. As Alexander Hamilton eloquently framed the issue in *Federalist Paper* No. 1: "It has been frequently remarked that it seems to have been reserved to the people of this country, by their conduct and example, to decide the important question, whether societies of men are really capable or not of establishing good government from reflection and choice, or whether they are forever destined to depend for their political constitutions on accident and force."

The Constitutional Convention was a maelstrom of compromised "reflections." It gave birth to a proposal, but without the consent of the people—without the element of free "choice"—this proposal was nothing but a piece of meaningless parchment, barren of the smallest particle of power. Madison was a maestro of understanding this new species of power that did not originate in royal courts and monarchical palaces.

And yet, he was always hesitant to be the one actually using it.

After the convention was over and the time for the ratification process began, Madison's first inclination was not to attend the Virginia ratification debate. Instead, he had to be coaxed and convinced that his attendance was both necessary and advantageous to the cause of the new Constitution.

At different times during the Virginia ratification debate when it became obvious that a grand orator was needed to counter the grandiloquence of Patrick Henry, Madison would defer to men of more oratorical prowess and grace. When he did speak, which he consistently did throughout the convention except for a few days in which he was suffering from a migraine, his manner was always humble and understated. He had no talent for the theater of speechifying. As the Harvard Law School professor Noah Feldman has observed, "Madison did not deal in grand pronouncements, nor did he have Henry's gift for oratory."[15]

But nowhere is Madison's propensity for stepping aside or working behind the scenes more pronounced than in his friendship with Jefferson. While Jefferson is perhaps the most celebrated American to have ever lived, behind much of this success is the genius of Madison. Jefferson urged Madison to challenge Hamilton's pro-British stance during the Washington administration, which he did in a series of essays using the pseudonym Helvidius. They drafted the Virginia and Kentucky resolutions together in opposition to John Adams's Alien and Sedition Acts. Most significantly, Madison worked steadily behind the scenes to help forge the new Democratic-Republican Party. When the party successfully defeated Adams in 1800, the first president representing the new party was Jefferson, not Madison.

Their friendship was both authentic and intensely productive. At its core, both men had a deep affection for each other. As John Quincy Adams wrote, "[The] mutual influence of these two mighty minds upon each other is a phenomenon, like the invisible and mysterious movements of the magnet in the physical world."[16] Both were from the same area of Virginia. Both were deeply committed to ensuring that the American experiment differentiated itself in both form and content from European monarchical society. As one biographer brilliantly observes, "Each was likeliest the smartest person the other ever met (with the possible exception of Alexander Hamilton)."[17]

They, of course, did not always agree. Jefferson's insistence that a Bill of Rights was necessary was a constant thorn in Madison's side during his battles with Henry. Jefferson would sometimes take philosophic flights of fancy more reminiscent of Platonic dialogues than realistic discourses such as his cockamamie—or "eccentric" if we choose to be kind—notion that constitutions should be rewritten or discarded every twenty years or so. Jefferson had a romanticized view of the French Revolution. He was closer and more adamant in his belief in direct democracy than any other founding father.

But, frankly, both men knew and recognized their own strengths.

A counterfactual national history in which Madison and Jefferson switch their most famous achievements, with Madison writing the Declaration of Independence and Jefferson designing the Constitution, is an alternative that stretches the boundary of historic imagination. The poetic gloss of the Declaration of Independence with its lyrical prose and broad historic pronouncements about natural law and human rights would have been a much different document had it been written by Madison. "The American Mind" beautifully elucidated by Jefferson would have instead sounded clunky, scientific, and formulaic.

Likewise, a constitution designed by Jefferson would have been utterly incompatible with the broad distrust of popular sentiment of the time. Jefferson famously argued for a "natural aristocracy," yet he believed in a benign human nature grounded in an innate moral sensibility and rationality that the rest of the founders found disturbingly naïve, especially John Adams.

And yet, Madison frequently saw himself as the junior partner in the relationship. Jefferson was the older man and more distinguished in early-American history, primarily because he was responsible for the document that embodies the apotheosis of the nation's soaring idealism, the Declaration of Independence. Jefferson carried himself with a form of intellectual and personal élan that forever eluded Madison. In many of the political battles that defined early-American history, Jefferson was an intellectual general, Madison his pragmatic and strategic foot soldier.

Madison's lack of self-regard or vainglory is a powerful lesson for Americans today. His quiet, subtle virtues of humility, selflessness, and modesty perhaps do not resonate the way they once did. But they should.

The novel *Goodbye, Mr. Chips*, about a beloved Latin teacher who spends his entire working life as a teacher at an English prep school for boys, gives eloquent voice to the power of being quietly valuable to a specific community or cause. At the end of his career Mr. Chips comes to a powerful realization about himself: "For the first time in his life he felt *necessary*—and necessary to something that was nearest his heart. There is no sublimer feeling in the world, and it was his at last."[18]

If ever there was a necessary but underappreciated American, it is James Madison.

CHAPTER 10

Theodore Roosevelt

Always Take the Stairs

Once in a while a pupil will ask me for a book recommendation. Sometimes, the student wants to dig deeper into the life of a specific American from the past or discover a unique era and its epochal idiosyncrasies. But when a student simply wants to be dazzled and inspired, yearning for a lively entrée to the world of American history and politics, I always suggest what I consider to be the greatest biography of the twentieth century: Edmund Morris's 1979 Pulitzer Prize–winning *The Rise of Theodore Roosevelt.*

"You mean the *Night at the Museum* guy?" they ask.

"Yes," I answer, "he was quite a guy."

So much so that the binding of my copy, which I initially read late at night when my first daughter was an infant and stubbornly refused to go back to sleep, now has multiple layers of masking tape keeping it in one piece. I have purchased so many copies for students over the years that Morris's estate should be paying royalties to me. It is a book that never fails to evoke a deep state of awe for Theodore Roosevelt (TR) neophytes and future enthusiasts. A reader encountering Morris's prologue for the first time is likely to remember it forever.

In just a few dozen pages, a reader confronts a human being who is the "fastest handshaker in history" (averaging fifty encounters a minute, 8,150 in a single day), the first American winner of the Nobel Peace Prize who also happens to be the youngest chief executive in the history of the republic, a maestro of conversation who can converse with anybody at intellectual depths normally reserved for specialists and scholars, a skinny-dipper in the Potomac, a reader of at least one book a day, a prolific writer of nearly forty books, including authoritative classics such as *The Naval War of 1812* and *The Winning of the West.*

And this is just the prologue.

No wonder my students are quickly smitten.

Anybody who decides to take a deep dive into the life and lore of Roosevelt is immediately struck by the fact that many of the classic books written about him are narrowly devoted to a single segment or narrow theme of his life. Morris, who is most famous for *Dutch,* an unorthodox and highly controversial 1999 biography of Ronald Reagan, later went on to pen two more dense volumes about Roosevelt, one devoted to his presidency, *Theodore Rex,* and the last one focused on his post-presidency years, *Colonel Roosevelt.* The late David McCulloch, the most popular and famous American historian of the past half century, won a National Book Award for *Mornings on Horseback,* yet the book covers a mere seventeen years of TR's early life, from 1869 to 1886. Doris Kearns Goodwin's biography *The Bully Pulpit* narrowly focuses on the relationship between TR and William Howard Taft and the evolving nature of journalism.

Every year of Roosevelt's life seemed to roar with ebullience and adventure, every phase brimmed with consequence. Historians have written and students have read endless volumes about TR because he personifies the American preoccupation with enormity. As Roosevelt himself admitted, "Like all Americans, I like big things; big prairies, big forests and mountains, big wheat-fields, railroads—and herds of cattle, too—big factories, steamboats, and everything else."

Quotes about TR from his contemporaries lend themselves to high hyperbole because if ever there was a hyperbolic human walking the earth, it was Roosevelt. As the historian Patricia O'Toole observed, "Whether one loved or despised Theodore Roosevelt, he was electricity in the flesh."[1]

Men and women with even the briefest of interactions with him could not deny the enormity of the impression he made: "I met in him a man of such extraordinary power that to find a second at the same time on the globe would have been an impossibility." "Do you know the two most extraordinary things I've seen in your country? Niagara Falls and the President of the United States—both great wonders of nature." "Theodore Roosevelt is a strong, tough man; hard to hurt and harder to stop."

The self-help version of Roosevelt is easy to discover. Unlike his more muted and unassuming presidential neighbors on Mount Rushmore, he never hesitated to tell people what they should do and how they should live, liberally dispensing advice to anybody who would listen. As early as the 1880s he was writing for *Youth's Companion*, "telling tales of his own adventures and giving advice on how people should conduct their lives."[2] Later in life, as a colossus in the realms of political and world affairs, he was universally known as an impresario of "the strenuous life," an idolizer of "the man in the arena," a denouncer of languid living and any "human being who led an easy life."

Thus, the difficulty of studying TR is not in the discovery but in the distilling.

Like all historic beings, the closer we look at the nuances of his life, the more likely we are to occasionally flinch or guffaw at some of his actions or opinions: all but abandoning his firstborn daughter for the first few years of her life, his lack of courage during the epic 1912 presidential election in confronting racial inequality and the deep injustices in the American South despite the justness of his private opinions, his belief that citizens who don't have children are guilty of "crimes of ease and self-indulgence, of shrinking from pain and effort and risk."[3] In other ways he seems eerily oracular, especially in his adoration of fellow New Yorker Alexander Hamilton and his disdain for Thomas Jefferson.

An audacious playwright hoping to emulate the success of *Hamilton* should consider the treasure trove of dramatic material available in any telling of TR's life.

His advice for living was never cloaked in mystical undertones. He was direct and confident and always—always!—eager to share what he possessed. In fact, the lesson for this chapter is so simple and straightforward that it might well be the best way of summing up his determination to always take the harder route. He rarely saw a choice between stairs and an elevator and didn't take the stairs.

Let us allow Theodore Roosevelt to enrich us.

Lesson #1: The Hard Is What Makes It Great

Although the classic film *A League of Their Own* was released seventy-three years after the death of Roosevelt, Tom Hanks's most meaningful line, a climactic peroration in which, as the fictional baseball player Jimmy Dugan, he explains to his star player what makes baseball so magical, could just as easily have come from the mouth of our twenty-sixth president explaining the central truth of the human condition: "The hard is what makes it great."

If ever there was a cardinal and sacral credo that guided the life of Roosevelt, it was the conviction that the most important things in life—love, purpose, faith, health, friendship, real achievement—are almost always the most difficult things to endure. Without an iron will there is no real way. Modern men and women certainly love a good hack or shortcut—to wealth, to weight loss, to love. A bevy of billion-dollar industries exist to stoke such desires because an abbreviated path to excellence and contentment is always appetizing in the moment.

But a shortcut almost never reaches its desired long-term goal. Americans, TR insisted, must intentionally embrace the arduous paths in life if they are to experience genuine joy and nourishing happiness.

To powerfully punctuate this point to his own children, TR would lead his family on adventures that he called "scrambles." These were deliberately long and laborious hikes through hills, mountains, and even creeks. A lot of fathers certainly enjoy taking their progeny through daunting landscapes. But what made these outings unique was Roosevelt's insistence on a strategy he called "point-to-point." He would point out a landmark in the distance and then insist that everyone in the party walk directly to it—"Over, under or Through—But Never Around."⁴

The consequence of this strategy was that sometimes his party had to climb cliffs or tunnel under fallen trees or even swim across the Potomac when ice was still floating in the early spring. These point-to-point outings would sometimes last for hours and leave everyone utterly exhausted. Not only did TR subject his own children to these excursions but on occasion hilariously drafted foreign diplomats into the adventures as well. He might explain these jaunts as an ingenious form of exercise or as a chance to bond as a family. But the undercurrent of this point-to-point activity was pedagogical in nature.

Sometimes arriving at a desired destination requires a level of effort few are willing to make—most people will go to great lengths to "go around" the highest hurdles in front of them. But TR was not most people, nor did he want his children or fellow Americans to be. He wanted us to understand that dreams and aspirations are mere whims if they are not firmly wedded to a steely resolve. Ambition is vacuous unless it is fervently reinforced by a steady determination to continue the climb of success, no matter the degree of difficulty, no matter the height of the mountain, the width of the forest, or the frigidity of the water we encounter.

Roosevelt's belief in the value of struggle might be assumed by a modern reader to be a benefit of a life of privilege, but in fact, suffering was no abstraction for him, even from his early childhood. Americans, Roosevelt believed, are not pawns of cosmic circumstance. Americans are agents of their own design. Nothing in his life demonstrated this conviction more than his titanic battle with debilitating poor health as a child. Starting at the age of three, "asthma and his consequent invalidism began to dominate Theodore's childhood."[5] The asthma was dire enough that it could have killed him. The attacks were sudden, dramatic, and highly unpredictable.

The doctors were of almost no use. He was forced to endure painful or voodoo treatments, such as swallowing "ipecac, quinine with iron, magnesia, rhubarb pills, and arrowroot."[6] He spent much of his youth enfeebled and weak, a source of almost constant anxiety for his parents who feared the worst at any moment. His mother was forever in search of new destinations where the young man, known in his youth as "Teedie," could fill his lungs with clean air and healthy living.

She sampled multiple resorts, baths, and springs, all of them imperfect stabs at relief for her son. One upshot of his frailty was that he had ample time for exploring books, including one of the most influential books he ever read, David Livingstone's *Missionary Travels and Researches in South Africa*, filled with illustrations of a world of zebras and hippopotami and elephants and enormous flies.[7] Reading the book helped to spawn an interest in the natural world that would stretch into adulthood.

He struggled with bad health his entire childhood, culminating in one of the most famous scenes of Roosevelt's young life. His frustrated father called his son into the room and sternly said to him, "Theodore, you have the mind, but you have not the body, and without the help of the body the mind cannot go as far as it should."[8]

His father continued with a charge that would change young Theodore's life forever: "You must *make* your body. It is hard drudgery to make one's body, but I know you will do it." His mother was a witness to the exchange. Her son's immediate reaction was steely, muttered through clenched teeth, "I'll make my body."[9] Theodore did what he promised to do. He committed to the drudgery, he "pulled and hauled, hoisted the weights up from the floor, then let them ride slowly back down again, time after time." The second-floor piazza of their home became the famous Roosevelt family gymnasium, where he continued the process by battering punching bags and endlessly swinging dumbbells.[10]

The apex of his efforts occurred from 1870 to 1871—"Fiber by fiber, his muscles tautened, while the skinny chest expanded by degrees perceptible only to himself."[11] He became more vigorous, climbing mountains, jumping into rapids, and was healthy enough by August 1871 to have an authentic, in-person encounter with the wilderness he had only read about in books. His visit to the Adirondacks and the White Mountains resulted in numerous new acquisitions for the Museum of Natural History that fall, including "one bat, twelve mice, a turtle, the skull of a red squirrel, and four birds' eggs," all "presented by Mr. Theodore Roosevelt, Jr."[12]

These were the birth pangs of the TR who would eventually spend years of his life chasing adventure in the Badlands in the aftermath of his wife's unexpected death, who climbed the Matterhorn, who led a well-funded expedition through Africa for an entire year after his time as president, who later took a harrowing trip down the uncharted River of Doubt in the Amazon, which nearly killed him.

By the time he was twenty-three, this once-frail boy was the youngest member of the New York State Assembly. He had married the year before, but his marriage would only last for four brief years. As difficult as it was to will his body to physical health, nothing was more torturous than recovering from the unexpected death of his first wife, Alice. During her pregnancy, TR was absent for long stretches of time, in Albany performing his duties as an assembly member. On February 13, 1884, he received an upbeat telegram reporting that his wife had delivered a healthy baby girl the night before. Apparently, the first telegram was reason to celebrate, but not necessarily a reason to come home. Later that day, however, a second telegram arrived. This one was anything but celebratory in tone. After receiving it he immediately rushed to catch the next train to New York City. The news in the second telegram was almost incomprehensible: His mother and his wife were dying at the same time.

His mother, frequently ill herself, was suffering from typhoid fever. His wife was dying of Bright's disease, a painful and fatal affliction of the kidneys that had somehow gone undiagnosed. After enduring what had to be a long and excruciating five-hour train ride, Roosevelt made his way through the rainy and foggy streets of New York City to find that Alice barely recognized him. He took her in his arms. He left her side only briefly to walk downstairs and say his final goodbye to his mother, who died at three in the morning. He walked back upstairs to his wife. Alice survived another eleven hours before passing in the early afternoon. They had both died on Valentine's Day. In his diary, TR drew a large X and wrote but a single sentence, "The light has gone out of my life."[13]

Roosevelt did not bemoan the vexatious Fates or raise his fist in rage at God. Neither did he go through other rituals of grief. Rather, he stoically refused to react at all to what had happened. The duet of deaths on the same day reinforced what he already knew to be true: Life can be utterly capricious, halted at any moment; no one is owed any amount of time. His own "asthmatic childhood had shown that life could be stifled, cut off, unless one fought back, and all Papa's admonitions to get action, to seize the moment, had the implicit message that there was not much time after all."[14]

Roosevelt was taught by his father to rebel against any form of weakness and thus he seems to have struggled with knowing how to grieve or even behave in the aftermath of his wife's death. His behavior, by modern standards, appears odd and, frankly, a little cold. He showed virtually no interest in his baby daughter for the first few months of her life—when he escaped to Dakota, he didn't ask a single question about her in his letters home. He was back at work in Albany three days after the funerals of his wife and mother. And most fascinating of all, "like a lion obsessively trying to drag a spear from its flank, Roosevelt set about dislodging Alice Lee from his soul." A prominent dictum of the

TR canon of quirks—and there are many to be sure—was his steadfast refusal to mention her name ever again. While not entirely true, the legend is hardly different from the facts. He never spoke of Alice to his daughter. When he wrote his own *Autobiography*, he failed to write a single sentence about his first wife and marriage.[15]

He largely succeeded in dislodging Alice from his soul and writing a narrative of his life as if she had never lived. As obtuse as TR's behavior might seem to modern sensibilities, it was perhaps necessary for him to move on to the next chapter of his life. Despite his stilted and maladroit response to her untimely death, TR never gave up on marriage and the deep commitments of family life. His second marriage to his childhood friend Edith Kermit Carow is one of the most successful marriages in presidential history, and he later became a deeply devoted, engaged, and affectionate father to his six children.

Lesson #2: It Is Not the Critic Who Counts

The most famous speech of Roosevelt's life wasn't delivered during his time as president. It wasn't even given on American soil.

It was *performed* (smacking his right fist into his left palm for maximum effect) in Paris at the Sorbonne.[16] The theme was citizenship in a republic. Whenever anyone encounters a poster featuring a picture of a jolly or intense Roosevelt, there is a good chance a quote from this speech is printed somewhere on it. It is quintessential TR and one of the most eloquent statements about the essence of the American character:

> It is not the critic that counts; not the man who points out how the strong man stumbles, or where the doer of deeds could have done them better. The credit belongs to the man who is actually in the arena, whose face is marred by dust and sweat and blood; who strives valiantly; who errs, and comes up short again and again, because there is no effort without error and shortcoming: but who does actually strive to do deeds, who knows the great enthusiasms,

the great devotions: who spends himself in worthy causes, who at best knows in the end the triumph of high achievement, and who at the worst, if he fails, at least fails while daring greatly, so that his place shall never be with those cold and timid souls who know neither victory or defeat.[17]

If ever there was an American Sermon on the Mount replete with its own set of inspiring temporal beatitudes stirring enough to last through the democratic ages, it is surely from this passage. Not only is it a passage of eloquent self-help; it is also a form of political philosophy.

A free people in a republic, TR perfectly understood, are expected to behave differently than a subjected or hierarchical people. With the bounty of freedom at hand comes the duty of cultivating self-reliance and the obligation to exercise liberty within the bounds of law. Europe was historically filled with state-oriented regimes, centered on an almost endless parade of monarchical pageantry, an expansive assortment of kings, queens, dukes, and lords keeping average people in their places. But America, as Alexis de Tocqueville eloquently pointed out, had been "born free" of such a tyrannical arrangement.

Thus, Roosevelt oratorically paints a vivid and inspiring picture of how men and women are to behave in a society whose vitality originates not in the mystique of royal families, bloodlines, and cryptic titles but through the efforts and energies of the common citizen. Our King Arthurs don't pull a sword from a stone, they study the law in log cabins and become the Great Emancipator, or they defy the weakness of their body and become the hero of San Juan Hill.

If a republic is to succeed, if the American dream is to become a foundational societal aspiration, then average Americans must resist the smug and easy exhilaration of redundant self-congratulations. Great devotions and worthy causes demand an ethic of self-creation and steady renewal. Yes, petty amusements and the mindless ornamentations of leisure have their place in the rich canvas of life. But at their core they are distractions, mere respites from the striving of the self toward grander and nobler ends.

Key to this self-created life, however, was openness to failure. TR could have reveled in his global celebrity in the aftermath of his presidency. He was, perhaps, the most famous and respected man in the entire world at the time. And yet, to his credit, Roosevelt lived grandly on both sides of the ledger of life, positive and negative. He followed his own advice. His résumé of successes is almost endless. But the other side of the ledger, the side of losses and grand disappointments, awaited him just two years after delivering his "man in the arena" speech at the Sorbonne; he would "err" and "come up short" and "fail while daring greatly."

Many use TR's quote about defying critics as an endorsement for any type of self-indulgent expression, no matter what it. "Ignore the haters, make any decision boldly" is the sort of modern advice that frequently leads people over cliffs. On examining Roosevelt's doomed 1912 presidential campaign, this may seem to be precisely what he did. However, we should note that even in his speech about defying critics, he argues not for the righteousness of *any* cause but praises rather the one "who spends himself in worthy causes."

He thought this last campaign was such a cause. The election of 1912 is one of the most studied elections in presidential history for a variety of reasons, chiefly because it is the closest the United States ever came to a genuine multiparty system. Much of the commentary around the election is not complimentary of TR—how he betrayed his friend Taft by entering the race, how he split the Republican vote and handed the election to Woodrow Wilson in the process, how he possessed "insane ambition," how he had "high-minded rationales for entering the fight but not a single credible insight into his motives."[18]

However, TR was utterly convinced that America's social fabric was at risk of unraveling, and that the dangerous times rivaled the turbulence of the years leading up to the Civil War. The successes of industrial capitalism were undeniable: the "unprecedented scale in manufacturing, technological innovation, a transportation revolution, ever-greater efficiency in production, the birth of the modern corporation."[19]

But the successes came at an immense social cost. Cities had become polluted and overcrowded. Working conditions bordered on inhumane. There was a palpable sense that the maldistribution of wealth inordinately favoring the wealthy was due to broad corruption in government and widespread mistreatment of powerless workers, who, in theory, were equal members of American society. The "collusion flowed back and forth between secretive boardrooms and secretive halls of government."[20]

Roosevelt was no socialist, but he increasingly believed that the role of government was to face and ameliorate the problems afflicting civil society. He wanted robust regulation, not widespread nationalization of industry. He wanted to expose and end public and plutocratic corruption. He wanted more electoral power for the average, everyday voter. The different planks of his domestic program came to be known as the Square Deal, yet much of what he wanted to achieve was blocked by members of his own party during his second term as president.

Thus, he decided to run for a third presidential term, knowing perhaps that his efforts would ultimately be in vain.

He insisted on entering the arena, even if it was against his old friend, even if the odds were against him, even if there were detractors aplenty. By 1912, the nomination process of winning delegates was a complex amalgamation of counting primary voters and extracting commitments from different elements of the party machinery. TR won the popular vote from rank-and-file voters but failed to secure the nomination as Taft dominated the delegate count from members of the Republican National Committee. TR believed that what he had "won at the ballot box had been snatched from him in Chicago by 'naked theft.'"[21]

But TR decided not to leave the arena, believing that the principles of progressive Republicanism and "New Nationalism" were worth fighting for in the general election. Running as a "Bull Moose," the results were absolutely disastrous from an electoral standpoint as Republicans famously split their vote and handed the election to the Democrat, despite the fact Wilson only garnered 41.8 percent of the popular vote. The election seemed to confirm the later observation of the historian

Richard Hofstadter that "third parties are like bees: once they have stung, they die."

And to many, TR's 1912 efforts were pure ego and vainglory. Taft described him as "a freak, almost, in the zoological garden."[22] But whether or not one's political sympathies lie with Taft's conservatism or TR's progressivism, the lesson for us is that by entering the arena, and then staying in the arena and allowing himself to be "marred by dust and sweat and blood," many of Roosevelt's ideas eventually came to fruition, including an eight-hour workday, minimum wage for women, and an amendment for a federal income tax.

The campaign was ultimately about ideals, not ego. He was willing to endure the savage cut and thrust of the presidential campaign to bolster his hopes of renegotiating America's fraying social contract. He may have made a political miscalculation in the short term, but his principles were in the right place.

His efforts demonstrate—in a perfect Hamiltonian fashion—how personal ambition and national progress can go hand in hand. By contrast, the types of men and women who are attracted to public life today often revel in spectacle and bathe in outrageousness. As the theologian David Bentley Hart has written, "sensationalism sells better than sense."[23] They simply behave as if the aim of public service is fame—or notoriety—unmoored from real civic achievement, with one eye on power and the other on a future cable news contract. Public officials who are never embarrassed by their online shenanigans, who trade in innuendo and cheap social media posts knowing they will vanish into the electronic ether, are not the types of souls generally described in *The Federalist Papers* or in tracts of high-minded republican theory. They are not "in the arena" in the spirit of Roosevelt.

In many ways, the 1912 election was TR's paean to his own belief in the "strenuous life." Twelve years earlier, as the governor of New York, he famously observed, "I wish to preach, not the doctrine of ignoble ease, but the doctrine of the strenuous life, the life of toil and effort, of labor and strife; to preach that highest form of success which comes, not to the man who desires mere easy peace, but to the man who does not shrink from danger, from hardship, or from bitter toil, and who out of these wins the splendid ultimate triumph."

There is nobility in resisting "easy peace." It is the only way Roosevelt, or any of us, will ever experience a "splendid ultimate triumph." It is the only way we will escape the harsh finitude of insignificance.

Maybe the triumph we seek is personal—acquiring a new skill, shedding a few pounds, finding a way to beautify a local park or help those who are homeless. Maybe it is professional in nature—attaining the position we seek, fueling a commercial success, starting a business. Or, maybe it is even spiritual—practicing gratitude, accepting the annihilation of the self, praying or meditating more often with more intensity. But before there is any hint of triumph in our lives, we must look in the mirror. We must ask what truly matters, what is worthy of our most colossal efforts, and then embolden and fortify ourselves by remembering it is never the critic that counts.

It is only the voice within.

Lesson #3: Never Stop Moving

In the pantheon of historical assassinations and assassination attempts, TR's is perhaps the most revealing of his inner character.

In mid-October, just a few weeks before the 1912 election, Roosevelt's campaign was unfolding at a breakneck pace, with the candidate sometimes delivering up to twenty speeches a day. The editor in chief of *The Outlook* described TR as "an electric battery of inexhaustible energy."[24]

Roosevelt was a battery that refused to die. Even a bullet in the chest couldn't kill him.

On October 14, 1912, as he was entering a car about to take him to his next speaking engagement, a gunman opened fire from about four or five feet away. Roosevelt fell backward. His stenographer immediately disarmed the would-be assassin, John Schrank, with a half nelson and appeared to be trying to break his neck.[25]

Roosevelt was able to stand up and yelled out, "Don't hurt him. Bring him here. I want to see him." He cupped Schrank's face in his hands, stared into his eyes, and was met with a gaze of unbridled lunacy. The man was wearing oversize shoes and filthy clothes, a paranoid schizophrenic who was utterly convinced that Roosevelt's attempt to win a third presidential term would lead the nation to ruin. Schrank believed that the former president William McKinley had been speaking to him at night through his dreams. He later said at his trial, "I did not intend to kill the citizen Roosevelt. I intended to kill Theodore Roosevelt, the third termer."[26]

When TR eventually made it into the car, he shocked everyone by forbidding his driver from taking him to the hospital. "You get me to that speech," he insisted.

But the bullet had done real damage. The lethality of the bullet was famously hindered by the fact that it traveled through his overcoat, suspenders, glasses case, and thick folded papers constituting the speech he was scheduled to give. When he arrived at the auditorium, he finally allowed himself to be examined. The bullet had made a dime-size hole under his right nipple. A rib was broken, he was bleeding, and the entire right side of his body had turned black.

Yet he insisted on delivering the speech. Nothing could stop his efforts on behalf of the campaign.

The man who introduced TR in front of ten thousand people told the crowd that Roosevelt had been the victim of an assassination attempt and was promptly met with pockets of skepticism from the crowd—"Fake! Fake!"[27] Roosevelt stepped forward and delivered the famous line: "It takes more than that to kill a bull moose." He then unbuttoned his vest and displayed a blood-soaked dress shirt to the crowd. He warned the audience, "I'm going to ask you to be very quiet. I'll do the best I can."

It wasn't until he unfurled his fifty pages of paper that he realized his loquaciousness might have saved his life. "You see," he gleefully intoned, "I was going to make quite a long speech." The bullet had seared a hole through the entire block of papers formerly ensconced in his jacket pocket. With a bullet lodged in one of his ribs and blood steadily oozing out of his body, TR spoke for a full eighty minutes, audaciously utilizing every page he had brought with him until finally surrendering to the reality that he desperately needed to go to the hospital.

TR's choice to give the speech with a bullet wedged in his body was genuinely shocking in the moment, with most audience members looking askance. Yet, to truly know Roosevelt is to recognize he was a relentless mover, an ardent believer that movement is the essence of life. Movement is the assurance of vitality. It is the great perpetuator of a distinct form of human hope—the hope of new and untrodden destinations for ardent seekers of beauty and truth. Movement is a reminder that we still walk the earth and the darkness of the grave is not yet at hand. It is a commandment to recapture the magical hum and buzz of our youth when movement seemed second nature.

If Roosevelt's life, in toto, can teach us anything, it is the lesson that we should never stop moving, never stop asking "what's next," never cull the surprising fork in the road or squash the desire to discover the utterly unexpected. It is the belief that another jewel in life's treasure chest of riches lies right around the corner. It is the conviction that some of life's deepest mysteries are within our grasp of understanding. Movement is essential to the good life and the attainment of human flourishing. It delays the sorrows of decay and subtly quiets the voices of anguish.

Thus, movement, in all its forms, is how Roosevelt discovered the deepest and most poetic joys of his life. His commitment to new challenges and constant movement culminated in the distinction of becoming the youngest president in American history. In a brief amount of time—just two decades—he went from being a rowdy and pugnacious college student to occupying the White House.

The key was constant movement. As a student at Harvard, he moved toward knowledge and the enthrallment of deep study and reflection. Just a few months after graduating, he moved toward family life by marrying Alice Hathaway Lee on his twenty-second birthday.

At the age of twenty-three, he moved into the world of politics, winning election to the New York State Assembly as the youngest man ever elected to his office and sowing the seeds of a life of vigorous public service.

The next year he moved toward the pleasure of the written word, penning *The Naval War of 1812*, a book that would later become required reading at the US Naval Academy and was widely considered the definitive book on the subject. He would go on to write dozens of books, including classics such as *The Winning of the West*.

In 1883, in the wake of his first wife's death, he moved toward one of the most famous chapters of his life, his embrace of adventure and ranching in the Dakota Territory where he summons the spirit of Artemis and hunts buffalo, captures boat thieves, participates in saloon melees, and retreats from his former life to establish the Elkhorn Ranch.

By 1887, he moved toward another attempt at both domestic life and political power as he moves into his famed residence, Sagamore Hill, with his second wife and just a few months later welcomes his first son, Theodore Roosevelt Jr., into the world.

By the end of the 1880s, he helps move the national government away from a corrupt spoils system of patronage by becoming the first commissioner of the US Civil Service, where he promotes merit in hiring practices and investigates political abuse and fraud. In his time as commissioner, his wife gives birth to two more children and he publishes multiple books.

He famously moves into law enforcement, becoming the police commissioner of New York City at a time when the department was awash with corruption. He institutes multiple reforms to ensure the police were properly making their rounds, brings back the nightstick, and arms policemen with a firearm. He walks deep into the heart of the city, observing the everyday reality of New Yorkers experiencing pounding poverty, observations that help inform his later embrace of robust regulation of the economy. As he writes his sister, "I get a glimpse of the real life of the swarming millions."[28]

He moves into the administration of President McKinley as the assistant secretary of the navy but quickly jettisons his post the next year in order to join the 1st United States Volunteer Cavalry Regiment. During the Spanish-American War he forms the Rough Riders, earns the rank of colonel, and fights in the Battle of San Juan, which he later describes as "the great day of my life," riding up and down the hill while encouraging his men to "March!"[29]

Later in 1898, he moves back into politics, winning the election to become the governor of New York. Just two years later he becomes the vice president of the United States. A few months into his second term, President McKinley is assassinated by an anarchist in Buffalo, New York, making Roosevelt the youngest occupant of the White House.

His presidency was among the most consequential in American history. He revolutionized the office of chief executive, transforming it from a pedestrian constitutional office with limited enumerated powers into a more vigorous popular institution imbued with expansive powers. He is the great progenitor of using the "bully pulpit" to influence public opinion by appealing directly to the people, thus earning a reputation as "the strangest creature the White House ever held."[30] He altered the relationship between big business and government and is considered by many historians to be the first modern president.[31]

Roosevelt rarely stayed in one place long enough to master the skill of self-reflection. He appears to have had no interest in peering beyond metaphysical veils—he was too busy hunting large game, building the Panama Canal, or taming the surging excesses of Western industrialism. The notion of resting on laurels or suspending the vigor of life for any amount of time was utterly foreign to him. After all, the world was so big, with books to read, causes to pursue, and mountains to summit.

There is certainly a time for rest and a place in the carousel of life for quiet scrutiny of our lives and opinions; silence can nourish the soul.

But what TR understood, and what the tempest of his life can teach us today, is that it is difficult to be unhappy, despondent, or depressed when we are briskly traveling the road we passionately wish to be on. Rest stops on interstates are certainly necessary, but they should never be confused with the destination.

CONCLUSION

In the fall of 2022, I was on the brink of a significant career milestone. I was about to begin my twenty-fifth year as a classroom teacher. When my students wanted to playfully make me feel old, they would describe this milestone somewhat differently: "Whoa, Mr. Adams, you've been teaching for a quarter of a century!"

It didn't matter whether my tenure as a teacher was described as "twenty-five years" or "a quarter of a century." To be honest, I was excited to hit this particular marker for a variety of reasons. In my American government class, I was going to have my daughter as a student. While she wasn't thrilled about having her father as her civics teacher, I couldn't help but be a little excited to see my child in a new and different setting. It wouldn't be the first time this had happened in my family. I'd had my father as my freshman English teacher thirty-two autumns earlier, at the same high school, and it was magical. I came to see and admire my dad in a wholly different light, understanding for the first time why he was so beloved by generations of former students.

Deep down, maybe, just maybe, I was hoping for the same fairy-tale outcome with my own child.

But if I am being honest, the ultimate reason for my excitement had nothing to do with career milestones or my daughter. This was going to be the first school year without the specter of COVID-19 hanging over our heads. Two years earlier had been the year of remote learning, with instruction contorted into Zoom sessions instead of traditional class periods. The next year was admittedly much better, but it was still a year of mask mandates and armies of students disappearing for ten days at a time, canceled events and antiquated distancing requirements at school functions.

Now—*finally!*—our school and our society were ready for a rendez-vous with normalcy.

But on the first day of school, before the first bell had had a chance to commence the new year, I knew something was dreadfully wrong. I was walking to the office to gather roll sheets out of my teacher box when I witnessed a mother interacting with her daughter in a peculiar way. The daughter's eyes were looking down at the ground, her shoulders were slouched, and she wore a large black mask. She was vehemently shaking her head in defiance of whatever her mother was saying to her.

I inched closer to them. One of the school's security officers was talking quietly to the daughter. Finally, I could detect what the mother was saying. She wasn't simply talking to her daughter; she was *pleading* with her.

"You can do this, you can do this, I promise you can do this."

The daughter then clutched the fence as if to steady herself. She kept shaking her head and now she was crying softly. "No, no, no."

The security officer, who is known for his soft touch and kind de-meanor, also tried to encourage her. But it was to no avail. The mother's expression was one of colossal dejection. She kept repeating, "You can, you can, you can . . ."

I decided to step in. Maybe a teacher would be less menacing than a security officer. Maybe a nonparent presence would be helpful. And most of all, I had a new card to play.

"Hey," I said, "I'm Mr. Adams. I have been here for twenty-five years and nobody is gonna mess with me on this campus."

I decided to channel one of my favorite lines from the film *Good Morning, Vietnam*: "I'm the tallest hog in the trough around here. I know everyone on this campus. I know every square foot of it. Let me walk with you to the gym and help you get your schedule and then I will walk you to your first class myself. I swear it will be easy."

The tears stopped. She steadied herself. And for the smallest moment I thought I was going to have my first triumph of the new school year. Instead, she shook her head again and began to walk back to her mother's car. Anyone who has ever been a parent could recognize the expression of utter defeat that blazed across her mother's face.

This book was written to demonstrate and explain what successful Americans of the past told themselves about their own lives in order to assist Americans like this young woman today. We all have stories we tell ourselves about our inner angels and haunting demons—narratives of the self we believe to be true. The young woman whom I tried to help on the first day of school believed herself to be so vulnerable, so fragile, and so delicate that she couldn't will herself to walk onto a school campus.

But the difficult, dreary reality is that Americans from all backgrounds increasingly find it difficult to walk past their own open gates, to find the poetry and magic in their lives.

One of the unifying threads of the ten men and women we have gotten to know so well in this book is a steadfast refusal to fetishize catastrophe. From the harrowing childhood of poverty for Abraham Lincoln and Ben Nighthorse Campbell, to the barriers of potent prejudice encountered by Arthur Ashe, Daniel Inouye, and Ruth Bader Ginsburg, or the failed personal relationships endured by the likes of Thomas Jefferson and James Madison, none of our heroes saw themselves as calamitous victims of forces larger than themselves.

So much of our modern misery can be traced to a fashionable catastrophism that convinces people they are utterly powerless to command the wheels of their own lives. It is why the New York Times features articles with titles such as "Hospitals Are Increasingly Crowded with Kids Who Tried to Harm Themselves."[1] It is why the newspaper of record publishes opinion pieces from conservative commentators earnestly asking, "What if Kids Are Sad and Stressed Because Their Parents Are?"[2] It is why there are long articles in USA Today detailing the fact that "Students Are Increasingly Refusing to Go to School. It's Becoming a Mental Health Crisis."[3]

The execrable propensity to preach and believe the gospel of everlasting catastrophe is not a quirk of a particular ideological camp. These days the politics of misery has its iterations on both the right and the left. It is fueled by fear, anger, and the constant drumbeat of outrage.

There is a habit in progressive corners to view the world as an unrelenting merry-go-round of injustice and doomsday scenarios. Impending cataclysms of the climate are constant topics of conversation, as is the argument that income inequality is the sadistic by-product of malevolent corporate actors hell-bent on bringing back the industrial horrors of late eighteenth-century capitalism. Activists suggest that racism is both ubiquitous in its power but also somehow sinister in its opaqueness. In this view of the world, new incarnations of American fascism and sexism are always lurking.

The *Washington Post* technology columnist Taylor Lorenz captured the essence of this zeitgeist of doom when she famously tweeted in 2020, "People are like 'why are kids so depressed it must be their PHONES!' But never mention the fact that we're living in a late stage capitalist hellscape during an ongoing deadly pandemic w record wealth inequality, o social safety net/job security, as climate change cooks the world."

Fetishizing doom and valorizing gloom are not just actions based on factually incorrect premises; they are a stain on the human spirit that yearns to be productive and free. To believe the world is so utterly barren of beauty and hope that it exists in a perpetual vise of bleakness and despair, not only robs modern Americans of their God-given agency but, worse, saps any desire to use what agency they do possess in a way that might be constructive and life-affirming. As Douglas Murray observes in *The War on the West*, "These notions are not just ahistorical. At this stage, they are completely self-destructive. For if the land you are on is simply stolen, the Founding Fathers were simply 'slave owners,' the Constitution needs to be re-written, and no figure in your history deserves respect, then what exactly holds this grand quarter-millennial-long project together?"[4]

Catastrophism, however, is not the exclusive domain of the political left. There is a conservative variety that can be equally debilitating, usually rooted in a potent fear that the traditional American way of life is under constant assault by sinister forces. As a result, deep suspicion abounds. Conspiracy takes root. Conservatives assert that different American institutions are deliberately trying to subvert civil society—the American media with its biases, distortions, and sometimes outright lies; the American academy, which has purportedly been captured by neo-Marxists more interested in indoctrination than actual instruction; the deep state and its law enforcement apparatus targeting conservatives and right-wing activists; left-wing politicians deliberately facilitating a porous border; young American educators who seem to mirror many of the people posted on the popular X account Libs of TikTok who see themselves less as instructors and more as pedagogic activists.

To be sure, both sides of the ideological spectrum have a significant body of facts on their side. And there is some truth, of course, in every claim of alarm. Income inequality has deepened in the past half century. Environmental degradation is a real concern. Elite American universities have become echo chambers of a rigid and often dogmatically progressive worldview. The relentless push to decriminalize a hodgepodge of crimes has left American cities virtually dystopian at times.

Consequently, a deep well of unease resides in many of us today in light of a modern culture in which there are no more North Stars. We look around and see a world lacking any transcendent gyroscope of absolutes—morality, nationhood, relationships, even human biology has no orienting device. A world where truth can be known, virtue can be practiced, and beauty can be perceived seems increasingly out of reach, a relic from a bygone era where right was right and wrong was wrong.

Social media sophisticates scoff at outdated notions of decency, standards, and moral consequence, deeming them bourgeoise or Boomer values. Young Americans have learned to decouple duty from honor and have thus detached commitment from fulfillment. Yet the truly transcendent moments available in the human walk of life—experiencing love, knowing truth, recognizing beauty—are anchored to a well-ordered soul.

Peddlers of catastrophism forget that the world's imperfection has nothing to do with the individual soul's fulfillment. The world has always been broken. It will always be broken. The insights of poets, philosophers, and prophets stretching across multiple millennia are not wrong. The words of Hamlet's soliloquy ring as true today as when Shakespeare wrote them more than four hundred year ago: "How weary, stale, flat, and unprofitable, / Seem to me all the uses of this world!"

A serious argument could be made that the material and political conditions of modern Westerners are the best they have ever been in the history of our species. And yet, if we are to believe modern research about happiness and well-being, we are more miserable than we have ever been. We are miserable because we have forgotten that the world's imperfections should never prevent its occupants from experiencing profound waves of gratitude. We have forgotten that the United States' imperfections are not grave enough to take passionate patriotism off the table. We have forgotten that the imperfections of our family and friends does not mean we should not love them beyond measure.

The world inhabited by the ten men and women of this book was just as broken and just as flawed as the world we are living in today. Perhaps more so. Despite this they found a way to live lives of deep and passionate meaning. This talent for human flourishing imbues them with a form of authority we should welcome in the modern age. It should command our attention and pique our interest. They exude authority in the best possible spirit of the word. Their authority is not a restriction of liberty but a guide on how to use it well. Their authority scaffolds the moral and aspirational framework for a life of achievement by way of sacrifice.

For as much as Americans love to say they are naturally born free, we have forgotten that the knowledge of how to use our freedom for purposeful and benevolent ends is not natural at all. We are not born with it. It is not innate. We all must be tutored and trained in the different lessons of liberty, becoming pupils of human freedom in the process, ultimately accepting that we are responsible for our own lives.

The alternative is what we are witnessing today—a variety of liberty that is licentious and a form of freedom that often tilts toward moral chaos and political tribalism.

Such wisdom must be acquired from others. It must be taught and received. It must be passed down from those who have experienced the rich spectrum of human possibilities, from the deepest pangs of sorrow to the sweetest jubilations of joy, and everything in between. The arrows and agonies of life do not spare any of us. Waiting for politicians to be honest or for global temperatures to drop before we embark on the enterprise of cultivating our truest and best selves is a strategy laden with disappointment. Instead, we should embrace what the ten American titans of this book always understood: Meaning, purpose, and joy don't simply happen *to us*, but must be discovered and cultivated *within us*.

As the great Sanskrit dramatist Kalidasa wrote more than fifteen hundred years ago:

The bliss of growth,
The glory of action,
The splendor of achievement
Are but experiences of time

Bliss.
Glory.
Splendor.
Big words reserved for serious people living serious lives. Not every era and civilization exalts human liberty as its paramount value. We do. It is time to get serious about it.

ACKNOWLEDGMENTS

The ten-to-fifteen-year career mark is often decisive in the life of a teacher. Many educators decide they want a different challenge, so they begin a new professional chapter—sometimes they change schools or teach a different grade level or get a graduate degree or, most frequently, decide they want to have a broader impact and go into the world of school administration.

But I have always believed in the enchantment of the written word, always believed that words and ideas can trigger metamorphoses of the individual soul and the collective consciousness. And I have never yearned to leave the classroom. So instead of just teaching about politics, I decided I wanted a second career as a professional writer about education and politics. Maybe, just maybe, I prayed, my own words could echo beyond my classroom.

Talk about taking the tough and often thankless path . . .

But what an incredible journey it has been to be afforded the extraordinary opportunity to write this book. It is truly the cumulation of every hope I have ever harbored as a teacher-writer. And the people who have traveled with me on this boat were not passive bystanders—their oars of encouragement, insight, and wisdom often propelled me forward more than I ever could have on my own.

To my agent, Linda Konner, I know actors and actresses frequently talk about the "big break" of their careers. My big break will always be your generous decision to believe in my writing and to fight for this humble high school teacher's voice to be heard. You are my megaphone and my "big break" rolled into one.

To my wife, Jennifer, we have a hectic life, but thank you for always understanding my drive and dream of writing this book.

To my brothers, Howard and Will, you are, of course, wise older brothers, but more than that, you are *believing* older brothers, believing that this book could and would happen someday, believing that it would have an impact, and believing that your younger brother was the one to write it.

To Craig Holliday, no one has been there every single step of the way like you. Your contributions are too many to list—I would have to write another book to name all of them. To Kevin Reynier, no one is ever more eager to read my work and encourage me than you. To Auguste Meyrat, my fellow occupant of this maddening but exhilarating writing trench reserved for teacher-writers, you are the only person who truly "gets it." To Shane Trotter, thank you so much for believing in this project and for being a fellow traveler, for reading sections of this book, and for believing that America's better days are in front of us. And to my oldest friend in all the world, Cory Irwin, thank you for your sharp insights about our fellow citizens as you travel the country as an airline pilot—your perspective proved invaluable.

My colleagues and students at Bakersfield High School have inspired me for twenty-six years. Without their support, inspiration, and encouragement to speak the truth this book never would have been written. Thank you also to the library staff at the Walter W. Stiern Library at California State University, Bakersfield, for supplying me with the best office with the best view and for helping me navigate COVID outbreaks, carpet repairs, and leaky ceilings during the course of the writing of the book.

To Hannah Long, yes, you are an exquisitely talented editor, and yes, you made this book so much better every step of the process. But I also feel like I made a friend along the way. And I hope that lasts for a long time. Everyone at Broadside Books has been everything an author could hope for and more. I am forever in your debt.

My mom and dad are no longer with me. But they are never far from my thoughts. I genuinely hope this book would have made them proud of their youngest child.

And finally, to my children, Lauren, Emma, and Benjamin, I don't know if you will ever read *Lessons in Liberty*, but I hope you make it to this acknowledgment page someday. Please know that though I love being a teacher and a writer, being your father is the defining love of my life. If I never taught another class or wrote another word, my life would still be complete having you as my children.

NOTES

Chapter 1: George Washington: Have Good Manners in Every Setting

1. Richard Brookhiser, *Founding Father: Rediscovering George Washington* (New York: Free Press, 1997), 9.
2. John E. Ferling, *The First of Men: A Life of George Washington* (Knoxville: University of Tennessee Press, 1989), 10.
3. Willard Sterne Randall, *George Washington: A Life* (New York: Holt, 1997), 28.
4. Ron Chernow, *Alexander Hamilton* (New York: Penguin Press, 2004), xx.
5. Harry Schenawolf, "General George Washington's Explosive Temper Helped Shape the Man Who Forged a New Nation," *Revolutionary War Journal* (March 23, 2022), https://www.revolutionarywarjournal.com /general-george-washingtons-temper-shaped-the-man-who-forged-a -new-nation/.
6. Randall, *George Washington*, 3.
7. Chernow, *Alexander Hamilton*, 124.
8. Brookhiser, *Founding Father*, 110.
9. Stephen Brumwell, *George Washington: Gentleman Warrior* (New York: Quercus, 2016), 2.
10. Chernow, *Alexander Hamilton*, 281.
11. "John Adams describes George Washington's ten talents, 1807," www .gilderlehrman.org/sites/default/files/inline-pdfs/00424_FPS_0.pdf.
12. Washington and Lee University, "University History," www.wlu.edu /the-w-l-story/university-history/.
13. Eric Sterner, "Joseph Addison's Cato: Liberty on the Stage," *Journal of the American Revolution* (October 25, 2016), https://allthingsliberty.com /2016/11/joseph-addisons-cato-liberty-stage/.

14. Joseph J. Ellis, *The Quartet: Orchestrating the Second American Revolution, 1783–1789* (New York: Vintage Books, 2016), 107.

15. Francis Rufus Bellamy, *The Private Life of George Washington* (New York: Thomas Y. Crowell, 1951), 353.

Chapter 2: Daniel Inouye: Be a Joiner

1. Emma Brown, "Daniel K. Inouye, U.S. Senator, Dies at 88," *Washington Post*, December 17, 2012, https://www.washington post.com/local/obituaries/daniel-k-inouye-us-senator-dies-at -88/2012/12/17/61030936-b259-11e0-9a80-c46b9cb1255f_story .html.

2. Paul Niwa, *Inouye* (self-pub., June 21, 2017), Apple Books, https:// books.apple.com/us/book/inouye/id1250916586.

3. Daniel Inouye, "McKinley High School Commencement Address," April 13, 2019, https://dkii.org/speeches/june-01-1975/.

4. Tom Brokaw, *The Greatest Generation* (New York: Random House, 2005), 354.

5. Inouye, "McKinley High School Commencement Address."

6. Jane Goodsell and Haru Wells, *Daniel Inouye* (New York: Crowell, 1977), 15.

7. "Daniel Inouye," www.readinga-z.com/books/leveled-books/book /?id=3733&langId=1.

8. Larry Smith, *Beyond Glory: Medal of Honor Heroes in Their Own Words: Extraordinary Stories of Courage from World War II to Vietnam* (New York: Norton, 2004), 39.

9. Goodsell and Wells, *Daniel Inouye*, 2.

10. Brokaw, *The Greatest Generation*, 351.

11. Smith, *Beyond Glory*, 40.

12. Brokaw, *The Greatest Generation*, 351.

13. Smith, *Beyond Glory*, 49.

14. "Remarks by the President at the Funeral Service for Senator Daniel Ken Inouye," National Archives and Records Administration, https:// obamawhitehouse.archives.gov/the-press-office/2012/12/21/remarks -president-funeral-service-senator-daniel-ken-inouye.

15. Smith, *Beyond Glory*, 37.
16. "Democratic National Convention Keynote Address," Daniel K. Inouye Institute, https://dkii.org/speeches/august-26-1968/.
17. Catalina Camia, "Praise for Sen. Daniel Inouye as He Lies in State," *USA Today*, December 20, 2012, https://www.usatoday.com/story/news/politics/2012/12/20/inouye-lies-in-state-capitol-memorial/1781941/.
18. "Senator Robert 'Bob' Dole Talks about His Friendship with Senator Daniel Inouye," YouTube, June 27, 2016, https://www.youtube.com/watch?v=1yBiqjAeFc8.
19. Niwa, *Inouye*, 70.
20. Ibid., 71.
21. Ibid.
22. "A Democrat to Watch by George Will," Daniel K. Inouye Institute, https://dkii.org/speeches/january-05-1981/.
23. James Fallows, "Daniel Inouye: A Genuine Hero," *The Atlantic*, December 18, 2012, https://www.theatlantic.com/politics/archive/2012/12/daniel-inouye-a-genuine-hero/266425/.
24. Audrey McAvoy, "LBJ Pushed Humphrey to Mull Inouye as VP Candidate," *San Diego Union-Tribune*, December 6, 2008.
25. "Senator Daniel Inouye & Family: Watergate Changed His Life," Daniel K. Inouye Institute, https://dkii.org/speeches/november-11-1973/.
26. Ibid.
27. "Maiden Speech," Daniel K. Inouye Institute, https://dkii.org/speeches/maiden-speech/.
28. Niwa, *Inouye*, 21.
29. "Remarks on Signing the Bill Providing Restitution for the Wartime Internment of Japanese-American Civilians," Ronald Reagan Presidential Library, https://www.reaganlibrary.gov/archives/speech/remarks-signing-bill-providing-restitution-wartime-internment-japanese-american.
30. "Inouye, Daniel Ken," US House of Representatives: History, Art & Archives, https://history.house.gov/People/Detail/15647.
31. Niwa, *Inouye*, 27.
32. Ibid., 26.

33. "Speech Recalls December 7th," Daniel K. Inouye Institute, https://
    dkii.org/speeches/speech-recalls-dec-7/.
34. "Sen. Inouye's Office Says His Final Word Was 'Aloha,'" *Hawaii
    News Now*, December 18, 2012, https://www.hawaiinewsnow.com
    /story/20366609/sen-inouyes-office-releases-statement-on-his-passing/.

Chapter 3: Clara Barton: It's Not Someone Else's Problem

1. Barbara A. Somervill, *Clara Barton: Founder of the American Red Cross*
   (Minneapolis, MN: Compass Point Books, 2007), 18.
2. Cathy East Dubowski, *Clara Barton: Healing the Wounds* (Englewood
   Cliffs, NJ: Silver Burdett Press, 1991), 55.
3. "Clara Barton's Nursing Career," Clara Barton Museum website, May 10,
   2018, https://clarabartonmuseum.org/nurse/#:~:text=My%20little
   %20hands%20became%20schooled,almost%20too%20ill%20to%20
   recover.%E2%80%9D.
4. Somervill, *Clara Barton*, 42.
5. Dubowski, *Clara Barton*, 55.
6. Stephanie Spinner and David Groff, *Who Was Clara Barton?* (New
   York: Grosset & Dunlap, 2014), 100.
7. Kieran Setiya, *Midlife: A Philosophical Guide* (Princeton, NJ: Princeton
   University Press, 2018), 12.
8. Dubowski, *Clara Barton*, 27.
9. *Massachusetts Passes First Education Law*, www.massmoments.org
   /moment-details/massachusetts-passes-first-education-law.html#:~:text
   =When%20John%20Adams%20drafted%20the,pass%20a%20
   comprehensive%20education%20law.
10. Dubowski, *Clara Barton*, 36.
11. Spinner and Groff, *Who Was Clara Barton?*, 29.
12. Elizabeth B. Pryor, *Clara Barton: Professional Angel* (Philadelphia:
    University of Pennsylvania Press, 1988), 148.
13. Ibid., 201.
14. "Public Speaking in an Outspoken Age: Oratory in 19th Century
    America," *E Pluribus Unum Project*, http://www1.assumption.edu/ahc
    /rhetoric/oratory.html.
15. Dubowski, *Clara Barton*, 95.

16. Harry Enten, "American Happiness Hits Record Lows," CNN, February 2, 2022, https://www.cnn.com/2022/02/02/politics /unhappiness-americans-gallup-analysis/index.html.

17. Dubowski, *Clara Barton*, 91.

18. Pryor, *Clara Barton*, 135.

19. Somervill, *Clara Barton*, 59.

20. Pryor, *Clara Barton*, 135.

21. Ibid., 140.

Chapter 4: Thomas Jefferson: Don't Specialize, Be a Generalist

1. "Thomas Jefferson Legacy," Library of Congress, https://www.loc .gov/exhibits/jefferson/jeffleg.html#:~:text=At%20key%20points%20 in%20his,Though%20critics%20questioned%20his%20role.

2. "Jefferson's Gravestone," Monticello, https://www.monticello.org /research-education/thomas-jefferson-encyclopedia/jeffersons -gravestone/#:~:text=A%20joint%20resolution%20of%20 Congress,at%20Monticello%20the%20next%20year.

3. Cara Giaimo, "Thomas Jefferson Built This Country on Mastodons," *Atlas Obscura* (June 10, 2021), https://www.atlasobscura.com/articles /thomas-jefferson-built-this-country-on-mastodons.

4. "Thomas Jefferson's Mockingbird Named Dick," Presidential Pet Museum, https://www.presidentialpetmuseum.com/pets/thomas -jefferson-mockingbird/.

5. James Parton, *Life of Thomas Jefferson: Third President of the United States* (Boston: James R Osgood and Company, 1874), 165, https://tjrs .monticello.org/letter/1440.

6. Dumas Malone, *Jefferson, the Virginian* (Boston: Little, Brown, 1948), 56.

7. "Jefferson's Life at School," William & Mary, https://www.wm.edu/about /history/tj/tjlife/index.php.

8. "Jefferson and Music," Monticello, https://www.monticello.org /thomas-jefferson/a-day-in-the-life-of-jefferson/a-delightful-recreation /jefferson-and-music/#:~:text=Jefferson%20played%20violin%20 %2D%2D%20and,while%20a%20student%20in%20Williamsburg.

9. Michael Knox Beran, *Jefferson's Demons: Portrait of a Restless Mind* (New York: Free Press, 2003), xv.

10. Alys Matthews, "Hooves Through History: The Untold Story of Thomas Jefferson's Daily Rides," *Richmond Times-Dispatch*, September 20, 2017, https://richmond.com/hooves-through-history-the-untold-story-of -thomas-jefferson-s-daily-rides/article_cc8f45bc-9e24-11e7-8a3a-cb8c1 e71659d.html.

11. "Spanish Language," Monticello, https://www.monticello.org/research -education/thomas-jefferson-encyclopedia/spanish-language/#:~:text =Jefferson%20supposedly%20learned%20the%20Spanish,Quixote %20and%20a%20Spanish%20grammar.

12. "Jefferson's Views on Mathematics," University of Virginia, https:// math.virginia.edu/history/Jefferson/jefferson.htm.

13. Andrew Burstein, *The Inner Jefferson: Portrait of a Grieving Optimist* (Charlottesville: University Press of Virginia, 1996), 19.

14. Gordon S. Wood, *Revolutionary Characters: What Made the Founders Different* (London: Penguin Books, 2007), 204.

15. Mary Bellis, "Thomas Jefferson's Life as an Inventor," ThoughtCo, March 28, 2018, https://www.thoughtco.com/thomas-jefferson -inventor-4072261.

16. "Wheel Cipher," Monticello, https://www.monticello.org/research -education/thomas-jefferson-encyclopedia/wheel-cipher/.

17. "About the APS," American Philosophical Society, https://www .amphilsoc.org/about.

18. "Founders Online: From John Adams to Benjamin Rush, 21 June 1811," National Archives and Records Administration, https://founders .archives.gov/documents/Adams/99-02-02-5649.

19. "Founders Online: From John Adams to Thomas Jefferson, 22 January 1825," National Archives and Records Administration, https:// founders.archives.gov/documents/Adams/99-02-02-7939.

20. "Adams Papers Digital Edition," Massachusetts Historical Society, https://www.masshist.org/publications/adams-papers/index.php/view /ADMS-04-08-02-0106.

21. Joseph J. Ellis, *Passionate Sage: The Character and Legacy of John Adams* (New York: W. W. Norton, 2001), 122.

22. Ibid., 129.

23. Dumas Malone, *Jefferson and His Time: The Sage of Monticello* (Boston: Little, Brown, 1948), 6:104.

24. Gregory S. Schneider, "Saving Thomas Jefferson's Soul," *Washington Post*, July 2, 2019, https://www.washingtonpost.com/history/2019 /07/03/saving-thomas-jeffersons-soul/.

25. "Founders Online: Thomas Jefferson to Miles King, 26 September 1814," National Archives and Records Administration, https:// founders.archives.gov/documents/Jefferson/03-07-02-0495.

26. Ibid.

27. Reem Nadeem, "How U.S. Religious Composition Has Changed in Recent Decades," Pew Research Center's Religion & Public Life Project, September 13, 2022, https://www.pewresearch.org/religion/2022/09/13 /how-u-s-religious-composition-has-changed-in-recent-decades/.

28. "Atheism Doubles among Generation Z," Barna Group, https://www .barna.com/research/atheism-doubles-among-generation-z/.

29. Sara Atske, "What Americans Know about Religion," Pew Research Center's Religion & Public Life Project, July 23, 2019, https://www .pewresearch.org/religion/2019/07/23/what-americans-know-about -religion/.

30. Jacob Siegel, "Michel Houellebecq's Sexual Apocalypse," UnHerd, December 8, 2022, https://unherd.com/2022/12/michel-houellebecqs -sexual-apocalypse/.

Chapter 5: Arthur Ashe: Don't Let Other People Pick Your Fights

1. Raymond Arsenault, *Arthur Ashe: A Life* (New York: Simon & Schuster, 2019), 383.

2. Arthur Ashe and Arnold Rampersad, *Days of Grace: A Memoir* (New York: Ballantine Books, 1994), 1.

3. Arsenault, *Arthur Ashe*, 12.

4. Alexandre Sokolowski, "When Connors and McEnroe Almost Came to Blows in Chicago," Tennis Majors, January 10, 2023, https://www .tennismajors.com/others-news/january-10-1982-connors-and-mcenroe -nearly-come-to-blows-in-chicago-315352.html.

5. Ashe and Rampersad, *Days of Grace*, 68.

6. Ibid., 69.

7. Ibid., 84.

8. Ibid., 86.

9. Ibid.

10. "Grand Opening of Arthur Ashe Stadium," YouTube, https://www
.youtube.com/watch?v=r_S9byNySH4.

11. Ashe and Rampersad, *Days of Grace*, 89.

12. Ibid., 118.

13. Ibid., 127.

14. Ibid., 128.

15. Ibid., 124.

16. *Citizen Ashe*, directed by Rex Miller and Sam Pollard (CNN Films/
Magnolia Pictures, 2021).

17. Arsenault, *Arthur Ashe*, 39.

18. International Tennis Hall of Fame, https://www.tennisfame.com
/hall-of-famers/inductees/dr-robert-johnson.

19. Arsenault, *Arthur Ashe*, 131.

20. *Citizen Ashe*.

21. Ibid.

22. Paul Mantell, *Arthur Ashe: Young Tennis Champion*, illustrated by
Meryl Henderson (New York: Aladdin Paperbacks, 2006), 149.

23. Arthur Ashe and Neil Amdur, *Off the Court* (New York: New
American Library, 1982), 145.

24. Arsenault, *Arthur Ashe*, 286.

25. Ashe and Amdur, *Off the Court*, 148.

26. Ibid., 118.

27. Arsenault, *Arthur Ashe*, 329.

28. Ashe and Amdur, *Off the Court*, 115.

29. Ibid., 132.

30. Mantell, *Arthur Ashe*, 79.

31. Frank Deford, "Raised by Women to Conquer Men: The Journey of
Jimmy Connors," *Sports Illustrated*, August 1, 1978, https://www.si
.com/tennis/2014/11/25/raised-women-conquer-men-jimmy-connors
-frank-deford-si-60.

32. Albert Stampone, "16 Inspiring Quotes from U.S. Open Tennis
Legend Arthur Ashe," *Entrepreneur*, August 27, 2019, https://www
.entrepreneur.com/business-news/16-inspiring-quotes-from-us-open
-tennis-legend-arthur-ashe/338541.

33. Arsenault, *Arthur Ashe*, 378, 379.

34. Ibid.

35. Ibid., 616.

36. Carroll Rogers Walton, "Remembering Arthur Ashe's AIDS Announcement 25 Years Later," *Atlanta Journal-Constitution*, April 12, 2017, https://www.ajc.com/sports/remembering-arthur-ashe-hiv-announcement-years-later/x6pVAE7ESvmSTrAuiDkmEK/#:~:text=But%20here%20was%20a%20buttoned,it%20could%20happen%20to%20anybody.

37. Ashe and Rampersad, *Days of Grace*, 326.

Chapter 6: Abraham Lincoln: Read for Pleasure and Purpose

1. Abraham Lincoln papers, Library of Congress, https://tile.loc.gov/storage-services/service/mss/mal/4¹⁰/41019⁰⁰/4101900.pdf.

2. David Herbert Donald, *Lincoln* (New York: Simon & Schuster, 1995), 15.

3. Allen C. Guelzo, *Lincoln: A Very Short Introduction* (Oxford: Oxford University Press, 2009), 1.

4. Doris Kearns Goodwin, *Team of Rivals: The Political Genius of Abraham Lincoln* (New York: Simon & Schuster, 2005), 99.

5. Donald, *Lincoln*, 336.

6. "Abraham Lincoln Birthplace: Kentucky Boyhood Home at Knob Creek Unit Cultural Landscape," National Park Service, https://www.nps.gov/articles/975192.htm.

7. Michael Burlingame, *Abraham Lincoln: A Life* (Baltimore, MD: Johns Hopkins University Press, 2008), 1:598–99.

8. "*Politics* by Aristotle," The Internet Classics Archive, http://classics.mit.edu/Aristotle/politics.8.eight.html.

9. Goodwin, *Team of Rivals*, 51.

10. Guelzo, *Lincoln*, 21.

11. "Washington and Lincoln: The Weems Connection," *Presidential History Blog*, April 7, 2020, https://featherfoster.wordpress.com/2015/01/26/washington-and-lincoln-the-weems-connection/.

12. Guelzo, *Lincoln*, 23.

13. Doris Kearns Goodwin, *Leadership in Turbulent Times* (New York: Simon & Schuster, 2018), 13.

14. Ibid., 15.

15. "President Lincoln Dreams About His Assassination," History.com, https://www.history.com/this-day-in-history/lincoln-dreams-about-a -presidential-assassination.

16. Donald, *Lincoln*, 184.

17. Ibid., 185.

18. *Field of Dreams*, directed by Phil Alden Robinson, written by W. P. Kinsella and Phil Alden Robinson, IMDb, https://www.imdb.com/title /tt0097351/characters/nm0000044.

19. Harry V. Jaffa, *A New Birth of Freedom: Abraham Lincoln and the Coming of the Civil War* (Lanham, MD: Rowman & Littlefield, 2000), 74.

20. Lewis E. Lehrman, *Lincoln at Peoria: The Turning Point: Getting Right with the Declaration of Independence* (Mechanicsburg, PA: Stackpole Books, 2008), 224.

21. Ibid., 8.

22. Donald, *Lincoln*, 149.

23. "Speech at Peoria," https://www.ucl.ac.uk/USHistory/Building/docs /peoria.htm.

24. Goodwin, *Leadership in Turbulent Times*, 116.

25. Michael J. Gerhardt, *Lincoln's Mentors: The Education of a Leader* (Boston: Mariner Books, 2022), 248.

26. Ibid., 249, 250.

27. John P. Diggins, *The Lost Soul of American Politics: Virtue, Self-interest, and the Foundations of Liberalism* (Chicago: University of Chicago Press), 305.

28. "We Are More in Common," More in Common, https://www .moreincommon.com/.

29. Joseph J. Ellis, *American Creation: Triumphs and Tragedies at the Founding of the Republic* (New York: Random House, 2007), 15.

Chapter 7: Ben Nighthorse Campbell: Don't Worry About the Best, Worry About *Your* Best

1. GovInfo, U.S. Government Publishing Office, 18, https://www.gov info.gov/content/pkg/CDOC-108sdoc21/pdf/CDOC-108sdoc21.pdf.

2. Herman J. Viola, *Ben Nighthorse Campbell: An American Warrior* (New York: Orion Books, 1993), 9.

3. Ibid., 12.

4. Ibid., 8.

5. Aedan Hannon, "Former Sen. Ben Nighthorse Campbell Inducted into the National Native American Hall of Fame," *Durango Herald*, November 13, 2021, https://www.durangoherald.com/articles/former -sen-ben-nighthorse-campbell-inducted-into-the-national-native -american-hall-of-fame/.

6. Viola, *Ben Nighthorse Campbell*, 203.

7. Ibid., 297.

8. John Norton, "Campbell: Rose Parade a Plus," *Pueblo Chieftain*, January 16, 1992, https://www.chieftain.com/story/special/1992/01/17 /campbell-rose-parade-plus/8652153007/.

9. Ibid., 236.

10. Congressional Record (Bound Edition), Volume 150 (2004), Part 18. Pages 24213–24225. https://www.govinfo.gov/content/pkg/CRECB-2004 -pt18/html/CRECB-2004-pt18-Pg24213-2.htm.

11. Viola, *Ben Nighthorse Campbell*, xi.

12. "The Judo Story of Ben Campbell," Judo Info, https://judoinfo.com /campbell/.

13. Ibid., 71.

14. Viola, *Ben Nighthorse Campbell*, 33.

15. Ibid., 39.

16. Ibid., 43.

17. "Ben Nighthorse Campbell," United States Judo Federation, https:// www.usjf.com/ben-nighthorse-campbell/.

18. Viola, *Ben Nighthorse Campbell*, 45.

19. Ibid., 227.

20. *Wired* staff, "Black Horse Homecoming," *Wired*, November 16, 2002, https://www.wired.com/2002/11/black-horse-homecoming/.

21. Viola, *Ben Nighthorse Campbell*, 171.

22. Ibid., 174, 175.

23. "Ben Nighthorse Campbell." *Dancing Rabbit Gallery*. Accessed December 18, 2023. https://www.thedancingrabbitgallery.com/2010/08 /25/ben-nighthorse-campbell/?dr_sort=130

24. Viola, *Ben Nighthorse Campbell*, 180.

25. Ibid., 184.

26. Ben Nighthorse Campbell, https://bennighthorseconsultants.com
    /bennighthorseconsultants.com/About_Ben.html.

27. "Colorado Experience: Ben Nighthorse Campbell," YouTube, https://
    www.youtube.com/watch?v=yD0pkYt2Qxo.

28. Viola, *Ben Nighthorse Campbell*, 45.

29. Michael Janofsky, "G.O.P. Senator Campbell of Colorado Will Retire,"
    New York Times, March 4, 2004, https://www.nytimes.com/2004
    /03/04/us/gop-senator-campbell-of-colorado-will-retire.html.

30. Phillip M. Bailey and Terry Collins, "What Is the State of American
    Democracy? As July 4th Nears, Poll Shows Voters Are Worried,"
    USA Today, June 27, 2023, https://www.usatoday.com/story/news
    /nation/2023/06/27democracy-in-america-voter-july-4-poll/70337
    592007/.

31. "Tributes to Hon. Ben Nighthorse Campbell," U.S. Government
    Printing Office, 2005, vii, https://www.govinfo.gov/content/pkg
    /CDOC-108sdoc21/pdf/CDOC-108sdoc21.pdf.

32. Ibid.

33. Viola, *Ben Nighthorse Campbell*, 199.

34. Ibid., 217.

35. "Nighthorse Campbell Switches to GOP," *The Morning Call*, last
    modified October 3, 2021, https://www.mcall.com/1995/03/04
    /nighthorse-campbell-switches-to-gop/.

36. Katherine Tully-McManus, "Secret Service Buying a Harley-Davidson,
    despite Trump's Calls for Boycott," *Roll Call*, December 13, 2019,
    https://rollcall.com/2018/09/13/secret-service-buying-a-harley
    -davidson-despite-trumps-calls-for-boycott/.

37. Linda Wheeler, "Lawmaker Turns Lawman," *Washington Post*,
    November 16, 1995, https://www.washingtonpost.com/archive/local
    /1995/11/16/lawmaker-turns-lawman/82db754f-a9f3-4ba2-b00a-68ed0
    943cb47/.

38. "Places," National Park Service, https://www.nps.gov/sand/learn
    /historyculture/places.htm.

39. "Sand Creek Massacre National Historic Site," National Park Service,
    https://www.nps.gov/places/sand-creek-massacre-national-historic-site
    .htm#:~:text=Sand%20Creek%20Massacre%20National%20Historic

%20Site%20comemorates%20the%20November%2029,about%20
170%20miles%20southeast%20of.

40. "Custer Falls Again as Site Is Renamed," *New York Times*, November 27,
1991, https://www.nytimes.com/1991/11/27/us/custer-falls-again-as-site
-is-renamed.html.

41. Viola, *Ben Nighthorse Campbell*, 270.

Chapter 8: Ruth Bader Ginsburg: Prioritize Relationships

1. Ted Johnson, "Donald Trump Tells Reporters He Hadn't Heard of Ruth
Bader Ginsburg's Death: 'You Are Telling Me Now for the First Time.
She Led an Amazing Life,'" Deadline, September 20, 2020, https://
deadline.com/2020/09/donald-trump-ruth-bader-ginsburg-1234579988/.

2. Brad Wilcox, "Why Are Liberals Less Happy Than Conservatives?,"
UnHerd, October 10, 2022, https://unherd.com/thepost/why-are
-liberals-less-happy-than-conservatives/.

3. Jane Sherron De Hart, *Ruth Bader Ginsburg: A Life* (New York: Alfred
A. Knopf, 2018), 77.

4. Antonia Felix, *The Unstoppable Ruth Bader Ginsburg: American Icon*
(New York: Sterling, 2019), 21.

5. Jeremy S. Adams, "Three Life Lessons for Young Americans on Ruth
Bader Ginsburg's 86th Birthday," *Educator's Room*, March 15, 2019,
https://theeducatorsroom.com/three-life-lessons-for-young-americans
-on-ruth-bader-ginsburgs-86th-birthday.

6. Felix, *The Unstoppable Ruth Bader Ginsburg*, 32.

7. De Hart, *Ruth Bader Ginsburg*, 417.

8. U.S. Census Bureau, "Historical Marital Status Tables," Census.gov,
https://www.census.gov/data/tables/time-series/demo/families/marital
.html.

9. "The Share of Never-Married Americans Has Reached a New High,"
Institute for Family Studies, https://ifstudies.org/blog/the-share-of
-never-married-americans-has-reached-a-new-high.

10. Daniel A. Cox et al., "Does Marriage Make Us Happier?," The Survey
Center on American Life, October 14, 2021, https://www.american
surveycenter.org/newsletter/does-marriage-make-us-happier/#:~:text

=A%20heap%20of%20academic%20work,unmarried%20people%20
is%20growing%20larger.

11. Richard Fry, "A Record-High Share of 40-Year-Olds in the U.S. Have
    Never Been Married," Pew Research Center, June 28, 2023, https://
    www.pewresearch.org/short-reads/2023/06/28/a-record-high-share-of
    -40-year-olds-in-the-us-have-never-been-married/.

12. "New Census Data: Key Takeaways on Divorce, Marriage, and Fertility
    in the U.S," Institute for Family Studies, https://ifstudies.org/blog
    /new-census-data-key-takeaways-on-divorce-marriage-and-fertility-in
    -the-us.

13. "Actually, Most People Love Being Parents," Institute for Family
    Studies, https://ifstudies.org/blog/actually-most-people-love-being
    -parents.

14. "What a Decades-Long Harvard Study Tells Us About Mental Health,"
    Wilson Quarterly, https://www.wilsonquarterly.com/quarterly/_/what
    -can-decades-long-harvard-study-tell-us-about-mental-health.

15. Laura Collins-Hughes, "After the Play, a Supreme Encore from Ruth
    Bader Ginsburg." *New York Times*, July 30, 2018, https://www
    .nytimes.com/2018/07/30/theater/ruth-bader-ginsburg-the-originalist
    -antonin-scalia.html.

16. Felix, *The Unstoppable Ruth Bader Ginsburg*, 87.

17. Ruth Bader Ginsburg, "Eulogy for Justice Antonin Scalia—March 1,
    2016," Iowa State University, Archives of Women's Political
    Communication, https://awpc.cattcenter.iastate.edu/2017/03/21
    /eulogy-forjustice-antonin-scalia-march-1-2016/.

18. Chris D'Angelo, "Ginsburg Says Supreme Court 'A Paler Place'
    Without Her Dear Friend Scalia," *HuffPost*, May 27, 2016, https://
    www.huffpost.com/entry/ginsburg-judicial-conference-speech-scalia
    _n57489d0ee4b03ede4414d23e.

19. Molly Longman, "Justice Scalia's Son Says Ruth Bader Ginsburg's
    Friendship with His Dad Teaches Valuable Lessons," *Bustle*, August 24,
    2018, https://www.bustle.com/p/justice-scalias-son-says-ruth-bader
    -ginsburgs-friendship-with-his-dad-teaches-valuable-lessons-10228737.

20. Lyman Stone and Brad Wilcox, "Now Political Polarization Comes for
    Marriage Prospects," *The Atlantic*, June 11, 2023, https://www.the

atlantic.com/ideas/archive/2023/06/us-marriage-rate-different-political
-views/674358/.

21. Charles Homans and Alyce McFadden, "Today's Politics Divide Parties,
    and Friends and Families, Too," *New York Times*, October 18, 2022,
    https://www.nytimes.com/2022/10/18/us/politics/political-division
    -friends-family.html.

22. Ruth Bader Ginsburg, *My Own Words* (New York: Simon & Schuster,
    2020), 144.

23. Akhil Reed Amar, *America's Unwritten Constitution: The Precedents
    and Principles We Live By* (New York: Basic Books, 2015), 254.

24. Ruth Bader Ginsburg, *United States v. Virginia et al.*, 518 U.S. 515
    (1996), Legal Information Institute, June 26, 1996, https://www.law
    .cornell.edu/supct/html/94-1941.ZO.html.

25. Felix, *The Unstoppable Ruth Bader Ginsburg*, 188.

Chapter 9: James Madison: Do What Others Are Unwilling to Do

1. Noah Feldman, *The Three Lives of James Madison: Genius, Partisan,
   President* (New York: Random House, 2017), 45.

2. Ralph Ketcham, *James Madison: A Biography* (Charlottesville:
   University Press of Virginia, 1992), 53.

3. "Kitty Floyd," History of American Women, https://www.womenhistory
   blog.com/2011/08/kitty-floyd.html.

4. Joseph J. Ellis, *The Quartet: Orchestrating the Second American
   Revolution, 1783–1789* (New York: Vintage Books, 2016), 108.

5. David O. Stewart, *Madison's Gift: Five Partnerships That Built America*
   (New York: Simon & Schuster, 2016), 59.

6. Feldman, *The Three Lives of James Madison*, 75.

7. Ellis, *The Quartet*, 130.

8. Jeffrey Rosen, interview with Akhil Reed Amar, *Live at the National
   Constitution Center*, December 16, 2016, https://podcasts.apple.com
   /us/podcast/akhil-amar-on-timeless-constitutional-lessons/id103742
   3300?i=1000503806929.

9. Feldman, *The Three Lives of James Madison*, 253.

10. Ellis, *The Quartet*, 206.

11. Robert V. Remini, *The House: The History of the House of Representatives* (New York: Smithsonian Books, 2007), 32.

12. Arthur C. Brooks, "Changing Your Mind Can Make You Less Anxious," *The Atlantic*, February 8, 2023, https://www.theatlantic.com /family/archive/2021/03/to-get-happier-admit-when-youre-wrong /618245/.

13. Ibid.

14. *Scene at the Signing of the Constitution of the United States*, https:// encyclopediavirginia.org/383hpr-5adeb3c3ea80ee4/.

15. Feldman, *The Three Lives of James Madison*, 225.

16. Stewart, *Madison's Gift*, 125.

17. Ibid., 124,

18. James Hilton, *Goodbye, Mr. Chips* (London: Hodder, 2016), 88.

Chapter 10: Theodore Roosevelt: Always Take the Stairs

1. Patricia O'Toole, *When Trumpets Call: Theodore Roosevelt After the White House* (New York: Simon & Schuster, 2006), 14.

2. Ibid., 4.

3. Ibid., 86.

4. "Theodore Roosevelt of Rock Creek Park," *Scary DC*, https://scarydc .com/blog/theodore-roosevelt-of-rock-creek-park/.

5. Kathleen M. Dalton, *Theodore Roosevelt: A Strenuous Life* (New York: Vintage Books, 2004), 35.

6. Ibid., 36.

7. Edmund Morris, *The Rise of Theodore Roosevelt* (New York: Modern Library, revised edition, 2001), 15.

8. David G. McCullough, *Mornings on Horseback* (New York: Simon and Schuster, 2003), 112.

9. Morris, *The Rise of Theodore Roosevelt*, 32.

10. McCullough, *Mornings on Horseback*, 112.

11. Morris, *The Rise of Theodore Roosevelt*, 33.

12. McCullough, *Mornings on Horseback*, 118.

13. Morris, *The Rise of Theodore Roosevelt*, 230.

14. McCullough, *Mornings on Horseback*, 285.

15. Morris, *The Rise of Theodore Roosevelt*, 270, 232, 233.

16. Edmund Morris, *Colonel Roosevelt* (New York: Random House, 2010), 47.

17. O'Toole, *When Trumpets Call*, 86.

18. Ibid., 137.

19. Kirsten Swinth, "The Square Deal: Theodore Roosevelt and the Themes of Progressive Reform," History Resources, Gilder Lehrman Institute of American History, https://www.gilderlehrman.org/history-resources/essays/square-deal-theodore-roosevelt-and-themes-progressive-reform.

20. Morris, *Colonel Roosevelt*, 108.

21. Lewis Gould, "Why TR Lost the Republican Nomination in 1912: What New Research Shows," History News Network, https://historynews network.org/article/49468.

22. Dalton, *Theodore Roosevelt*, 392.

23. David Bentley Hart, *Atheist Delusions: The Christian Revolution and Its Fashionable Enemies* (New Haven, CT: Yale University Press, 2009), 220.

24. "When Teddy Roosevelt Was Shot in 1912, a Speech May Have Saved His Life," History.com, https://www.history.com/news/shot-in-the-chest-100-years-ago-teddy-roosevelt-kept-on-talking.

25. Morris, *Colonel Roosevelt*, 244.

26. "When Teddy Roosevelt Was Shot in 1912."

27. Morris, *Colonel Roosevelt*, 245.

28. "How Teddy Roosevelt Ascended in New York Politics," History.com, https://www.history.com/news/theodore-roosevelt-new-york-politics-governor-police-commissioner.

29. "T.R. the Rough Rider: Hero of the Spanish American War," National Park Service, https://www.nps.gov/thrb/learn/historyculture/tr-rr-spanamwar.htm.

30. Edmund Morris, *Theodore Rex* (New York: Random House, 2001), 108.

31. Sidney Milkis, "Theodore Roosevelt: Impact and Legacy," University of Virginia, Miller Center, https://millercenter.org/president/roosevelt/impact-and-legacy.

Conclusion

1. Ellen Barry, "Hospitals Are Increasingly Crowded with Kids Who
   Tried to Harm Themselves, Study Finds," *New York Times*, March 28,
   2023, https://www.nytimes.com/2023/03/28/health/pediatric-mental
   -health-hospitalizations.html#:~:text=Hospitalizations%20for%20
   pediatric%20suicidal%20behavior,in%20the%20United%20States
   %20found.

2. David French, "What if Kids Are Sad and Stressed Because Their
   Parents Are?," *New York Times*, March 19, 2023, https://www.nytimes
   .com/2023/03/19/opinion/teen-adult-depression-anxiety.html.

3. Adrianna Rodriguez, "Students Are Increasingly Refusing to Go to
   School. It's Becoming a Mental Health Crisis," *USA Today*, May 18,
   2023, https://www.usatoday.com/in-depth/news/health/2023/05/15
   /school-avoidance-becomes-crisis-after-covid/11127563002/.

4. Douglas Murray, *The War on the West* (New York: Broadside Books,
   2022), 96.

INDEX

American public
  as agent of their own design, 186
  apathy of, 55–56
  lost faith in institutions, 29
  satisfaction level with life, 147
  unhappiness of, 60–61
American Red Cross, 49
American soul, 3, 32, 38, 45, 109, 118
American spirit, 49, 122–123
Americanism, 34
America's founding generation
  academic background, 110
  Adams, John (*see* Adams, John)
  excesses of, 15
  fascination with ancient Rome,
    20–21
  Franklin, Benjamin, 15, 24, 73, 167,
    175
  Hamilton, Alexander, 15, 21, 67, 110,
    177, 184
  Jefferson, Thomas (*see* Jefferson,
    Thomas)
  Madison, James (*see* Madison, James)
  Monroe, James, 110, 173
  Plutarch's book as inspiration for, 4–5
  as "villains," 2
  Washington, George (*see* Washington,
    George)
ancient Rome, 20–21
Andersonville Confederate prison,
  62–63
Andersonville National Cemetery,
  63–64
Andrew, John A., 53
"Angel of the Battlefield." *See* Barton,
  Clara
Anthony, Susan B., 59
Antietam, battle of, 54–55
anxiety epidemic, 3
apartheid. *See* South Africa, apartheid in

apathy, 55–56
Appearances Matter, 16–20
aristocracies, 176, 179
Arsenault, Raymond, 88–89
Arthur Ashe Stadium, 94
Articles of Confederation, 23, 169–170
Ashe, Arthur
  activism of, 88–89, 97–100
  AIDS diagnosis, 104
  belief in power of persuasion, 100
  character formation, 87–88
  circles of significance, 89
  on confidence, 102
  Connors rivalry with, 102
  critics of, 100
  as Davis Cup team captain, 91–92
  facing death, 104–105
  on father's discipline, 96–97
  on finding your own voice, 90
  on his political passivity, 95–96
  Howard University speech, 94–95
  on individual belief preceding grand
    achievement, 102
  on inequality issues, 98–99
  Jackson, Jesse on, 95
  Kennedy, Robert and, 88, 98
  on loss of his mother, 96
  McEnroe and, 92–94
  memoir of, 87–88
  on nature of heroism, 100
  personality, 90–91
  post-tennis life, 104–105
  reticence of, 96–97
  on South Africa apartheid, 88,
    94–95
  South Africa visit, 99–100
  tennis clinics, 104
  on trappings of segregation, 96–97
  US Open win, 98–99
  Wimbledon finals, 86–87, 101–103

ABOUT THE AUTHOR

Jeremy S. Adams was the Daughters of the American Revolution 2014 California Teacher of the Year and a finalist for the Carlston Family Foundation Outstanding Teachers of America Award. He is a social studies teacher at Bakersfield High School and was a longtime political science lecturer at California State University, Bakersfield.